Great Crocheted Sweaters in a Weekend

Great Crocheted Sweaters in a Weekend

Nola Theiss
& Chris Rankin

A Sterling/Lark Book
Sterling Publishing Co., Inc.   New York

Art Director: Katheen Holmes
Production: Elaine Thompson, Kathleen Holmes
Editor: Dawn Cusick
English Translation: Networks, Inc.
Proofreading: Diane Murphy, Julie Brown

Library of Congress Cataloging-in-Publication Data
Theiss, Nola.
    Great crocheted sweaters in a weekend / Nola Theiss & Chris Rankin.
      p.   cm.
    "A Sterling/Lark book."
    Includes bibliographical references and index.
    ISBN 0-8069-0441-0
    1. Crocheting--Patterns.   2. Sweaters.   I. Rankin, Chris.
TT825.T44   1993
    746.9'2--dc20   93-24608
                                            CIP

10 9 8 7 6 5 4 3

A Sterling/Lark Book

Produced by Altamont Press, Inc.,
   50 College Street, Asheville, NC 28801 USA

Published in 1993 by Sterling Publishing Co., Inc.,
   387 Park Avenue South, New York, NY 10016 USA

Photos and instructions copyright Ariadne/Spaarnestad, Utrecht, Holland
English Translation © 1993, Altamont Press

Distributed in Canada by Sterling Publishing,
   c/o Canadian Manda Group, P.O. Box 920, Station U,
   Toronto, Ontario, Canada M8Z 5P9
Distributed in the United Kingdom by Cassell PLC
   Villiers House, 41/47 Strand, London WC2N 5JE, England
Distributed in Australia by Capricorn Link Ltd., P.O. Box 665,
   Lane Cove, NSW 2066

ISBN 0-8069-0441-0

Contents

Introduction

In a sense, crochet is the craft most akin to the family traditions of patchwork quilting and early knitting. A crocheter determined to learn new stitches usually learns them from another crocheter, or by examining samples of work she admires. Lacking a written literature, American crochet has relied on folk tradition for subsistence. It has been handed down, literally, from one generation to the next. It is a skill often taught by a next-door neighbor or to a child who is fascinated by the flash of a working crochet hook. American crocheters, like early quilters, enjoy the challenge of making something whole from left-over scraps, often producing unique color and pattern combinations. The items American crocheters produce are usually quite functional — an afghan or a baby blanket — and are often presented as gifts to celebrate important occasions.

European crochet is quite different. Because knitting is so popular in Europe, crocheters usually lack the helpful next-door neighbor for instruction, relying instead on written directions. Most European crocheters are also fervent knitters, so it's not unusual for them to use knitted borders and edgings in their crochet projects. European crocheters, eager to create garments as fashionable as their knitting counterparts, have designed new crochet stitches and patterns that make truly wonderful sweaters.

Like most crochet projects, the garments in this book are quick to make and do not require extensive knowledge. A bibliography has been included for reference if you can't find someone to help you with the stitches. The patterns are labeled with their level of difficulty, so you may want to begin with an easy sweater and work your way up to a more challenging one.

Stitches, Tips, and Techniques

Many experienced crocheters have never had to work with row-by-row instructions, and may find them intimidating. The abundance of abbreviations, though, often makes the instructions appear more complicated than they actually are. The pages that follow explain the stitches and abbreviations used in this book, and a few minutes of study time will pay off when it comes time to begin your first project. (British crocheters should refer to the terminology translation table on page 17.)

When following the instructions, it is very important to read carefully and to pay attention to the position of the hook at all times. Make a sample gauge to learn the stitch and check measurements and tension (more about this later). Often you will be called upon to place the hook at the back or front of the work; but remember, unless specified, always insert the hook in the front of the stitch under both loops and work from right to left. Frequently it will be necessary to skip stitches and then come back to them. Position of the hook is very important in this case because you must know whether to work in front or in back of the stitches worked after the skipped stitches. Use the photos as a guide.

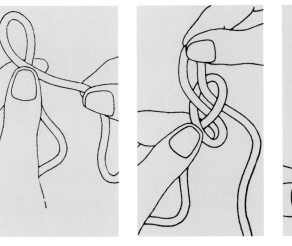
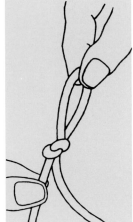
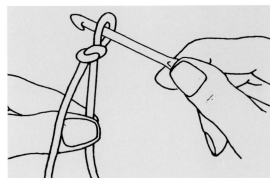

Making a Slip Knot

Asterisks

The asterisk symbol (,*,) is used in crochet as a repeat sign. All instructions included between two asterisks should be repeated the number of times indicated. To save space, the abbreviations rep, beg, and foll are used to indicate repeat, beginning, and following, respectively.

Yarn Over (yo)

A yarn over is technically not a stitch in itself, but no crochet stitch is possible without it. Wrap the yarn around the hook from back to front to form a loop. Depending on the stitch, more yarn overs are formed and drawn through loops. In essence, this is crochet — a very simple process that no machine can duplicate.

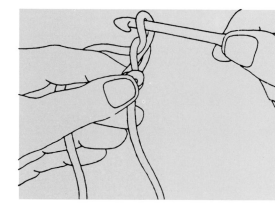 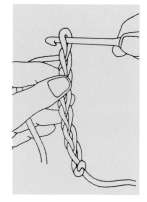

Chain Stitch (ch)

To start the chain, make a slip knot; insert the hook from right to left through the loop. With the hook in front of the yarn, wrap the yarn around the hook from back to front. With the hook pointing down, draw a new loop through the loop on the hook. One chain stitch has been completed.

 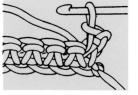

Slip Stitch (sl st)

Insert the hook into the chain or stitch; wrap the yarn over the hook from back to front; draw a loop through both the chain (or stitch) and the loop on the hook. One slip stitch has been completed.

Single Crochet (sc)

Insert hook into the second chain from the hook. Wrap the yarn around the hook from back to front. Draw the yarn through the chain, making two loops on the hook. Wrap the yarn around the hook from the back to front and draw the yarn through the two loops on the hook. One single crochet stitch has been completed. Continue by inserting the hook in the next chain. After the last stitch, chain 2 and turn. Insert the hook into the first stitch to begin the next row.

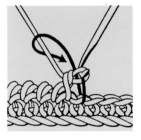

Shrimp Stitch

This stitch is used frequently as a finishing edge on necklines and other borders. It is worked like single crochet, but in the opposite direction, from left to right, instead of right to left. Keep the right side of the work facing you as you work. If you're doing it correctly, it will feel as if you are working backward. If it feels like you are doing single crochet, you have probably turned the work and you are doing single crochet.

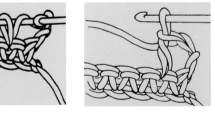

Half-Double Crochet (hdc)

Wrap the yarn around the hook from back to front. Insert the hook into the third chain from the hook. Wrap the yarn over the hook and draw the yarn through the chain, making three loops on the hook. Wrap the yarn around the hook from back to front and draw through the three loops on the hook. One half-double crochet stitch has been completed. Continue by wrapping the yarn around the hook and inserting the hook in the next chain. After the last stitch, chain 2 and turn. Wrap the yarn over

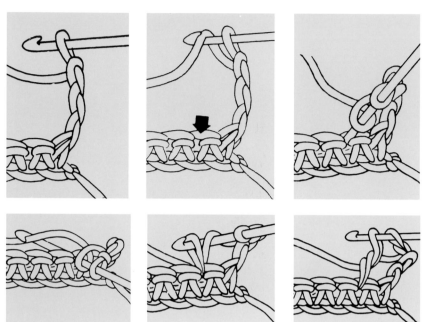

the hook, and insert the hook in the first stitch to begin the next row.

Double Crochet (dc)

Wrap the yarn around the hook from back to front; insert the hook into the fourth chain from the hook; wrap the yarn over the hook and draw the yarn through the chain, making three loops on the hook. Wrap the yarn over the hook and draw it through two loops. Wrap the yarn over the hook again and draw the yarn through the last two loops to complete the stitch. Continue by repeating the sequence in each chain stitch. After the last stitch, chain 3 and turn. Insert the hook in the second stitch to begin the next row.

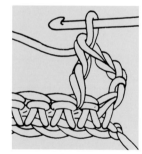

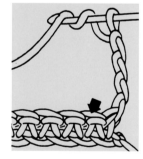

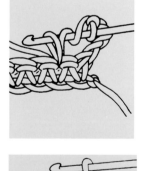

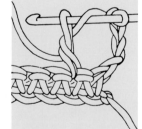

Treble Crochet (tc)

Wrap the yarn around the hook from back to front twice, and insert the hook in the fifth chain from the hook. Wrap the yarn over the hook and draw a loop through the chain, making four loops on the hook. Wrap the yarn over the hook and draw the yarn through two loops. Wrap the yarn over the hook and draw the yarn through two more loops. Last, wrap the yarn over the hook again and draw through the yarn through last two loops to complete the stitch. Continue by repeating the sequence in each chain. After the last stitch, chain 4 and turn; insert the hook into the second stitch to begin the next row.

Afghan Stitch

Using an afghan crochet hook, make a chain equal to the desired number of stitches, plus 2.

Row 1: Insert the hook into the second chain from the hook. Wrap the yarn over the hook and draw through a loop through the chain. Continue by wrapping the yarn over the hook, pulling a loop through each chain in the row. Do not turn the work — you will always be working with the right side facing you.

Row 2: This next row is worked by wrapping the yarn over the hook and pulling a loop through the first loop on the hook. Then wrap the yarn over the hook and draw a loop through the next two loops on the hook. Repeat until there is one loop left on the hook. The remaining loop forms the first stitch of the next row.

Row 3: Skip the first vertical loop in the previous row and insert the hook from right to left through the second vertical loop. Wrap the yarn over the hook and draw the loop through, making two loops on the hook. Continue across the row. Note: Insert the hook through the center of the last loop leaving two strands of yarn at the edge.

Row 4: Same as row 2.

Repeat rows 3 and 4 until the desired length is reached.

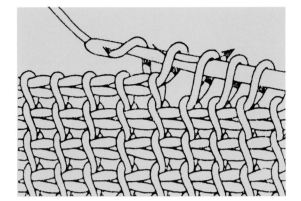

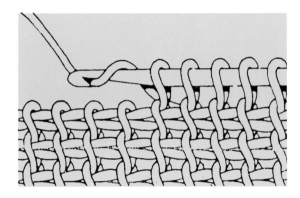

Filet Stitch

There are many versions of the filet stitch, but this is the most common. To make beautiful motifs, fill in the desired squares with 1 stitch.

Row 1: *1 Dc, ch 1*, rep * to * across, end with 1 dc.

Row 2 and all following

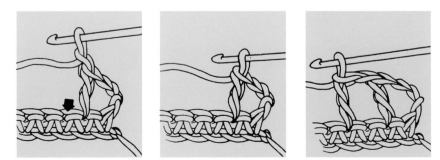

rows: Chain 4 to turn (beginning of the first square). Always work 1 double crochet in the double crochet of the previous row, and chain above the chain of the previous row.

Relief Stitches

All relief stitches are basically the same. Just insert the hook around the post (the length of the stitch found in a previous row), and work the desired stitch. The resulting texture depends on the stitch, which previous row is worked, and whether the stitch is worked on the back or front. We've listed a few variations to give you the general idea.

Front Relief Single Crochet

This stitch is worked in single crochet by working around the post of the stitch below. For front relief stitches, insert the hook from right to left around the post of the indicated stitch at the front of the work. Yarnover, and draw through loop; yarnover and draw through both loops.

Back Relief Single Crochet

This stitch is worked in single crochet by working around the post of the stitch below. For back relief stitches, insert the hook from right to left around the post of the indicated stitch at the back of the work. Yarnover, and draw through loop; yarnover, and draw through both loops.

Front Relief Double Crochet

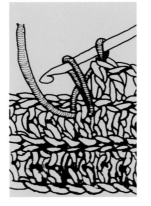

This stitch is worked in double crochet by working around the post of the stitch of the previous row. Yarnover over the hook, and insert the hook from right to left around the post of the indicated stitch at the front of the work. Yarnover, and draw through the loop; yarnover, and continue as you would a double crochet.

Back Relief Double Crochet

This stitch is worked in double crochet by working around the post of the stitch of the previous row. Yarnover over the hook, and insert the hook from right to left around the post of the indicated stitch at the back of the work. Yarnover, and draw through the loop; yarnover and continue as you would a double crochet.

Border Stitches

Most American crocheters are not accustomed to the term border stitch. The first and last stitches, usually the chain at the beginning of the row and the last stitch of the row, are considered border stitches by Europeans because they are worked into the seams and are not part of the pattern. In most cases, they are worked in the same colors as adjoining stitches in most cases. On jacquard patterns, they are usually not included on the chart. When border stitches are used, some explanation will be given in the pattern. Often, when joining seams, one sews or crochets between the border stitch and the adjoining stitch.

Some of the patterns use a knitted ribbing rather than a

crocheted edging. We have included a description of all the stitches used here, as well as some alternatives. Again, a glance at other crochet reference books will provide you with additional ideas. Feel free to substitute your own preferred edgings. Knitted ribbings are more elastic, but don't let a knitted edge stop you from making a design; crochet your edgings instead.

1/1 ribbing

Row 1: *K1, pl*. Rep * to * across.

Row 2 and all following rows: Work the stitches as established in the previous row by knitting the stitches which were purled in the previous row and look flat on the second row, and purling the stitches which were knitted in the previous row and have a loop next to the needle.

2/2 ribbing

Row 1: *K2, p2*. Rep * to * across.

Row 2 and all following rows: Work the stitches as established in the previous row.

Crochet Ribbing - Post Stitch Ribbing (single crochet)

This stitch is worked on an even number of stitches. The idea is always to work a back relief post stitch in a front relief post stitch of the previous row so that alternate ridges are formed on the back and front of the work.

Row 1: 1 Sc in each ch.

Row 2: Ch 1 (= 1 border st) *1 front relief sc, 1 back relief sc*, 1 sc in last space (= 1 border st).

Row 3: Ch 1, *1 back relief sc, 1 front relief sc*, 1 sc in last space.

Repeat Rows 2 and 3.

Post Stitch Ribbing (double crochet)

This stitch is the same as the single crochet post stitch with longer posts.

Row 1: 1 Dc in each st.

Row 2: Ch 2 (=1 border st) *1 front relief dc, 1 back relief dc*, rep * to * across row, end with 1 front relief dc, 1 hdc (=1 border st).

Row 3: Ch 2, *1 back relief dc, 1 front relief dc*, rep * to * across row, end with 1 back relief dc, 1 hdc.

Always rep rows 2 and 3.

Crochet Ribbing - Ridge Stitch Ribbing

Note: The ridges are formed horizontally and they form a ribbing when turned sideways. Chain the desired depth of ribbing. When used as a ribbing on a garment, the ridge stitch is usually crocheted separately to the desired length and then attached to the garment.

Row 1: Skip 1 ch, 1 sc in each ch to end of row, ch 1, turn.

Row 2: 1 sc in back loop of each st to end of row, ch 1 turn.

Repeat row 2 for the pattern.

Establishing Gauge

The correct gauge is important for the proper size of a garment. If you are used to making afghans only, it may not have mattered if the finished piece was a few inches larger or smaller than you planned. Those inches can be critical on a garment, so be careful. Each pattern has a specific gauge — the number of stitches and rows that equal a 4-inch (10 cm) square. It is important to crochet a sample square using the yarn and hook size specified before starting the garment. If your square measures less than 4 inches, try a larger hook size. If your square measures larger than 4 inches, try a smaller hook size. Be sure to measure your swatch on a flat surface and avoid the temptation to stretch it.

Increasing

To make a single increase, work 2 stitches in one stitch. To make a double increase, work 3 stitches in one stitch. You may want to work in the back loop for one increase and the front loop for the next. To add more stitches at the end of a row, make an additional chain stitch for each additional stitch needed plus the required number of turning chain stitches. On the next row, crochet a pattern stitch in each added chain. Some of the patterns give specific directions for increasing in that pattern stitch. The goal is to make as smooth an edge as possible and to get the correct number of stitches.

Decreasing

To decrease a single stitch, insert the hook in a stitch, and draw through a loop. Insert the hook into the next stitch, and draw through a loop. Wrap the yarn over the hook and then draw the yarn through all 3 loops. To decrease 2 stitches in single or half double crochet, first insert the hook in a stitch. Draw through a loop and skip the next stitch. Insert the hook in the following stitch and draw up through a loop. Wrap the yarn over the hook and draw through the yarn through all 3 loops. This process is called slip stitching across stitches and is the most common way to decrease at the beginning of a row. To decrease at the end of a row, work across until you have the specified number of stitches unworked at the end of row. Turn and continue as directed across the next row. Be sure to work the correct number of turning chains to begin the following row. To avoid a staircase effect at the edge, you may wish to leave one less stitch unworked than specified, then slip stitch across the first stitch of the following row to give a slanted edge.

Reversing Shapings

Although both sides of a neckline are generally shaped the same, keep in mind that they're in mirror image of each other. Usually, the directions will be very specific for the right side of the neckline and then say to reverse shaping for the left side. This simply means that the shapings that were worked at the beginning of the row will now be worked at the end of the row and vice versa. If you slip stitched across 6 stitches at the beginning of a row on the right edge before, now work to the last 6 stitches of the row and leave them unworked, and so on. Increases will also be worked on the opposite edge on the second half.

On a cardigan, directions are only given for one half of the front and you will reverse the instructions so that the two fronts will correspond in shaping. Keep the completed half nearby so that you don't forget which half you are working on.

Jacquard charts and pattern stitch motifs may also reverse pattern placement from one side of the front to the other or from the back to the front. The directions may tell you to work the chart beginning at the left edge for the back and to begin the chart from the right edge on the front so that the motifs will match at the side seams.

Always try to visualize the finished garment as you work and the logic of the design will guide you.

Yarns and Substitutions

When possible, the names of specific yarns have been included in the directions for the garment. For the best results, please use those yarns. Always choose a comparable yarn when making a substitution. When it was not possible to name a specific yarn, a description of the type, weight, and yardage has been given to help you choose an appropriate yarn.

Making Buttonholes

Horizontal crocheted buttonholes can be made by single crocheting at the desired buttonhole location; then crochet chain stitches equal to the buttonhole length. Skip the corresponding number of stitches in the previous row and continue with single crochet. On the following row, work the same number of stitches across the chained stitches.

To make knitted buttonholes, bind off the desired number of stitches on the right side of the work row. Work to the end of the row. On the wrong side of the work row, work to where you have bound off the stitches. Cast the number of stitches that were bound off onto the right hand needle and continue working to the end of the row.

Finishing Techniques

Blocking and pressing are two crucial finishing techniques. Always check the yarn label before proceeding and heed the manufacturer's recommendations. Most crocheted garments need very little blocking. If it is necessary to block, block the individual sections of the garment separately. Using the correct measurements, draw an outline of the finished section on heavy paper. Place the paper on a flat surface padded with several soft towels. Using rustproof pins, pin the crocheted piece to the paper. Carefully work the piece to the correct size and shape. Cover the piece with a very damp cloth and gently mold it to the correct size by weighting it down with towels and a wood board. Leave the towels and the board in place until the piece dries thoroughly. Another way to mold a piece to its correct size is to steam it. Keep the weight of the iron above the work and allow the steam to gently touch the piece. Remove the damp cloth and leave the piece in position to dry thoroughly.

Joining Methods

Garment pieces may be joined together using several methods. To join pieces with the backstitch method, first pin the right sides of the pieces together. Use a yarn or tapestry needle and a piece of the crochet yarn. Working from right to left with small, even stitches, insert the needle back through the pieces at the point where it emerged on the previous stitch, bringing the needle through to the front slightly to the left of where it entered.

To slip stitch pieces together, first pin the right sides of the pieces together. Using a crochet hook and yarn, insert the hook through both pieces of the garment and draw through a loop through the fabric and the loop on the hook. Repeat until the seam is completed.

To secure pieces together with invisible vertical weaving, lay the edges to be joined next to one another with their right sides facing up. With a yarn needle and yarn, insert the needle up through the lower half of the end stitch on one piece and draw the yarn through. From the front, insert the needle through the upper half of the edge stitch on the other piece and draw the yarn through. Continue inserting the needle through alternate sides.

To secure pieces together with invisible horizontal weaving on the final row edges, lay the edges to be joined next one another, aligning the corresponding stitches. Using a yarn needle and yarn, insert the needle under one stitch of one piece and under the corresponding stitch of the second piece. Continue across all stitches and fasten off.

Pieces can also be secured with crocheted seams. First hold two pieces with their right sides together (unless specified otherwise). Insert the hook through both thicknesses and draw up a loop. Insert the hook in the next stitch and draw up a loop, yarnover, and draw through both loops. Continue along the seam.

Using Two of More Colors

Single crochet — Work to the last stitch of the first color. Insert the hook in the next stitch, wrap the yarn over the hook and draw through a loop. Drop the first color to the wrong side of the work and with the second color, wrap the yarn over the hook and draw through a loop. It is important to always change to a different color in the same manner.

Half double crochet — Yarn colors in half double crochet are changed in the same manner as single crochet. Always work the last wrap over the hook with the new color so that the stitch before the new color is completed with the new color.

Double color work — The new color is also used to complete the previous stitch before starting the stitch with the changed color. The color not being used is carried across the top of the previous row and the new row is worked over it making the fabric reversible. Do not draw through the new colored yarn too tightly when using it again or it will distort your work.

Block of color — Two colors worked alternately across a row can be carried along the wrong side of the work when not in use as described above. If you are using large blocks or isolated motifs, separate the balls or bobbins needed for each section. The bobbins or balls of yarn hang at the back of the work and the colors are changed by dropping the first

color to the back and using the second color to wrap the yarn over the hook to complete a stitch and start the new stitch with the second color. Either weave the ends in or work over the ends when you change to a new color. These directions apply to changing yarns as well as to changing the colors of threads.

Hooks

Crochet hooks are made of plastic, coated aluminum, steel, and wood in a range of sizes. The three sizing systems are the U.S. system, the British system, and the Metric system. Since all of these patterns were originally worked with Metric size hooks, we are including an interchange chart for Metric-U.S.-U.K. size hooks. If possible, we tested the yarn on a U.S. hook; thus you may sometimes find that there is a slight discrepancy between the chart interchanges and the ones given in the instructions, or that another chart in another book is slightly different. In any case, you should use the chart as a guide only and always check your gauge and change hooks accordingly.

Steel hooks are generally used with lightweight yarns and threads to create finer, lacier work. Aluminum and plastic hooks are used with most popular weight yarns. Wood hooks are usually found only in the larger and longer lengths. A special hook called an afghan hook is made of aluminum and has a straight shaft with a knob or cap at one end and a hook at the other. They are sized like the aluminum and plastic hooks.

Crochet Hook Translation Table

Metric	U.S.	U.K.
2.5	B/1	12
3	C/2	11
3.25	D/3	10
3.5	E/4	9
4	F/5	8
4.5	G/6	7
5	H/8	6
5.5	I/9	5
6	J/10	4
7	K/10.25	2

Terminology Translation Table

American terms	British terms
Slip st (sl)	Single crochet (sc)
Single crochet (sc)	Double crochet (dc)
Half double crochet (hdc)	Half treble crochet (htr)
Double crochet (dc)	Treble crochet (tr)
Treble crochet (tr)	Double treble (dtr)
Double treble crochet (dtr)	Treble treble (trtr)

Note: For exact measurements, use centimeters.
Conversions to inches from centimeters
may cause discrepancies up to 1/4 inch.

PULLOVERS

Striped Pullover

Level: Easy

Size
- Woman's Small (Medium, Large), bust 30-32 (33-35, 36-38) in. — 76-81.5 (84-89, 91.5-97) cm
- Finished bust measurements: 41-1/2 (44-1/2, 48) in. — 104 (112, 120) cm
- Length: 26-1/4 in. (66 cm)
- Sleeve seam: 16-3/4 in. (42 cm)

Materials
- Scheepjeswol Voluma (approx. 209 yds per 50 g skein) 7 (8, 8) skeins color gray and 1 skein color white
- Crochet hooks U.S. size B/1 and C/2 (Metric size 2.5 and 3) or size needed to obtain gauge To save time, take time to check gauge!

Gauge
19 dc and 14 rows in pat st = 4 in. (10 cm) using larger hook

Stitches
Chain (ch), single crochet (sc), half double crochet (hdc), double crochet (dc).
Relief hdc: Worked around the post of the underlying hdc.
Front relief hdc: Insert hook right to left from front to back around post, yo and work 1 hdc.
Back relief hdc: Insert hook right to left from back to front around post, yo and work 1 hdc.

Border pat:
Row 1: 1 hdc in the 4th ch from the hook, 1 hdc in each foll ch.
Row 2: Ch 2 = border st, *1 front relief hdc, 1 back relief hdc*, rep * to *, end with 1 hdc for border st.
Row 3 and all foll rows: Rep row 2, alternating 1 front relief and 1 back relief hdc. Work a back hdc over a front hdc and vice versa to create pattern.
Pattern stitch: *1 row dc, 1 row sc*, rep * to *. Beg each row of sc with ch 1. Beg each row of dc with ch 3.

Note: See "Stitches and Techniques" for detailed instructions on stitches and shapings.

Back
With smaller size hook and gray, ch 80 (84, 88) + ch 2 to turn = 1 hdc. Work in border pat for 2-3/4 in. (7 cm). Change to larger size hook and continue by foll chart, working first row in sc and inc 21 (25, 29) sts across row = 99 (107 115) sc. Work in pat st. Beg every row of sc with ch 1 and every row of dc with ch 3. Work 1 border st at each edge which is not shown on chart. Work 85 rows of pat st = 26 in. (65 cm). End with 1 row of gray, alternating 1 front relief hdc and 1 back relief hdc. Fasten off.

Front
Work same as back.

Sleeves
With smaller size hook and gray, ch 48 (50, 52) + ch 2 = 1 hdc. Work in pat st for 2 in. (5 cm). Change to larger size hook and continue in pat st by foll chart, inc 7 (9, 11) sts evenly spaced across first row = 53 (57, 61) dc. At each edge of every 3rd row, inc 1 st 17 times = 87 (91, 95) sts + 1 border st at each edge. After 55 rows of pat st, sleeve will measure 16-3/4 in. (42 cm). Fasten off.

Finishing
Block pieces to indicated measurements. Sew shoulder seams over 7 (7-1/2, 8) in. - 18 (19, 20) cm at each edge. Sew sleeves to armholes, matching center of sleeve with shoulder seams. Sew side and sleeve seams.

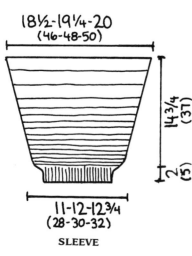

18½-19¼-20
(46-48-50)

14¾
(37)

2
(5)

11-12-12¾
(28-30-32)

SLEEVE

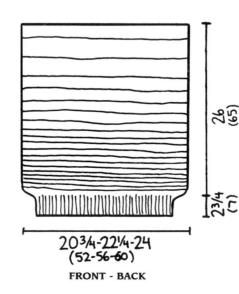

26
(65)

2¾
(7)

20¾-22¼-24
(52-56-60)

FRONT - BACK

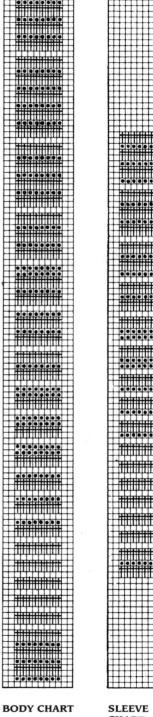

BODY CHART

SLEEVE CHART

Key to Chart

· = 1 sc in gray

+ = 1 dc in gray

☐ = 1 sc in white

19

Filet Pullover

Level: Easy

Size

❖ Woman's Small (Medium, Large), bust 30-32 (33-35, 36-38) in. — 76-81.5 (84-89, 91.5-97) cm
❖ Finished bust measurements: 42-1/2 (45-1/2,48) in. — 106 (114, 120) cm
❖ Length: 24 (24-1/2, 24-3/4) in. — 60 (61, 62) cm
❖ Sleeve seam: 17 in. (43 cm)

Materials

❖ Mohair worsted weight yarn (approx. 110 yds per 50 g skein) 7 (8, 9) skeins color black
❖ Crochet hook U.S. size F/5 (Metric size 4) or size needed to obtain gauge
❖ Knitting needles U.S. size 6 (Metric size 4)
❖ Circular needle U.S. size 6 (Metric size 4).
To save time, take time to check gauge!

Gauge

9 squares and 7 rows = 4 in. (10 cm)

Stitches

Chain (ch), double crochet (dc).
Filet st: Each open square = 1 dc and ch 1, skip 1 ch. Beg open square row with ch 4. Work dc above dc of previous row.
1/1 ribbing: Row 1: *K1, p1*. Rep * to * across.
Row 2 and all foll rows: Work sts as established in previous row.

Note: See "Stitches and Techniques" for detailed instructions on stitches and shapings.

Back

With crochet hook, ch 97 (103, 109) + ch 4 = first open square. Row 1: 1 dc in the 7th ch from the hook, *ch 1, skip 1 ch, 1 dc in the foll ch*, rep * to *, end with 1 dc = 48 (51, 54) open squares with 1 dc at each edge as border sts. Work until piece measures 21-1/2 (22, 22-1/4) in. - 54 (55, 56) cm = 38 (39, 40) rows. Fasten off.

Front

Work same as back, until piece measures 13-1/2 (14, 14-3/4) in. - 34 (35.5, 37) cm = 24 (25, 26) rows. Shape V neck: Leave the center square unworked for medium size. Work each side separately. Work across first 24 (25, 27) squares. At each neck edge of every row, dec 1 square 9 times. Work 5 rows over rem 15 (16, 18) squares. Fasten off. Work 2nd half to correspond.

Sleeves

With crochet hook, ch 55 (57, 59) + ch 4 = first open square. Row 1: 1 dc in the 7th ch from the hook, *ch 1, skip 1 ch, 1 dc in the foll ch*, rep * to * across = 27 (28, 29) squares. At each edge alternately every 2nd and 3rd row, inc 1 square 8 times. Row 2: Ch 3 to turn, 1 dc in the first dc. Work row in open squares and end with 2 dc in the last st. Row 3: Ch 4, 1 dc in the foll dc. Work row in open squares. In the last dc, ch 1, 1 dc to inc 1 dc = 1 square inc at each edge. Continue in this way until you have 43 (44, 45) squares and 27 rows = 15 in. (38 cm) from beg. Fasten off.

Finishing

Block pieces to indicated measurements. Sew shoulder seams. With knitting needles, pick up and knit 66 (72, 78) sts along lower edge of back and work 2-1/2 in. (6 cm) in 1/1 ribbing. Bind off loosely. With knitting needles, pick up and knit 36 (38, 40) sts along lower edge of each sleeve and work 2 in. (5 cm) in 1/1 ribbing. Bind off loosely. With circular needle, pick up and knit 82 (88, 94) sts around neck, beg and end at center front and working back and forth, work 1-1/4 in. (3 cm) in 1/1 ribbing. Bind off loosely. Overlap right edge over left edge and sew in place. Sew sleeves to armholes, matching center of sleeve with shoulder seams. Sew side and sleeve seams.

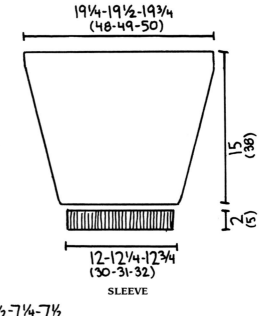

19¼-19½-19¾
(48-49-50)

15
(38)

2
(5)

12-12¼-12¾
(30-31-32)

SLEEVE

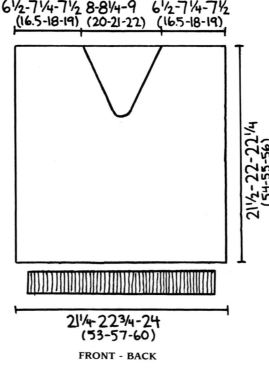

6½-7¼-7½ 8-8¼-9 6½-7¼-7½
(16.5-18-19) (20-21-22) (16.5-18-19)

21½-22-22¼
(54-55-56)

21¼-22¾-24
(53-57-60)

FRONT - BACK

Shawl Collar Pullover

Level: Challenging

Size
❖ Woman's Small (Medium/Large), bust 30-32 (33/38) in. — 76-81.5 (84/97) cm
❖ Finished bust measurements: 40 (44) in. — 100 (110) cm
❖ Length: 22-1/2 in. (56.5 cm)
❖ Sleeve seam: 19-1/4 in. (50.5 cm)

Materials
❖ Mohair/acrylic worsted yarn (approx. 155 yds per 50 g skein) 4 (5) skeins color fuchsia, 2 (3) skeins each color dark blue, dark red, and lilac
❖ Crochet hook U.S. size G/6 (Metric size 4.5) or size needed to obtain gauge
❖ Knitting needles U.S. size 6 (Metric size 4).
To save time, take time to check gauge!

Gauge
16 dc and 7 1/2 rows = 4 in. (10 cm)

Stitches
Chain (ch), double crochet (dc).
Block pat: Each block is 5 sts wide and 2 rows high. Use a separate ball for each section of color. When changing colors, work the last loop of the last st with the color of the next st.
2/2 ribbing: Row 1: *K2, p2*. Rep * to * across.
Row 2 and all foll rows: Work sts as established in previous row.

Note: See "Stitches and Techniques" for detailed instructions on stitches and shapings.

Back
With fuchsia, ch 80 (88). Break yarn. Work in dc in foll colors: Row 1: 5 dc in dark blue, *5 dc in dark red, 5 dc in dark blue*, rep * to * 3 times, end with 35 (43) dc in dark red. Work 2nd row in established color. Row 3: 5 dc in lilac, *5 dc in fuchsia, 5 dc in lilac*, rep * to * 3 times, end with 35 (43) dc in fuchsia. Row 4: Work in established colors. Rep these 4 rows 2 more times. Then work in

vertical stripe pat by repeating rows 3 and 4 of block pat until piece measures 9-1/2 in. (24 cm) from beg. Dec 5 dc at each edge of foll row. Work until armhole measures 4-3/4 in. (12 cm), then rep rows 1 to 4 as at lower edge. When armhole measures 9-3/4 in. (24.5 cm), after 10 rows in block pat, fasten off.

Front
Beg front same as back, but rev colors on first row: Row 1: 35 (43) dc in dark red, 5 dc in dark blue, 5 dc in dark red, etc. Shape armholes as on back. Work 2 rows after armhole, right side facing, work 25 (28) dc in fuchsia and leave rem dc unworked. When armhole measures 4-3/4 in. (12 cm), work 2 rows in dark red, 2 rows in fuchsia. Work 3 vertical stripes in dark red and end with 1 stripe in fuchsia. When the armhole measures 10-3/4 in. (27 cm), fasten off. Leave the center 20 (22) sts unworked and work last 25 (28) sts until armhole measures 4-3/4 in. (12 cm). Work in block pat. At neck edge, work 0 (3) dc in dark blue, 5 sts in dark red, *5 dc in dark blue, 5 dc in dark red*, rep * to * once. Work foll row in established colors. Rows 3 and 4: Work lilac above dark blue and fuchsia above dark red. When piece measures same as first half, fasten off.

Left Sleeve
With fuchsia, ch 55. Break yarn. Work in dc in foll colors: *5 dc in dark blue, 5 dc in lilac*, rep * to * 4 times, end with 5 dc in dark blue. Work until sleeve measures 8 in. (20 cm). Inc 1 dc at each edge 14 times as foll: Inc in the first and 2nd row, work 3rd row without inc. Rep these 3 rows until you have 83 sts. At the same time, when piece measures 8 in. (20 cm) over center 45 dc in block pat, work in stripe pat at each edge as foll: Rows 1 and 2: Work in dark red above dark blue and fuchsia above lilac. Rows 3 and 4: Work in dark blue above dark red and lilac above fuchsia. Rep rows 1 to 4. Work until sleeve measures 16-3/4 in. (42 cm), end with 1 row in dark red and fuchsia. Work next 2 rows as foll: Fuchsia above the first and last 20 dark red dc,

above the 5 fuchsia dc work in lilac and above the 5 dark red dc work in dark blue. Fasten off.

Right Sleeve

Work same as left sleeve, but beg with block pat, then stripe pat. When sleeve measures 8 in. (20 cm), work as foll: Rows 1 and 2: 5 sts in dark blue, *5 dc in lilac, 5 dc in dark blue*, rep * to * 4 times. Rows 3 and 4: Work in dark red above dark blue and fuchsia above lilac. Work 16 rows in block pat, then work in vertical stripes by rep rows 1 and 2 of block pat. At each edge of center 45 dc, work in dark blue. Work last 2 rows as on left sleeve, but work in lilac above dark blue sts at edges and work in established colors.

Finishing

Block pieces to indicated measurements. With knitting needles and fuchsia, pick up and knit 82 (88) sts along lower edge of front and work in 2/2 ribbing. Bind off loosely. Work same ribbing on back. With knitting needles and fuchsia, pick up and knit 42 sts from each sleeve end and work 2-1/2 in. (6 cm) in 2/2 ribbing. Bind off. Neckband: With knitting needles and fuchsia, cast on 122 sts and work 5-1/4 in. (13 cm) in 2/2 ribbing, end with k2. Bind off loosely. Sew shoulder seams. Sew neckband to neck edges, lapping the right over left end at center front. Sew ends in place. Sew sleeves to armholes, matching center of sleeve with shoulder seams. Sew side and sleeve seams.

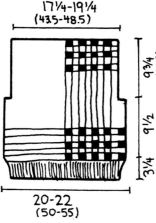

17¼-19¼
(43.5-48.5)

9¾
(24.5)

9½
(24)

3¼
(8)

20-22
(50-55)

BACK

6-7 5-5¼
(15.5-17.5) (12.5-13.5)

10¾
(27)

9½
(24)

3¼
(8)

20-22
(50-50)

FRONT

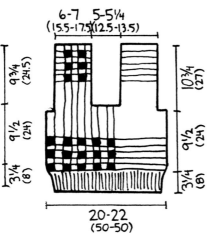

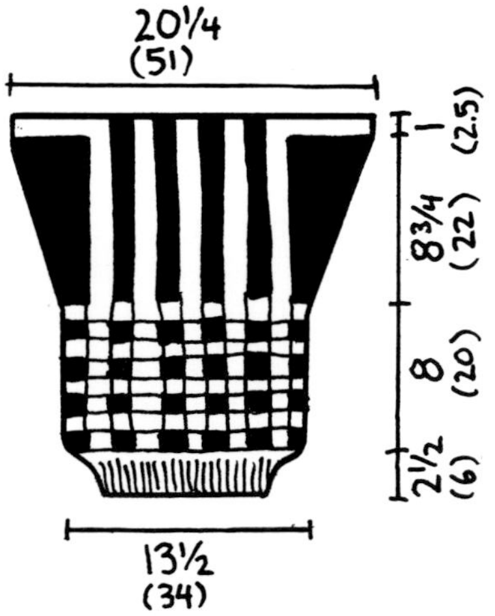

20¼
(51)

1
(2.5)

8¾
(22)

8
(20)

2½
(6)

13½
(34)

RIGHT SLEEVE 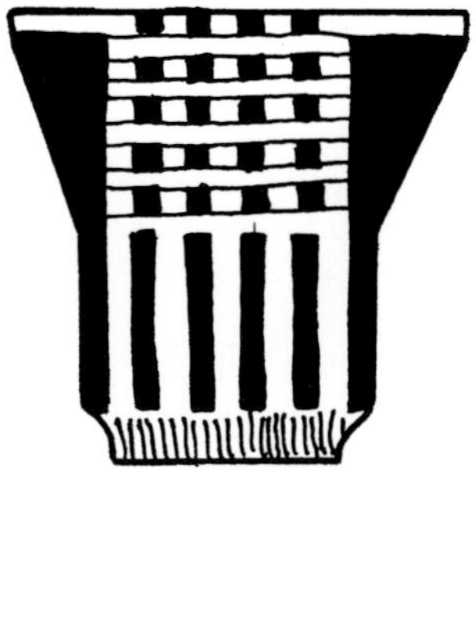   **LEFT SLEEVE**

V-Neck Pullover

Level: Intermediate

Size
❖ Woman's Small (Medium, Large, X Large), bust 30-32 (33-35, 36-38, 39-42) in. — 76-81.5 (84-89, 91.5-97, 99-107) cm
❖ Finished bust measurements: 35 (38-1/2, 41-1/2, 44-1/2) in. — 88 (96, 104, 112) cm
❖ Length: 26-1/4 (26-3/4, 27, 27-1/2) in. — 66 (67, 68, 69) cm

Materials
❖ Sport weight novelty cotton yarn (approx. 150 yds per 50 g skein) 7 (7, 8, 8) skeins color ecru
❖ Crochet hook U.S. size C/2 (Metric size 3)
❖ Knitting needles U.S. size 2 (Metric size 2.5) or size needed to obtain gauge
To save time, take time to check gauge!

Gauge
10 motifs (1 motif = 1 hdc and 1 sc) and 16 rows = 4 in. (10 cm)

Stitches
Chain (ch), slip st (sl), single crochet (sc), half double crochet (hdc).
Pat st: Worked in a sc row.
Row 1: Ch 1 = 1 border st, *1 hdc and 1 sc in the foll sc, skip 1 sc*, rep * to *, end with 1 hdc = 1 border st.
Row 2: Ch 1, *1 hdc and 1 sc in the foll sc, skip 1 hdc*, rep * to *, end with 1 hdc.
Repeat the 2nd row.
1/1 ribbing: Row 1: *K1, p1*. Rep * to * across.
Row 2 and all foll rows: Work sts as established in previous row.

Note: See "Stitches and Techniques" for detailed instructions on stitches and shapings.

Back
With knitting needles, cast on 90 (94, 98, 102) sts and work 2 1/2 in. (6 cm) in 1/1 ribbing. Bind off loosely. In the bound off row, with crochet hook work 88 (96, 104, 112) sc with 1 border st at each edge. Work in pat st, beg with row 1 = 44 (48, 52, 56) motifs with 1 border st at each edge. When piece measures 15-1/4 in. (38.5 cm), shape armholes. Dec 2 (2, 3, 3) motifs at each edge of every 2nd row once, dec 1 motif 1 (2, 2, 2) times, dec 1/2 motif twice. (Slip over the dec motifs at the beg of the row and leave the dec motifs at the end of the row unworked.) Work the rem 36 (38, 40, 44) motifs until armhole measures 10 (10-1/4, 10-3/4, 11) in. - 25 (26, 27, 28) cm. Leave the center 10 (10, 10, 12) motifs unworked. Work each shoulder separately. At neck edge of every row, dec 1 motif once, dec 1/2 motif twice. At the same time, at the shoulder edge of every row, dec 3 motifs 3 times, dec 2 (3, 4, 5) motifs once. Fasten off.

Front
Work same as back until piece measures 13-1/2 (14, 14, 14-1/4) in. - 34 (35, 35, 36) cm. Divide work into 2 parts. Work each side separately. At neck edge of every row, dec 1/2 motif 7 (7, 7, 8) times. At neck edge of every 4th row, dec 1/2 motif 7 (7, 7, 8) times. When piece measures 15-1/4 in. (38.5 cm), shape armholes. Dec 2 (2, 3, 3) motifs once, dec 1 motif 1 (2, 2, 2) times, dec 1/2 motif twice. Shape shoulders at same length as back.

Neckband
With knitting needles, cast on 160 (168, 168, 174) sts and work 1-1/4 in. (3 cm) in 1/1 ribbing. At the same time, at each edge of every row, inc 1 st. Bind off by knitting all sts.

Armbands
With knitting needles, cast on 158 (164, 168, 174) sts and work 1-1/4 in. (3 cm) in 1/1 ribbing. Bind off by knitting all sts.

Finishing
Block pieces to indicated measurements. Sew shoulder and side seams. Sew neckband to neck edge with inc edge at center front. Sew center seam. Sew the armbands to armhole edges and sew seams.

(continued on page 143)

Block Pullover

Level: Challenging

Size
❖ Woman's Small (Medium, Large), bust 30-32 (33-35, 36-38) in. — 76-81.5 (84-89, 91.5-97) cm
❖ Finished bust measurements: 38-1/2 (43, 48) in. — 96 (108, 120) cm, length: 23-1/4 in. (58 cm)
❖ Sleeve seam: 18 in. (45 cm)

Materials
❖ Mohair worsted weight yarn (approx. 110 yds per 50 g skein) 6 (7, 8) skeins color black, 2 skeins color purple, 1 (1, 2) skeins each color light green and blue, 1 skein each color pink, green, and yellow
❖ Crochet hook U.S. size H/8 (Metric size 5) or size needed to obtain gauge
❖ Knitting needles U.S. size 7 (Metric size 4.5). Circular knitting needle U.S. size 7 (Metric size 4.5).
To save time, take time to check gauge!

Gauge
11 dc and 7 rows = 4 in. (10 cm)

Stitches
Chain (ch), slip st (sl), double crochet (dc)
Jacquard st: When changing colors, work the last loop of the last st with the color of the next st. Do not carry unused yarn across wrong side of work. Work 4 rows in established colors.
2/2 ribbing: Row 1: *K2, p2*. Rep * to * across.
Row 2 and all foll rows: Work sts as established in previous row.

Note: See "Stitches and Techniques" for detailed instructions on stitches and shapings.

Body
Work the sweater in 1 piece, beg at lower edge of front. With knitting needles and black, cast on 54 (62, 66) sts and work 2 in. (5 cm) in 2/2 ribbing as foll: 1 border st, *k2, p2*, rep * to *, end with 1 border st. Bind off loosely. With

crochet hook, work in block pat, inc 1 (0, 1) st at each edge for border st = 56 (62, 68) sts. Work as foll: Row 1: Right side facing, 1 border st, *9 (10, 11) dc with black, 9 (10, 11) dc in yellow*, rep * to * across, end with 1 border st. Work border st in same color as adjacent st. Always beg with ch 3 = 1 border st. Rows 2 to 8: Work in established colors with 1 border st at each edge. Row 9: Right side facing, 1 border st, *9 (10, 11) dc in pink, 9 (10, 11) dc in black*, rep * to *, end with 1 border st. Rows 10 to 15: Work pink above black and black above pink. Row 16: Wrong side facing, 1 border st, *9 (10, 11) dc with red, 9 (10, 11) dc with black*, rep * to *, end with 1 border st. Rows 17 to 21: Work in established colors with 1 border st at each edge. When piece measures 14 in. (35 cm), ch 45 (45, 44) + ch 3 for the first dc. For the left sleeve, make a separate ch of 45 (45, 44) in black. Row 22: Wrong side facing, work over the ch for the right sleeve, work over the body and work over left sleeve sts. Work as foll: Work the first dc in the 4th ch from the hook, 9 (5, 0) dc with purple, *9 (10, 11) dc with black, 9 (10, 11) dc with purple*, rep * to *, end row with 9 (5, 0) dc with black, 1 border st. Rows 23 to 26: Work in established colors with 1 border st at each edge. Row 27: Right side facing, 1 border st, 9 (5, 0) dc with blue, *9 (10, 11) dc with black, 9 (10, 11) dc with blue*, rep * to *, end with 9 (5, 0) dc with black, 1 border st. Rows 28 to 30: Work in established

colors with 1 border st at each edge. Piece will measure 18-3/4 in. (48 cm). Leave the center 10 sts unworked. Work the right half first. At neck edge of every row, dec 2 (2, 3) sts once, dec 1 st 2 (3, 3) times. Row 31: Right side facing, 1 border st, 9 (5, 0) dc with black, *9 (10, 11) dc with green, 9 (10, 11) dc with black*, work * to * twice, end with 4 (5, 6) dc with green, turn. Rows 32 to 33: Work in established colors with 1 border st at sleeve edge. Row 34: Wrong side facing, 0 (0, 1) dc in black, *9 (10, 11) dc in light green, 9 (10, 11) dc in black*, rep * to *, end with 9 (5, 0) dc in light green, 1 border st. Row 35: Work in established colors with 1 border st at sleeve edge. Row 36: Work black above light green and light green above black with 1 border st at sleeve edge. Row 37: Work same as 35th row. For the back neck, make a chain in black of 18 (20, 22) sts. Break yarn. The piece measures 23-1/4 in. (58 cm) from beg. Work the left half same as right half, rev neck shapings. Join the right half, back neck and left half with a sl st and work in block pat across all sts for back. Row 38: Wrong side facing, 1 border st, 9 (5, 0) dc with black, *9 (10, 11) dc in light green, 9 (10, 11) dc in black*, rep * to *, end with 9 (5, 0) dc with light green, 1 border st. Row 39: Like row 35, with 1 border st at each edge. Row 40: Like row 36, but with 1 border st at each edge. Row 41: Like row 39. Row 42: Like row 38, but substitute green for light green. Rows 43 and 44: Work in established colors with

1 border st at each edge. Row 45: 1 border st, 9 (5, 0) dc with blue, *9 (10, 11) dc with black, 9 (10, 11) dc with blue*, rep * to *, end with 9 (5, 0) dc with black, 1 border st. Rows 46 to 48: Work in established colors with 1 border st at each edge. Row 49: Like row 27, but substitute purple for blue. Rows 50 to 53: Like rows 23 to 26. Sl st over 45(45, 44) sts, work center 56 (62, 68) sts for back and leave last 45 (45, 44) sts unworked. Row 54: 1 border st, *9 (10, 11) dc with red, 9 (10, 11) dc with black*, rep * to *, end with 1 border st. Rows 55 to 59: Work in established colors with 1 border st at each edge. Row 60: Like row 16, but substitute pink for red. Rows 61 to 66: Like rows 10 to 15. Row 67: Like row 9, but substitute yellow for pink. Rows 68 to 74: Like rows 2 to 8. Fasten off. Piece will measure 21-1/4 in. (53 cm) from back neck. With knitting needles and black, pick up and knit 54 (62, 66) sts from last row of crochet piece. Work in 2/2 ribbing as on front. Bind off loosely.

Finishing
Block pieces to indicated measurements. With knitting needles and black, pick up and knit 30 sts from each sleeve end and work in 2/2 ribbing as on front for 1-1/2 (1-1/2, 2) in. - 4 (4, 5) cm. Bind off loosely. With circular needle and black, pick up and knit 56 sts from around neck and work 1-1/4 in. (3 cm) in 2/2 ribbing as on front. Bind off loosely. Sew side and sleeve seams.

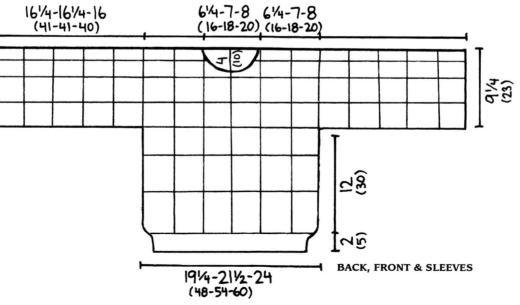

16¼-16¼-16 (41-41-40)   6¼-7-8 (16-18-20)   6¼-7-8 (16-18-20)

9¼ (23)

12 (30)

2 (5)

19¼-21½-24 (48-54-60)

BACK, FRONT & SLEEVES

Zigzag Jacquard Pullover

Level: Intermediate

Size

❖ Woman's Small (Medium, Large), bust 30-32 (33-35, 36-38) in. — 76-81.5 (84-89, 91.5-97) cm

❖ Finished bust measurements: 41-1/2 (44, 47) in. — 105 (112, 120) cm, length: 21-3/4 in. — 54 cm

❖ Sleeve length: 17 in. (43 cm)

Materials

❖ Mayflower Cotton 8 (approx. 186 yds per 50 g skein) 3 (4, 4) skeins color black, 3 skeins each color red and gray, 2 skeins each color pink and white.

❖ Crochet hook U.S. size C/2 (Metric size 3) or size needed to obtain gauge.

❖ Knitting needles U.S. size 3 (Metric size 3).

To save time, take time to check gauge!

Gauge

22 dc and 10-1/2 rows = 4 in. (10 cm).

Stitches

Chain (ch), double crochet (dc) Jacquard st: Work by foll chart in dc. When changing colors, work the last loop of the last st with the color of the next st. Hold the unused yarn against the back of work. When inserting hook, work around the unused yarn so that the new sts hold it against the work. The vertical lines on the chart indicate the pat rep. Beg row with ch 3 = first dc.

1/1 ribbing: Row 1: *K1, p1*. Rep * to * across.

Row 2 and all foll rows: Work sts as established in previous row.

Note: See "Stitches and Techniques" for detailed instructions on stitches and shapings.

Back

With crochet hook and black, ch 118 (126, 134) + ch 3 = first dc. Row 1: With black, work 1 dc in the 5th ch from hook, 1 dc in each ch = 118

(126, 134) dc. Row 2: Wrong side facing: *3 dc in pink, 1 dc in white*, rep * to * 28 (30, 32) times, end with 2 dc in pink. Continue by foll chart to point B. The total length is 18-1/2 in. (46.5 cm). Fasten off.

Front

Work same as back.

Sleeves

With crochet hook and gray, ch 62 (66, 70) + ch 3 = first dc. Row 1: With gray, work 1 dc in the 5th ch from the hook, 1 dc in each ch = 62 (66, 70) sts. Row 2: With pink, work in dc. Inc 1 st at each edge. Row 3: Right side facing, continue by foll chart, beg at point C. Center the chart at point X. Inc 1 st at each edge of every 2nd row 15 times. Inc 1 st at each edge of every row 4 times = 102 (106, 110) sts. Work to point D on chart, then work 5 rows in dc: 1 row in red, 1 row in gray, 1 row in pink, 2 rows in black. The sleeve will measure 15-1/2 in. (39 cm). Fasten off.

Finishing

Block pieces to indicated measurements. With knitting needles and red, pick up and knit 118 (126, 134) sts from lower edge of back and work in 1/1 ribbing as foll: 7 rows in red, 14

rows in black. Bind off. Along upper edge of back, with knitting needles and red, pick up and knit 151 (161, 171) sts and work 3/4 in. (2 cm) in 1/1 ribbing. Bind off. Work same along upper and lower edge of front. With knitting needles and red, pick up and knit 62 (66, 70) sts along each sleeve end and work as foll: 4 rows in red, 8 rows in black. Bind off loosely. Sew shoulder seams, leaving center 9-1/4 (9-1/2, 10) in. - 23 (24, 25) cm open for neck. Sew sleeves to armholes, matching center of sleeve with shoulder seams. Sew side and sleeve seams.

9¼-9½-10
(23-24-25)

3/4
(2)

18½
(46.5)

2½
(6)

20¾-22-23½
(52.5-56-60)

FRONT - BACK

18-18¾-19½
(45-47-49)

15½
(39)

½
(1)

10¼-11½-12¼
(27-29-31)

SLEEVE

Key to Chart

⬤ = black

• = pink

☐ = white

━ = red

⊠ = gray

B

D

C

X

JACQUARD CHART

CARDIGANS

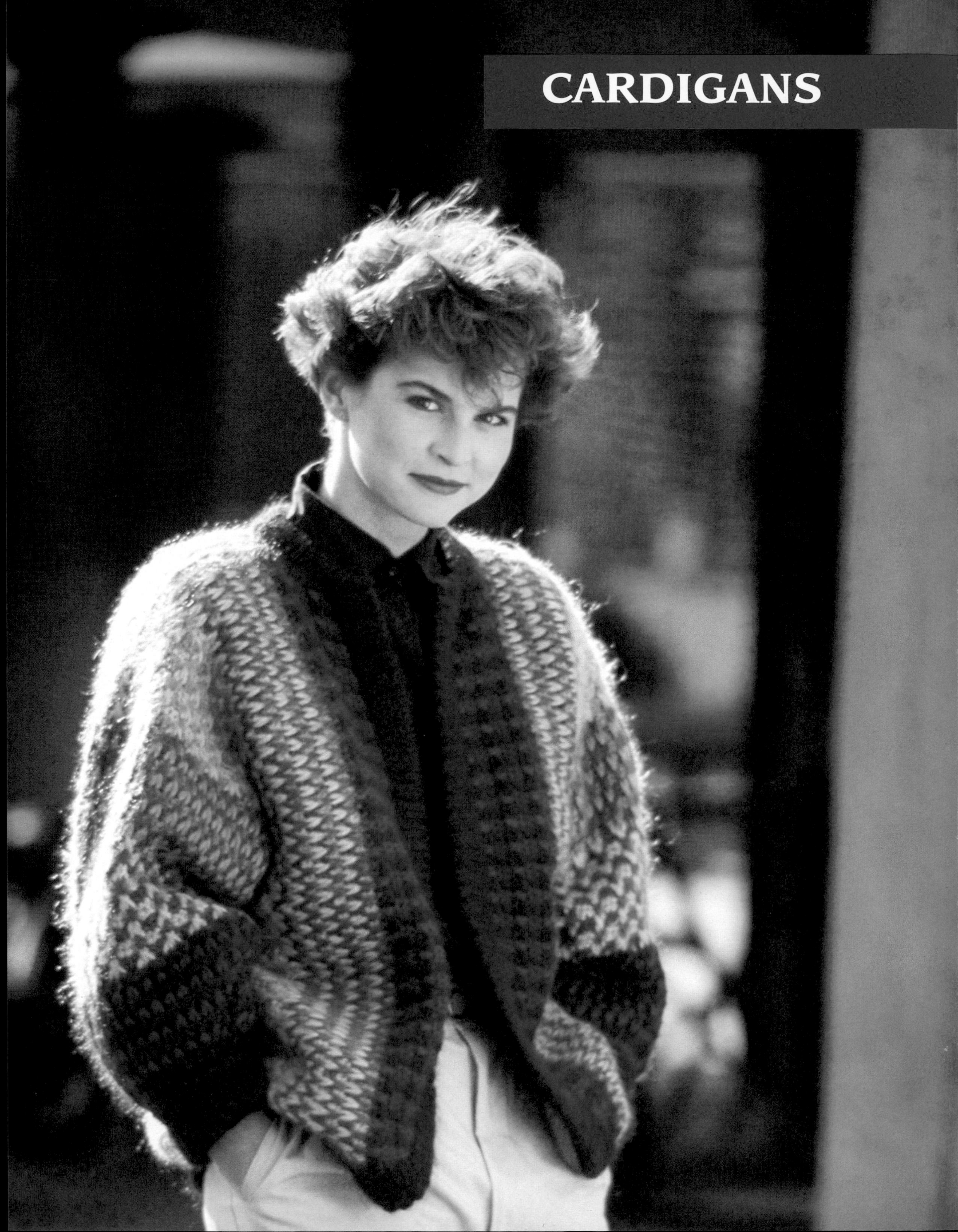

Sport Cardigan

Level: Challenging

Size

❖ Woman's Small (Medium, Large), bust 30-32 (33-35, 36-38) in. — 76-81.5 (84-89, 91.5-97) cm

❖ Finished bust measurements: 43-1/4 (47, 51) in. — 108 (118, 128) cm

❖ Length: 28 in. (70 cm)

❖ Sleeve seam: 17-1/4 in. (43 cm)

Materials

❖ Sport weight mohair yarn (approx. 165 yds per 50 g skein) 5 skeins color dark blue, 4 (4, 5) skeins color light blue, 3 (3, 4) skeins color green, 3 skeins each color light green and green/blue

❖ Crochet hook U.S. size E/4 (Metric size 3.5) or size needed to obtain gauge

❖ Knitting needles U.S. size 4 (Metric size 3.5)

To save time, take time to check gauge!

Gauge

16 sts and 16 rows = 4 in. (10 cm)

Stitches

Chain (ch), single crochet (sc), double crochet (dc)

Relief dc around sc of the previous row: Worked in dc by working around post of the st 2 rows below. Yo before inserting hook.

Relief dc around a relief dc 2 rows below: Insert hook around the post from back to front. Yo before inserting hook.

Relief motif: Worked on a multiple of 4. Beg sc rows with ch 1. Beg dc rows with ch 3.

Motif A: Row 1: With dark blue, work 1 sc in each ch, beg with the 3rd ch from the hook. Row 2: With dark blue, 1 dc in each st. Work the last loop with green/blue. Row 3: With green/blue, *1 sc in the foll dc, 1 relief dc in the foll sc 2 rows below*, rep * to *. Row 4: With green/blue, work 1 dc in each st, work last loop with dark blue. Row 5: With dark blue, *1 sc in the foll dc, 1 relief dc in the foll relief dc 2 rows below*, rep * to *. Row 6: With dark blue, 1 dc in each st. Work the last loop with green/blue. Row 7: With green/blue, *1 sc in the foll dc, 1 relief dc in the foll relief dc 2 rows below*, rep * to *. Always rep the 4th to the 7th row.

Motif B: Row 1: Wrong side facing, with green, 1 dc in each st. Work the last loop with light blue. Row 2: With light blue, *1 sc in the foll dc, skip 1 relief dc, 1 relief dc in the foll relief dc 2 rows below, 1 sc in the foll dc, 1 relief dc in the skipped relief dc*, rep * to *. Row 3: With light blue, 1 dc in each st. Work the last loop with green. Row 4: With green, like row 2. Rep 1st to 4th rows.

Motif C: Work rows 4 to 7 of motif A, but work in green instead of green/blue and light green instead of dark blue.

Motif D: Work 1st to 4th rows of motif B. Substitute light green for green.

Motif E: Work rows 4 to 7 of motif A, but work with green instead of green/blue and light blue instead of dark blue.

Motif F: Row 1: Wrong side facing, with dark blue, 1 dc in each st. Work the last loop in green/blue. Row 2: With green/blue, *1 sc in each of the foll 3 dc, 1 relief dc in the foll relief dc 2 rows below*, rep * to *. Row 3: With green/blue, 1 dc in each st. Work the last loop with dark blue.

Row 4: With dark blue, *1 sc in the foll dc, 1 relief dc in the center of the 3 sc 2 rows below, 1 sc in each of the foll 2 dc*, rep * to *. Row 5: with dark blue, 1 dc in each st. Work the last loop with green/blue. Row 6: With green/blue, *1 sc in each of the foll 3 dc, 1 relief dc around the center of the 3 sc 2 rows below*, rep * to *. Always rep rows 3 to 6.

Pat border: *K2, p1*, rep * to *. Work foll rows by working as established.

Note: See "Stitches and Techniques" for detailed instructions on stitches and shapings.

Body

With crochet hook and dark blue, ch 58 (60, 62). Work in motif A - 57 (59, 61) sc. Inc 1 st at each edge every 3/4 in. (2 cm) 6 (3, 0) times. Inc 1 st at each edge every 1/2 in. (1.5 cm) 15 (19, 23) times = 99 (103, 107) sts. Work inc sts in pat st. Work 5 in. (12.5 cm) in motif A, 5 in. (12.5 cm) in motif B, 4 in. (10 cm) in motif C and 1/4 in. (1 cm) in motif D, end on right side row. Piece will measure 14 -1/4 in. (36 cm). Work 99 (103, 107) sts in motif D. Ch 59 (57, 55) + ch 1 and slip st to beg of row. Make another ch and join to end of row = 217 sts and continue in motif D until sleeve measures 3-1/2 (4, 4 -1/4) in. - 8.5 (10, 11) cm. Now work 2-3/4 (3-1/4, 3-3/4) in. - 7 (8, 9.5) cm in motif E. Dec 1 st at left edge for lower edge of front. Work in motif E until body measures 6-1/4 (7-1/4, 8-1/4) in. - 16 (18.5, 21) cm from beg. Divide work in 2 parts for front. Work the first 106 sts in motif F. Dec alternately 1 and 2 sts at left edge 12 times = 18 dec sts. At the same time, at neck edge of every row, dec 2 sts twice. At neck edge of every 2nd row, dec 1 st twice. After the last dec on the left front, motif F measures 3 in. (7.5 cm). The body measures 9-1/4 (10-1/4, 11-1/4) in. - 23.5 (26, 28.5) cm. Fasten off. Ch 82 + ch 1 for the first sc in dark blue. Work in motif F, rev shapings of right front for neck and lower edge. On the first row you will have 82 sc in dark blue. Rep rows 3 to 6 of motif F until piece measures 3 in. (7.5 cm) = 106 sts. Work on back sts, leaving the first 3 sts unworked and work rem 107 sts in motif F. At neck edge every 1/2 in. (1.5 cm) inc 1 st once. Work until piece measures 8 in. (20.5 cm) from beg of neck. Inc 1 st at neck edge. Work until neck measures 8-3/4 in. (22 cm), ch 3 at neck edge, then sl st to sts of right front. Fasten off. Work over 216 sts in motif E, work the first 106 sts of right front, ch 3 and foll 107 sts of back. After 3/4 in. (2 cm) at left edge, inc 1 st. Work 3 (3-1/2, 4) in. - 8.5 (9.5, 11) cm in motif E and motif D. Leave 59 (57, 55) sts unworked at each edge. Work sleeve by rev shapings, dec at each edge instead of inc. Fasten off.

Finishing

Block pieces to indicated measurements. With knitting needles and dark blue, work in border pat. Beg first row with k2, p1, end row with k1. After 2-3/4 in. (7 cm), work 1 row of eyelets as foll: *k1, k2 tog, yo*, rep * to *, end with k1. On foll row, resume border pat. When border measures 5-1/2 in. (14 cm), bind off all sts. Along the front and lower edges of body, with knitting needles and dark blue, pick up 397 sts and work 10 rows of pat border. Work 1 row of eyelets, then work 10 rows of pat border. Bind off loosely. With knitting needles and dark blue, pick up and knit 50 sts around neck and work in pat border, beg and end first row with k2. Inc 3 sts at each edge of every 2nd row 4 times. Work new sts in pat = 74 sts. Work eyelet row as on sleeve. Dec 3 sts at each edge of every 2nd row 4 times. After 10 rows of pat border, after eyelet row, bind off rem 50 sts. Sew armhole border. Fold borders in half at eyelet row to inside and sl st in place. Sew side and sleeve seams.

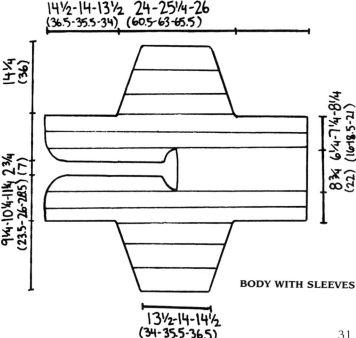

14½-14-13½
(36.5-35.5-34) 24-25¼-26
(60.5-63-65.5)

14¼
(36)

8¾ 6¼-7¼-8¼
(22) (16-18.5-21)

9¼-10¾-11¼ 2¾
(23.5-26-28.5) (7)

BODY WITH SLEEVES

13½-14-14½
(34-35.5-36,5)

Worsted Jacquard Cardigan

Level: Challenging

Size
❖ Woman's Small (Large), bust 30-32 (36-38) in. — 76-81.5 (91.5-97) cm
❖ Finished bust measurements: 43-1/4 (48) in. — 108 (120) cm
❖ Length: 27 (27-1/2) in. — 68 (69) cm
❖ Sleeve seam: 18 in. (45 cm)

Materials
❖ Mohair worsted weight yarn (approx. 110 yds per 50 g skein) 6 (7) skeins color blue, 2 (3) skeins each color yellow and pink and 1 (2) skeins color dark pink
❖ 5 buttons
❖ Crochet hook U.S. size H/8 (Metric size 5) or size needed to obtain gauge
❖ Knitting needles U.S. size 8 (Metric size 5)
To save time, take time to check gauge!

Gauge
12-1/2 hdc = 4 in. (10 cm). 5 rows = 2-1/2 in. (6 cm)

Stitches
Chain (ch), half double crochet (hdc)
Jacquard st: When changing colors, work the last loop of the last st with the color of the next st. Hold the unused yarn against the back of work. When inserting hook, work around the unused yarn so that the new sts hold it against the work. Work entirely in hdc. Beg each row with ch 2 to turn which counts as the first hdc.
1/1 ribbing: Row 1: *K1, p1*. Rep * to * across.
Row 2 and all foll rows: Work sts as established in previous row.

Note: See "Stitches and Techniques" for detailed instructions on stitches and shapings.

Body
With knitting needles and blue, cast on 145 (161) sts and work in 1/1 ribbing, beg and end with k1. When border measures 1-1/4 in. (3 cm), make a buttonhole 3 sts from right edge. Bind off the 4th and 5th sts. On the foll row, cast on 2 sts over bound off sts. When border measures 2-1/2 in. (6 cm), place 7 sts on each edge on holders = 131 (147) sts. Bind off loosely. With crochet hook, work in jacquard hdc by centering chart at point M. Inc 1 hdc at each edge for seam. These border sts are not shown on chart. When piece measures 18-1/4 in. (45.5 cm) from beg, work the first 31 (35) hdc for right front, inc 1 hdc at armhole for seam. Work until piece measures 24-3/4 (25-1/4) in. - 62 (63.5) cm. At neck edge of every row, dec 2 hdc 3 times, dec 3 hdc once, dec 2 hdc once. Fasten off. Work over last 31 (35) hdc for left front by rev shapings. Work over center 61 (69) hdc for back, leaving 5 hdc unworked at each edge for armholes. At each edge of first row, inc 1 hdc = 63 (71) hdc. Work to same length as fronts. Fasten off.

Sleeves
With knitting needles and blue, cast on 38 (42) sts and work 2 in. (5 cm) in 1/1 ribbing. Bind off loosely. With crochet hook, work 38 (42) hdc along top of ribbing and work by centering jacquard chart. Inc 1 hdc at each edge of every 3rd row 10 times = 58 (62) hdc. When sleeve measures 18 in. (45 cm) from beg, fasten off.

Finishing
Block pieces to indicated measurements. Sew shoulder seams. With knitting needles and blue, pick up and knit 7 sts from holder on left front and inc 1 st at inner edge. Work in 1/1 ribbing until piece fits to neck edge. Bind off 1 st at inner edge and place rem 7 sts on holder. Make same border on right front, making 3 buttonholes 2 sts wide. Place buttonholes at 7, 13-1/4, 19-1/4 (7-1/4, 13-1/2, 19-3/4) in. - 18, 33, 48 (18.5, 34, 49.5) cm. Sew borders to front edge. With knitting needles and blue, pick up and knit 83 (85) sts around neck, including sts from front borders, beg and end on right side of work with k1. After 1/4 in. (1 cm), make last buttonhole above previous ones. Bind off when ribbing measures 1-1/4 in. (3 cm). Sew sleeves to armholes, matching center of sleeve with shoulder seams. Sew sleeve seams. Sew on buttons.

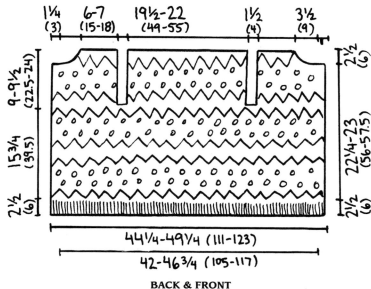

BACK & FRONT

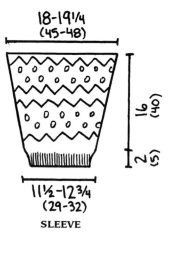

SLEEVE

Key to Chart

⊠ = blue
· = yellow
○ = pink
⊞ = dark pink

JACQUARD CHART

Colorful Jacquard Cardigan

Level: Challenging

Size

❖ Woman's Small (Medium, Large), bust 30-32 (33-35, 36-38) in. — 76-81.5 (84-89, 91.5-97) cm

❖ Finished bust measurements: 41-1/4 (44-3/4, 48-1/4) in. — 103 (112, 121) cm

❖ Length: 26 in. (65 cm)

❖ Sleeve seam: 17-1/2 in. (44 cm)

Materials

❖ Mohair worsted weight yarn (approx. 110 yds per 50 g skein) 3 skeins each color black and pink, 3(3, 4) skeins each color blue and red, 2 (3, 3) skeins each color yellow and turquoise

❖ Crochet hook U.S. size H/8 (Metric size 5) or size needed to obtain gauge

❖ Knitting needles U.S. size 8 (Metric size 5)

To save time, take time to check gauge!

Gauge

11 hdc and 8 rows = 4 in. (10 cm)

Stitches

Chain (ch), half double crochet (hdc).

Jacquard hdc: Work entirely in hdc. When changing colors, work the last loop of the last st with the color of the next st. Hold the unused yarn against the back of work. When inserting hook, work around the unused yarn so that the new sts hold it against the work. Foll the chart. Beg each row with ch 2 = 1 hdc and end each row with 1 hdc worked in the ch 2 of the previous row = 1 border st at each edge. These border sts are not shown on charts. Work border sts in the same color as the adjacent st. End the shoulders of both fronts with 1 row of hdc in black. Skip this row on the back.

1/1 ribbing: Row 1: *K1, p1*. Rep * to * across.

Row 2 and all foll rows: Work sts as established in previous row.

Note: See "Stitches and Techniques" for detailed instructions on stitches and shapings.

Back

With knitting needles and black, cast on 124 (134, 144) sts work 2-1/2 in. (6 cm) in 1/1 ribbing, making 1 buttonhole when border measures 1-1/4 in. (3 cm) 3 sts from right edge. For buttonhole, bind off 2 sts. On foll row, cast on 2 sts over bound off sts. When ribbing is complete, place 7 sts on each edge on holder and bind off rem sts.

With crochet hook, work 1 st in each bound off st by foll chart, inc 1 st at each edge = 1 border st at each edge = 112 (122, 132) sts. When piece measures 16 -3/4 (16-1/4, 16) in. - 42 (41, 40) cm divide work into 3 sections. Work the first 26 (28, 31) hdc for the right front, inc 1 st at armhole edge for border st = 27 (29, 32) hdc. Work foll chart until armhole measures 7 (7-1/2, 8) in. - 18 19, 20) cm. Shape Neck: At right edge of every row, dec 3

hdc once, 2 hdc once, 1 hdc twice. Work the rem 20 (22, 25) hdc until armhole measures 9-1/2 (10, 10-1/4) in. - 24 (25, 26) cm. Work 1 row of hdc in black, then fasten off. Slip st over the next 5 hdc and work foll 50 (56, 60) hdc, inc 1 st at each edge = 1 border st at each edge. Work in jacquard by foll chart until armhole measures same as right front and fasten off after last row of chart. Slip st over next 5 sts for armhole, work last 26 (28, 31) hdc as on right front, rev shapings. Fasten off.

Sleeves

With knitting needles and black, cast on 28 (32, 36) sts and work 1-1/2 in. (4 cm) in 1/1 ribbing. Bind off all sts. With crochet hook, work by foll chart, working 1 hdc in each bound off st, inc 1 st at each edge for border st. Beg at point A (B, C). Inc 1 st at each edge of every 3rd row 10 times = 50 (54, 58) hdc. Work to end of chart. The sleeve will measure 18-1/2 in. (46 cm) from beg. Fasten off.

Borders

With knitting needles and black, pick up 7 sts from left edge and cast on 1 st at inner edge and work until border fits along front edge. Bind off inner edge st and place rem 7 sts on holder.

Work same border on right edge, making 3 buttonholes evenly spaced along right border as on lower border, allowing for last buttonhole on neckband.

Finishing

Block pieces to indicated measurements. Sew borders to fronts. Sew shoulder seams. With knitting needles and black, pick up 61 (64, 69) sts around neck, including sts from holders and work 1-1/4 in. (3 cm) in 1/1 ribbing. Make last buttonhole above the previous ones when border measures 1/4 in (1 cm). Bind off loosely. Sew sleeves to armholes, matching center of sleeve with shoulder seams. Sew side and sleeve seams. Reinforce buttonholes and sew on buttons.

(continued on page 36)

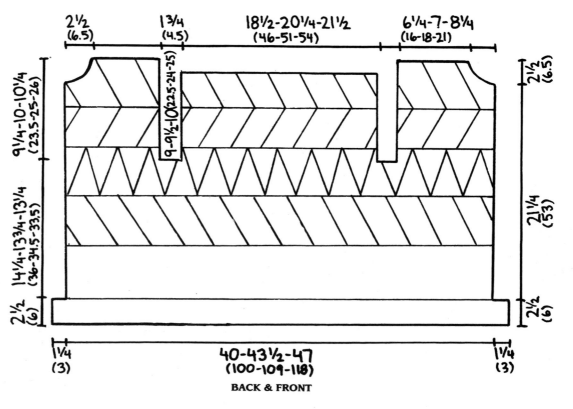

BACK & FRONT

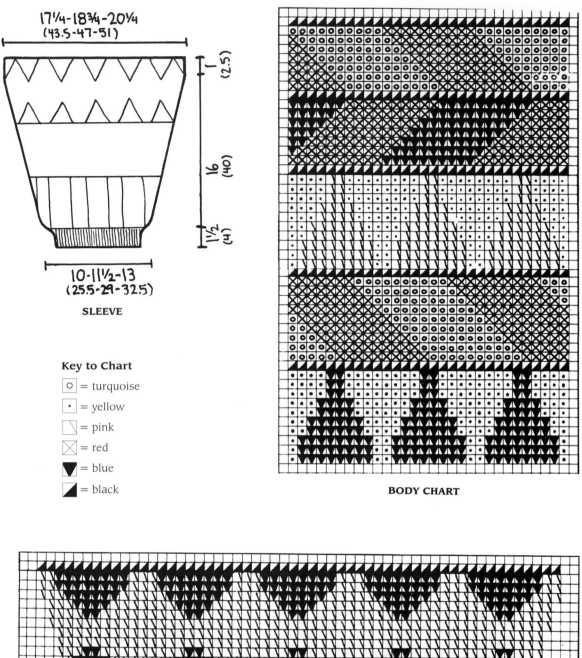

17¼-18¾-20¼
(43.5-47-51)

1
(2.5)

16
(40)

1½
(4)

10-11½-13
(25.5-29-32.5)

SLEEVE

Key to Chart

⊙ = turquoise

• = yellow

◸ = pink

⊠ = red

◢ = blue

◿ = black

BODY CHART

A B C

SLEEVE CHART

Jacket Cardigan

(photo on preceding page)

Level: Challenging

Size
❖ Woman's Large, bust 36-38 in. — (91.5-97) cm
❖ Finished bust measurements: 55 in. — (140) cm
❖ Length: 28 in. — (72) cm
❖ Sleeve seam to armhole: 17-1/4 in. — (44 cm)

Materials
❖ Mohair yarn worsted weight (approx. 110 yds per 50 g skein): 2 skeins color red, 5 skeins color rust, 3 skeins color black, 1 skein color moss green, 3 skeins color yellow brown, 1 skein each color dark red and bright red
❖ Neveda Gold (approx 257 yds per 50 g skein): 1 skein color gold.
❖ Worsted weight yarn (approx. 99 yds per 50 g skein): 2 skeins color black, 1 skein each color brown red and moss green
❖ 7 leather buttons
❖ Crochet hook U.S. size H/8 (Metric size 5) or size needed to obtain gauge
❖ Knitting needles U.S. size 6 (Metric size 4)
To save time, take time to check gauge!

Gauge
14-1/2 dc and 8 rows = 4 in. (10 cm)

Stitches
Chain (ch), slip st (sl), single crochet (sc), double crochet (dc)
Pat st: Skip 1 dc, *work 2 dc in the opening between the dcs, skip 2 dc,* rep * to *, end with 2 dc between the 2 dc, skip 1 dc, 1 dc in the last dc.
Bobble: For each bobble, *yo, insert hook in the foll st and draw up 1 loop, yo, drawing through 2 loops*, work * to * twice in the same st, yo and draw through the 4 loops on the hook.
Jacquard: Work the last loop of one color with a strand of the next color. Hold the unused yarn against the wrong side of work. When inserting hook, work around the unused yarn so that the new sts hold it against the back of work. Work by foll chart. Beg every dc row with ch 3 = 1 border st and end row with 1 dc worked in the turning ch of the previous row = 1 border st. Beg every sc row with ch 1 = 1 border st. End these rows with 1 sc in the turning ch = 1 border st. The border sts are not shown on chart. Work the border st in the same color as the adjacent color.
1/1 ribbing: Row 1: *K1, p1*. Rep * to * across.
Row 2 and all foll rows: Work sts as established in previous row.

Note: See "Stitches and Techniques" for detailed instructions on stitches and shapings.

Back and Front
With knitting needles and black worsted weight wool, cast on 171 sts and work 3/4-in. (2 cm) in 1/1 ribbing, beg and end with p1. At the right edge, bind off the 4th and 5th sts for buttonhole. On the foll row, cast on 2 sts over bound off sts. When the ribbing measures 2-1/2 in. (6.5) cm, place 7 sts at each edge on holders and loosely bind off the center 157 sts.
With crochet hook and black mohair, ch 205 and foll the chart. Work the first half by foll chart and work the 2nd half to correspond. Each dc is represented by two squares high and each sc in one square high on chart. Work as foll: Row 1: 1 dc in the 5th ch from the hook, 1 dc in each of the foll ch = 202 dc. Rows 2, 3, and 4: Dc, beg each row with ch 3. Rows 5 and 6: Work the motif with red in dc and the rem sts in pat st. Row 7: Sc. Row 8: Dc with bobbles in gold. Row 9: Sc. Rows 10, 11, and 12: Dc. Rows 13, 14, and 15: Work moss green sections in pat st and the rem sts in dc. Rows 16 to 29: Dc. Row 30: 1 border st, 45 dc, 6 sc (for the beg of the first armhole), 98 dc, 6 sc (for

the 2nd armhole), 45 dc, 1 border st. Divide work in 3 parts and work each part separately, beg with right front. Row 31: 1 border st, 43 dc, 1 sc, 1 border st, turn. Row 32: Sl 1, 1 border st, work the rem sts in moss green in pat st. Rows 33 and 34: Work in dc in moss green in pat st. Rows 35, 36, and 37: Dc. Row 38: Sc. Row 39: Work in dc with bobbles in gold over moss green sts. Row 40: Sc. Rows 41 to 45: Dc, but work the rust mohair sts in gold in pat st. Rows 46, 47, and 48: Dc. Row 49: 1 border st, 4 sc, complete row in dc. Row 50: 1 border st, 36 dc, 1 sc, 1 border st. Row 51: Sl 1, 1 border st, 1 sc, 34 dc, 1 border st. Row 52: Sc. Row 53: Sl 1, 1 border st, 1 sc, work in dc with bobbles in black to the end of the row. Row 54: Sc. Row 55: Dc. Row 56: Sc. Fasten off. Work the left front by rev shapings. Work the center 98 sts for the back, shaping armholes as on fronts.

Sleeves
With knitting needles and black worsted weight wool, cast on 39 sts and work 2-1/2 in. (6.5 cm) in 1/1 ribbing. Bind off loosely.
With crochet hook and rust mohair, ch 65 and work by foll chart. Row 1: Dc, working the first dc in the 5th ch from the hook. Row 2: Work in pat st. Beg with the 3rd row, inc at each edge, foll chart for place-

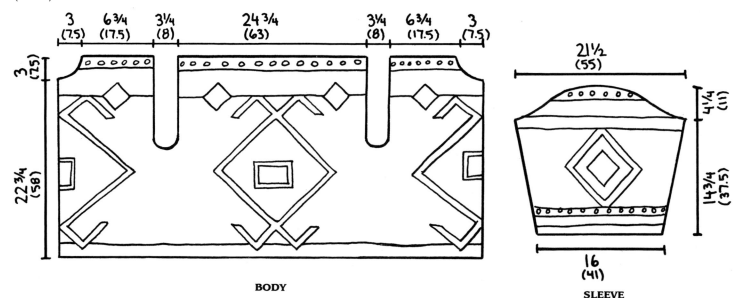

BODY

SLEEVE

ment of incs. Rows 3, 4, and 5:
Dc. Row 6: Sc. Row 7: Dc with
black bobbles. Row 8: Sc.
Rows 9 and 10: Dc. Rows 11
and 12: Work in dc, work in
moss green sections in pat st.
Rows 13 to 31: Dc. Beg dec for
sleeve cap, foll the chart. Row
32: Sc. Row 33: Dc with gold
bobbles. Row 34: Sc. Rows 35,
36, and 37: Work in pat st. Row
38: Dc. Row 39: Dc with black
bobbles. Rows 40 and 41: Dc.
Fasten off. Make a 2nd sleeve.

Front Bands

With knitting needles and
black worsted weight wool,
pick up the 7 sts from the left
border and inc 1 st at inner
edge. Work in 1/1 ribbing until
piece fits to front neck edge.
Place sts on holder. Work same
band on right border making 5
buttonholes like the buttonhole in the lower ribbing. Place
the last buttonhole 3-1/2 in. (9
cm) below neck edge, evenly
spacing the other 4 on front.

Finishing

Block pieces to indicated measurements. Sew the front bands
to fronts. Sew shoulder seams.
With knitting needles and black
worsted weight wool, pick up
75 sts along neck edge, including front bands and work 1-1/4
in. (3 cm) in 1/1 ribbing, making the last buttonhole after 1/4
in. (1 cm) on right front. Bind
off loosely. Sew sleeves to armholes. Sew sleeve seams. Sew
on the buttons. Embroider the
cross sts using double strand
of bright pink mohair, foll the
chart.

Key to Chart

O = red mohair

X = rust mohair

■ = black mohair

= = moss green mohair

V = dark red mohair

/ = 1 strand yellow brown/
    strand gold

I = 1 strand rust/1 strand gold

• = moss green wool

Z = brown red wool

⋮⋮ = gold

↘ = cross st in dark red mohair

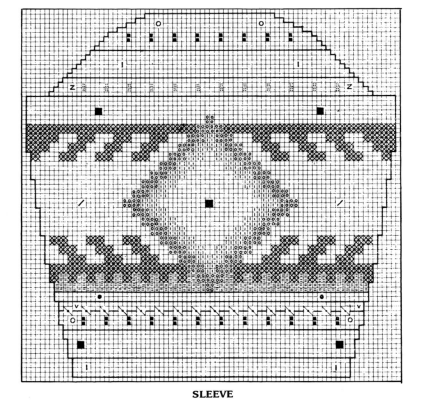

SLEEVE

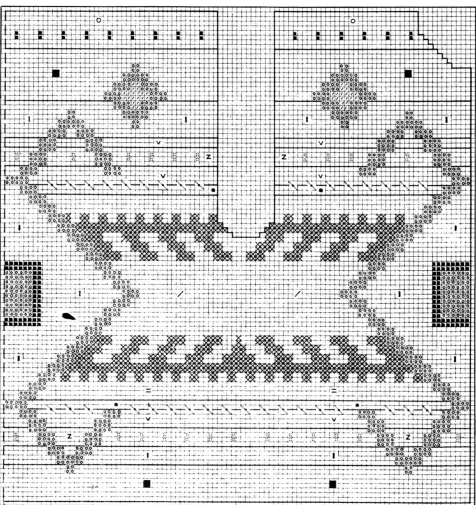

RIGHT FRONT & HALF BACK

Filet Cardigan

Level: Intermediate

Size

❖ Woman's Small (Medium, Large), bust 30-32 (33-35, 36-38) in. — 76-81.5 (84-89, 91.5-97) cm

❖ Finished bust measurements: 42-1/2 (45-1/2, 48) in. — 106 (114, 120) cm

❖ Length: 25-1/4 (25-1/2, 26) in. — 63 (64, 65) cm

❖ Sleeve seam: 17 in. (43 cm)

Materials

❖ Mohair worsted weight yarn (approx. 110 yds per 50 g skein) 9 (9, 10) skeins color green

❖ 7 buttons

❖ Crochet hook U.S. size F/5 (Metric size 4) or size needed to obtain gauge

❖ Knitting needles U.S. size 6 (Metric size 4)

To save time, take time to check gauge!

Gauge

9 squares and 7 rows = 4 in. (10 cm)

Stitches

Chain (ch), double crochet (dc). Filet St: Each open square = 1 dc, ch 1, skip 1 ch. Beg an open square row with ch 4. Work dc of foll row above dc of previous row.

1/1 ribbing: Row 1: *K1, p1*. Rep * to * across.

Row 2 and all foll rows: Work sts as established in previous row.

Note: See "Stitches and Techniques" for detailed instructions on stitches and shapings.

Body

With crochet hook, ch 195 (207, 219) + ch 3 = first dc. Row 1: 1 dc in the 5th ch from the hook, ch 1, skip 1 ch, 1 dc in the foll ch*, rep * to *, end with 1 dc = 96 (102, 108) squares with 1 dc at each edge as border sts. Beg and end row with 1 dc (each row has 1 extra dc at each edge for border st = 2 dc at each edge). When piece measures 14 (13-3/4, 13-1/2) in. - 35 (34.5, 34) cm, divide the work in 3 parts. Work the first 24 (25, 27) squares for the

right front. Dec the last dc at end of row so that the 23rd (24th, 26th) square is worked as foll: yo, work 1 dc in each of the foll 2 dc, working last 2 dc tog (= 1 dec square). Work rem 23 (24, 26) squares until armhole measures 7 (7-1/4, 7-1/2) in. - 18 (18.5, 19) cm. End on wrong side row. On foll right side row, dec as foll: Row 1: Work the first 18 (18, 19) squares, leave rem squares unworked. Row 2: Sl st across 2 squares, ch 3, work over rem sts = 16 (16, 17) squares. Work 2 rows even = 23-1/2 in. (59 cm). Fasten off. Work left front by rev shapings. Work center 48 (52, 54) squares for the front. Leave 1 square at each edge unworked for armhole. Work rem 46 (50, 52) squares to same length as fronts. Fasten off.

Sleeves

With crochet hook, ch 55 (57, 59) + ch 4 = first open square. Row 1: 1 dc in the 7th ch from the hook, *ch 1, skip 1 ch, 1 dc in the foll ch*, rep * to * across = 27 (28, 29) squares. At each edge alternately every 2nd and 3rd row, inc 1 square 8 times as foll: Row 2: Ch 3 to turn, 1 dc in the first dc. Work row in open squares and end with 2 dc in the last st. Row 3: Ch 4, 1 dc in the foll dc. Work row in open squares. In the last dc, ch

1, 1 dc to inc 1 dc = 1 open square inc at each edge. Continue in this way until you have 43 (44, 45) squares and 27 rows = 15 in. (38 cm) from beg. Fasten off.

Finishing

Block pieces to indicated measurements. Sew shoulder seams. With knitting needles, pick up and knit 137 (149, 161) sts along lower edge of body and work 2-1/2 in. (6 cm) in 1/1 ribbing. Bind off loosely. With knitting needles, pick up and knit 36 (38, 40) sts along lower edge of sleeve and work 2 in. (5 cm) in 1/1 ribbing. Bind off loosely. With knitting needles, pick up and knit 53 (57, 61) sts around neck and work 1 in. (2.5 cm) in 1/1 ribbing.

Beg and end at center front. Work back and forth. Bind off loosely. Along left front edge, work in sc as foll: Row 1: 9 sc along lower ribbing, 2 sc in each edge st, 4 sc along neck edge. Work 3 rows of sc. Fasten off. Work same border on right front, making 7 buttonholes on 3rd row, placing a buttonhole 1-1/4, 5-1/4, 9-1/4, 13-1/4, 17-1/4, 21-1/4, 25-1/4 in. - (3, 13, 23, 33, 43, 53, 63) cm from lower edge. For each buttonhole, ch 2, skip 2. On foll row, work 1 sc in each ch. Fasten off. Sew sleeves to armholes, matching center of sleeve with shoulder seams. Sew side and sleeve seams. Sew on buttons.

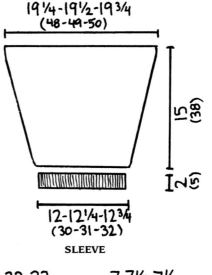

19 1/4-19 1/2-19 3/4
(48-49-50)

15
(38)

2
(5)

12-12 1/4-12 3/4
(30-31-32)

SLEEVE

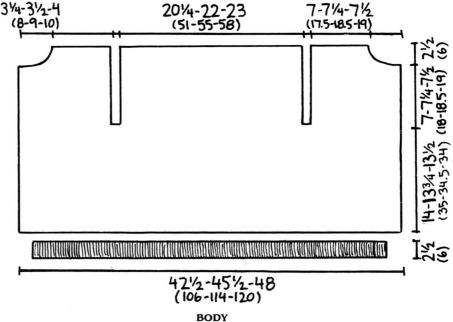

3 1/4-3 1/2-4
(8-9-10)

20 1/4-22-23
(51-55-58)

7-7 1/4-7 1/2
(17.5-18.5-19)

2 1/2
(6)

7-7 1/4-7 1/2
(18-18.5-19)

14-13 3/4-13 1/2
(35-34.5-34)

2 1/2
(6)

42 1/2-45 1/2-48
(106-114-120)

BODY

Pastel Striped Cardigan

Level: Challenging

Size
❖ Woman's Small (Medium, Large), bust 30-32 (33-35, 36-38) in. — 76-81.5 (84-89, 91.5-97) cm
❖ Finished bust measurements: 38-1/2 (40-1/2, 42-1/2) in. — 96 (102, 106) cm
❖ Length: 19-1/2 (21-1/4, 22-3/4) in. — 49 (53, 57) cm
❖ Sleeve seam: 14 (14-3/4, 15-1/2) in. — 35 (37, 39) cm

Materials
❖ Mayflower Cotton 8 (approx. 186 yds per 50 g skein) 6 (7, 8) skeins color black
❖ Kid Mohair sport weight yarn (approx. 90 yds per 50 g skein) 1 (2, 2) skeins each color lilac, light pink, salmon and 2 skeins each color light yellow, ecru and light blue
❖ 7 buttons
❖ Crochet hook U.S. size F/5 (Metric size 4) or size needed to obtain gauge
❖ Knitting needles U.S. size 2 (Metric size 2.5)
To save time, take time to check gauge!

Gauge
18 sts and 15 rows in pat st using 1 strand cotton and 1 strand of mohair

Stitches
Chain (ch), single crochet (sc).
Pat st: Multiple of 2 + ch 1 for the first st.
Row 1: 1 sc in the 3rd ch from the hook, *ch 1, skip 1 ch, 1 sc in the foll ch*, rep * to *. Row 2: Ch 1, 1 sc in the foll ch of the previous row, *ch 1, 1 sc in the foll ch*, rep * to *, ch 1, 1 sc in the last st. Rep these 2 rows.
Stripe pat: Use 1 strand of black cotton and 1 strand of mohair. Work as foll: *15 rows of black/light pink, 15 rows of black/lilac, 15 rows of black/light blue, 15 rows of black/ecru, 15 rows of black/light yellow, 15 rows of black/salmon*, rep * to *.
1/1 ribbing: Row 1: *K1, p1*. Rep * to * across.
Row 2 and all foll rows: Work sts as established in previous row.

Note: See "Stitches and Techniques" for detailed instructions on stitches and shapings.

Body
Worked sideways. Beg at lower edge of left sleeve. With crochet hook and black/lilac (black/lilac, black/light pink), ch 46 (48, 50) + ch 1 for the first st. Continue in pat st and stripe pat. Beg stripe pat with 10 (15, 5) rows of black/lilac (black/lilac, black/light pink). At each edge of every 5th (6th, 6th) row, inc 2 sts 8 times. Work inc sts in pat st. Work 78 (80, 82) sts for a total of 49 (52, 55) rows, end with 9 (7, 5) rows in black/light yellow. Piece will measure 13 (13-3/4, 14-1/2) in.-32.5 (34.5, 36.5) cm from beg. Inc 44 (50, 56) sts at each edge of foll row. Work inc sts in pat st = 166 (180, 194) sts until 22 (24, 26) rows from beg and body measures 5-3/4 (6-1/4, 7) in. - 14.5 (16, 17.5) cm. End with 1 row black/light pink. Work on 82 (90, 96) sts on the right edge for back for 28 rows total - 7-1/4 in. (18.5) cm, end with 14 rows

black/lilac. Lay aside work. Work on the 84 (90, 98) sts on left edge for left front. At right edge of every 2nd row, dec 4 sts twice, dec 2 sts twice. Work rem 72 (78, 86) sts for 12 rows total. Fasten off. Ch 72 (78, 86) + ch 1 for the first st with black/lilac. Work 12 rows in pat st. Shape neck by rev shapings, inc instead of dec. Work 84 (90, 98) sts until there are 12 rows in black/lilac. Join sts of front and back and work in pat st for 22 (24, 26) rows, end with the 6 (8, 10) rows of black/ecru. The back measures 19-1/4 (20-1/4, 21-1/4) in. - 48 (51, 53) cm. Dec 44 (50, 56) sts at each edge. Work rem 78 (80, 82) sts and continue in pat st for the right sleeve, rev shapings of left sleeve (dec instead of inc). Fasten off.

Finishing
Block pieces to indicated measurements. With knitting needles and black cotton, pick up and knit 113 (119, 125) sts along left front and work 1-1/4 in. (3 cm) in 1/1 ribbing. Bind off loosely. Work same border on right front. With knitting needles and black cotton, pick up and knit 1 st from every st

along right front edge and work 1 in. (2.5 cm) in 1/1 ribbing. Make 5 buttonholes. Place the first buttonhole 2-1/2 (2-3/4, 3) in.- 6.5 (7, 7.5) cm from neck edge and lower edge. Evenly space 3 more buttonholes between the edge ones. For each buttonhole, bind off 3 sts. On foll row, cast on 3 sts over bound off sts. When border measures 1-1/4 in. (3 cm), bind off. With knitting needles and black cotton, pick up and knit 44 (46, 48) sts along lower edge of each sleeve and work 1-1/4 in. (3 cm) in 1/1 ribbing. Bind off loosely. Sew side and sleeve seams. With knitting needles and black cotton, pick up and knit 103 sts around neck and work 1/4 in. (1 cm) in 1/1 ribbing. Make buttonhole above previous ones. Work border until it measures 1-1/4 in. (3 cm). Bind off loosely. With knitting needles and black cotton, pick up and knit 225 (241, 257) sts along lower edge and work 1/4 in. (1 cm) in 1/1 ribbing. Make buttonhole below previous ones. Work border until it measures 1-1/4 in. (3 cm). Bind off loosely. Sew on buttons.

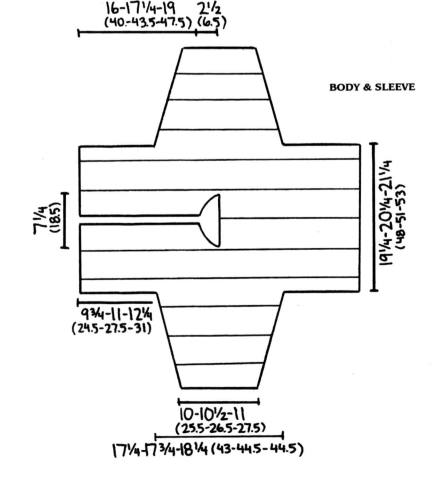

16-17 1/4-19 (40.-43.5-47.5) 2 1/2 (6.5)

BODY & SLEEVE

7 1/4 (18.5)

19 1/4-20 1/4-21 1/4 (48-51-53)

9 3/4-11-12 1/4 (24.5-27.5-31)

10-10 1/2-11 (25.5-26.5-27.5)

17 1/4-17 3/4-18 1/4 (43-44.5-44.5)

Worsted Cardigan

Level: Challenging

Size

❖ Woman's Small (Medium, Large), bust 30-32 (33-35, 36-38) in. — 76-81.5 (84-89, 91.5-97) cm

❖ Finished bust measurements: 42-1/2 (45-1/2, 49-1/2) in. — 106 (114, 124) cm

❖ Length: 23-1/2 (24, 24-1/4) in. — 59 (60, 61) cm

❖ Sleeve seam: 18 in. (45 cm)

Materials

❖ Worsted weight yarn (approx. 154 yds per 50 g skein) 19 (20, 22) skeins color ecru

❖ 7 leather buttons

❖ Crochet hook U.S. size G/6 (Metric size 4.5) or size needed to obtain gauge
To save time, take time to check gauge!

Gauge

16 dc and 7 1/2 rows in pat st = 4 in. (10 cm)

Stitches

Chain (ch), single crochet (sc), double crochet (dc), treble crochet (tr).

Front Relief dc: Work 1 dc in the front post of the st of the previous row, inserting hook right to left. Yo before inserting hook in st.

Back Relief dc: Work 1 dc in the back post of the st of the previous row, inserting hook right to left. Yo before inserting hook in st.

Pat st: Work by foll charts I and II.

Chart I: Worked on a ch base. Row 1: Right side facing, ch 3 = 1 dc, 1 tr in the 7th ch from hook, *1 dc in the 5th and 6th ch from hook (= long dc's), working behind the tr, skip 1, 2 long dc, 1 tr in skipped st working in front of 2 long dc, 1 dc, skip 2, 1 tr, 1 long dc in each skipped st working in back of tr*, rep * to *, end with 1 dc. Row 2: Wrong side facing, ch 3 = 1 dc, *skip 2, 1 tr, 1 long dc in each skipped st working in front of tr, skip 1, 2 long dc, tr in skipped st working in back of 2 long dc, 1 back relief dc in dc*, rep * to *, end with 1 dc. Row 3: Right side

facing: ch 3, *skip 2, 1 tr, 1 dc in each skipped st working in back of tr, skip 1, 2 dc, 1 tr in the skipped st working in front of the 2 long dc, 1 front relief dc in the relief dc*, rep * to *, end with 1 dc. Always rep the 2nd and 3rd row.

Chart II: Worked on a chain base.

Row 1: Ch 3 = 1 dc, 1 long dc in the 6th and 7th ch from hook, 1 tr in the 5th st working in front of the 2 long dc (all wrong side tr are worked from back to front), *1 dc in the foll ch, skip 2, 1 tr, 2 long dc in each of the skipped sts working in back of the tr*, rep * to *, end with 1 dc. Row 2: Ch 3 = 1 dc, *skip 1, 2 long dc, 1 tr in the skipped st working in back of the 2 long dc, 1 back relief dc, skip 2, 1 tr, 2 dc in the skipped sts working in front of the tr*, rep * to *, end with 1 dc. Row 3: Ch 3 = 1 dc, *skip 1, 1 long dc in the 2nd and 3rd st, 1 tr in the skipped st working in front of the 2 long dc, 1 front relief dc in the relief dc, skip 2, 1 tr in the 3rd st, 1 dc in the 2 skipped sts working behind the tr*, rep * to *, end with 1 dc. Always rep rows 2 and 3.

Note: See "Stitches and Techniques" for detailed instructions on stitches and shapings.

Back

Ch 86 (92, 100). Work in pat st foll chart II (I, II). Size small will have 11 motifs with half motif at each edge. Medium will have 13 full motifs and

will have 13 full motifs and large will have 13 motifs with half motif at each edge. Work until piece measures 12-1/4 in. (31 cm) from beg. Leave 6 sts unworked at each edge for armholes = 74 (80, 88) sts. For sizes small and large, at each edge work 1 relief dc and 1 dc for border sts. When armhole measures 9-1/4 (9-1/2, 10) in. - 23 (24, 25) cm, fasten off.

Right Front

Ch 41 (44, 48). Work in pat st foll chart I, but work 1 extra dc at center front edge as border st as foll: Row 1: Ch 3 = 1 border st, 1 dc in the 5th ch from hook, *skip 2, 1 tr, 1 long dc in each skipped st working in back of tr, skip 1, 2 long dc, 1 tr in skipped st working in front of 2 long dc, 1 dc in foll ch*, rep * to * = 5-1/2 (6 6-1/2) motifs. Work until piece measures 12-1/4 in. (31 cm) from beg. At left edge, leave 6 sts unworked for armhole. Work in pat until armhole measures 7 (7-1/2, 8) in. - 18 (19, 20) cm. At right edge of every row, dec 10 sts once, dec 1 st once = 1-1/2 motifs decreased. Work rem 24 (27, 31) sts until armhole measures 9-1/4 (9-1/2, 10) in. - 23 (24, 25) cm. Fasten off.

Left Front

Work same as right front, rev shapings. Work in pat st foll chart II (I, II). End at left edge after the extra relief dc (border st).

Sleeves

Ch 50 (57, 57). Work in pat st

foll chart I = 7 (8, 8) motifs. Inc 1 st at each edge every 1-1/4 in. (3 cm) 12 (10, 12) times. Work inc sts in pat = 74 (77, 81) sts. Work until piece measures 17-1/4 in. (43.5 cm) from beg. Fasten off.

Finishing

Block pieces to indicated measurements. Sew shoulder seams. Sew side seams. Along lower edge of body, work 1 row of dc, skipping every 4th st to obtain an odd number of sts. Work 4 rows of relief dc alternating back and front relief sts. Beg each row with ch 2 = first relief dc. Fasten off. Along lower edge of each sleeve, work 30 (34, 34) sc. Work 1 row of dc and 4 rows of relief dc as on body. Fasten off. Sew sleeves to armholes, matching center of sleeve with shoulder seams and sewing top of sleeve to armhole edges. Sew sleeve seams. Around the neck, work 65 (65, 67) sc with right side facing, then work 1 row dc and 1 row relief dc as on lower edge. Fasten off. Along center edge of left and right fronts, work 4 rows of sc as foll: Row 1: wrong side facing, work 2 sc per row, on borders work alternately 1 and 2 sc per row. Row 2: Sc. Row 3: Sc, but on the right front, make 7 buttonholes evenly spaced. For each buttonhole: Ch 2, skip 2 sc. Row 4: Work in sc, but on the right front, work 1 sc in each ch.

(continued on page 50)

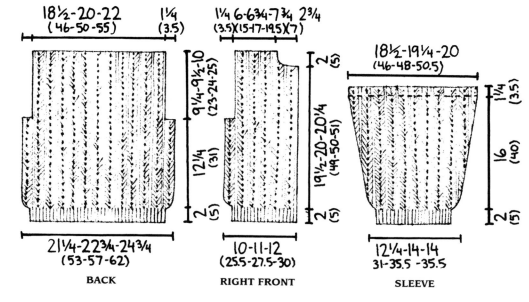

18½-20-22 (46-50-55)   1¼ (3.5)

9¼-9½-10 (23-24-25)

12¼ (31)

21¼-22¾-24¾ (53-57-62)

BACK

1¼ 6-6¾-7¾ 2¾ (3.5X15-17-19.5X7)

2 (5)

19½-20-20¼ (49-50-51)

2 (5)

10-11-12 (25.5-27.5-30)

RIGHT FRONT

18½-19¼-20 (46-48-50.5)

1¼ (3.5)

16 (40)

2 (5)

12¼-14-14 31-35.5 -35.5

SLEEVE

Soft Mohair Cardigan

Level: Intermediate

Size

❖ Woman's Small (Large), bust 30-32 (36-38) in. — 76-81.5 (91.5-97) cm
❖ Finished bust measurements: 40 (48) in. — 100 (120) cm
❖ Length: 26 in. (65 cm)
❖ Sleeve seam: 18 in. (45 cm)

Materials

❖ Mohair yarn (approx. 110 yds per 50 g skein) 3 skeins color gray, 4 (5) skeins each color yellow and pink
❖ Crochet hook U.S. size F/5 (Metric size 4) or size needed to obtain gauge
❖ Knitting needles 7 (Metric size 4.5 mm)
❖ 5 buttons
To save time, take time to check gauge!

Gauge

1 block of 10 dc and ch 1 in width x 5 rows of dc and 1 row of sc = 3-1/4 x 3-1/4 in (8 x 8 cm)

Stitches

Chain (ch), slip st (sl), single crochet (sc), double crochet (dc).
Pat st: Each block is worked in 10 dc and ch 1. After 5 rows of dc, work 1 row of sc. The chain sts will later be worked in gray. Alternate the blocks in yellow and pink. Work the sc row in gray. Beg all dc rows with ch 3 to turn which counts as the first dc, and beg all sc rows with ch 1 which counts as the first sc.
1 inc in 1 sc or 1 dc at the beg of row: Ch 1 or 3 to turn and work 1 sc or 1 dc in the same st.
1 inc in 1 sc or 1 dc at the end of a row: Work 2 sc or 2 dc in the last st of the row.
1 dec in 1 sc or 1 dc at the beg of the row: Sl 1 over the number of sts to be decreased, then work ch 1 or 3 to turn.
1 dec in 1 sc or 1 dc at the end of the row: Leave the sts to be decreased unworked.
1/1 ribbing: Row 1: *K1, p1*. Rep * to * across.
Row 2 and all foll rows: Work sts as established in previous row.

Note: See "Stitches and Techniques" for detailed instructions on stitches and shapings.

Body

Beg at lower edge of right sleeve. With crochet hook and pink (yellow), ch 46 + ch 3 to turn (= 1 dc). Row 1: 1 dc in the 5th ch from the hook, 4 dc, *ch 1, skip 1 ch, 10 dc*, work * to * 3 times, ch 1, skip 1 ch, 6 dc. Continue by foll the chart. The outside st is the border st. Inc 1 st at each edge of every 3rd row 7 times. Inc 1 st at each edge of every 2nd row once. Inc 1 st at each edge of every row 8 times. Sleeve will measure 16 in. (40 cm). With yellow (pink), make 2 chains 44 sts long and join one to each edge of sleeve. Continue in block pat across all sts = 15 blocks. Work for 10 (16) rows from side seams. Now work the right front. Work over the first 76 sts. Turn and dec at neck edge of every row 3 times. Work 3 rows without decreases. Work the last 2 rows in pink. Fasten off. Now work back. Leave 7 sts unworked at center, then work foll 81 sts. After 2 rows, at neck edge, dec 1 st = 80 sts. Work 14 rows even from neck dec. Inc 1 st at neck edge. Fasten off. Now work the left front. Ch 73 + ch 3 for the first dc. Work 3 rows in block pat (= 2 rows in dc with pink, 1 row of sc with gray). At each neck edge of every row, inc 1 st 3 times. Work 6 rows even. At the end of the 7th row, ch 7 for the neck and join with the first st of the back = 164 sts. Beg on wrong side of work. Work the 81 sts of back first, then ch 7, work 76 sts of left front. Work block pat for 10 (16) rows after the neck shaping. Leave 44 sts unworked at each edge for side seams and work on center 76 sts for left sleeve. At each edge of every row, dec 1 st 8 times. At each edge of every 2nd row, dec 1 st once. At each edge of every 3rd row, dec 1 st 6 times. Work 2 rows over 46 sts. Fasten off.

Finishing

Block pieces to indicated measurements. With crochet hook and gray, work chain rows as foll: Beg with right sleeve or right side seams on the right side of the work. Attach yarn to edge sts. Work over the ch sts as foll: *1 sc around the ch, ch 1*, rep * to *. Fasten off. Attach to the opposite edge. With gray, work 38 sc along the sleeve edge. Fasten off. With knitting needles and gray, pick up and knit 1 st from each sc and work 2 in. (5 cm) in 1/1 ribbing. Bind off loosely. Sew side and sleeve seams. With knitting needles and gray, pick up and knit 147 (169) sts along lower edge of body and work 2 in. (5 cm) in 1/1 ribbing. Bind off loosely. With knitting needles and gray, pick up and knit 79 sts along left front edge and work 3/4 in. (2 cm) in 1/1 rib-bing. Bind off loosely. Work same border on right front, making 4 buttonholes when border measures 1/4 in. (1 cm). Place the first buttonhole at the center of the lower ribbing and one at the center of every 2nd block. For each button-hole, bind off 2 sts. On foll row, cast on 2 sts over bound off sts. With knitting needles and gray, pick up and knit 87 sts around neck edge and work in 1/1 ribbing. Make a button-hole 3 sts from right edge when border measures 1/4 in. (1 cm). When neckband mea-sures 3/4 in. (2 cm), bind off. Sew on buttons. Bind off loosely. Sew sleeves to arm-holes, matching center of sleeve with shoulder seams. Sew side and sleeve seams. Reinforce buttonholes and sew on buttons.

(continued on page 50)

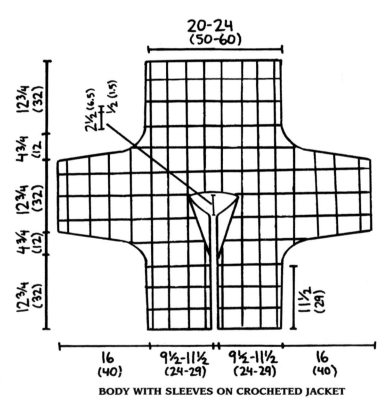

BODY WITH SLEEVES ON CROCHETED JACKET

Mohair Jacquard Cardigan

Level: Challenging

Size

❖ Woman's Medium, bust 33-35 in. — (84-89) cm
❖ Finished bust measurement: 46 in. (116 cm)
❖ Length: 29 in. (72 cm)
❖ Sleeve seam: 18-1/2 in. (46 cm)

Materials

❖ Mohair worsted weight yarn (approx. 130 yds per 50 g skein) 5 skeins color black, 2 skeins color sea green, 1 skein each color rose, ecru, cognac, and gray
❖ 9 buttons
❖ Crochet hook U.S. size F/5 (Metric size 4) or size needed to obtain gauge
❖ Knitting needles U.S. size 4 (Metric size 3.5)
To save time, take time to check gauge!

Gauge

14-1/2 hdc and 9 rows = 4 in. (10 cm)

Stitches

Chain (ch), half double crochet (hdc)

Jacquard st: Follow the chart in hdc. When changing colors, work the last loop of the last st with the color of the next st. Hold the unused yarn against the wrong side of work. When inserting hook, work around the unused yarn so that the new sts hold it against the work. Beg each row with ch 2 = first hdc.

1/1 ribbing: Row 1: *K1, p1*. Rep * to * across.

Row 2 and all foll rows: Work sts as established in previous row.

Note: See "Stitches and Techniques" for detailed instructions on stitches and shapings.

Body

With knitting needles and black, cast on 169 sts and work 1-1/4 in. (3 cm) in 1/1 ribbing. At the right edge of foll row, bind off the 3rd and 4th sts. On foll row, cast on 2 sts over bound off sts. Continue in 1/1 ribbing until ribbing measures 2-1/2 in. (6 cm). Place 5 sts at each edge on holders. Bind off center 159 sts. With crochet hook, work in jacquard hdc foll chart by working 1 hdc in each bound off st and inc 1 border st at each edge = 161 hdc. The border sts are not shown on chart. Work until piece measures 18-1/2 in. (46 cm) from beg. Work the first 36 sts for the first front, inc 1 st at armhole edge = 37 sts. At armhole edge of each row, dec 2 sts twice, dec 1 st twice. Fasten off. Work over the last 36 sts for the 2nd front and inc 1 st at armhole edge and work to correspond to first half. Work the center 71 sts for the back, leaving 9 sts unworked at each edge for armhole. Inc 1 st at each edge = 73 sts. Shape raglans as on fronts. Fasten off.

Sleeves

With knitting needles and black, cast on 40 sts and work 2-1/2 in. (6 cm) in 1/1 ribbing. Bind off loosely. With crochet hook, work 43 hdc in bound off edges + 1 border st at each edge = 45 hdc. Continue in jacquard st by foll chart (border sts not shown on chart). Inc 1 st at each edge every 1-1/4 in. (3.5 cm) 10 times = 65 sts. Work until piece measures 18-1/2 in. (46 cm) from beg. Dec 4 sts at each edge of every row once, dec 2 sts 4 times. Fasten off.

Yoke

With crochet hook, work across 29 sts of first front, 39 sts of sleeve, 59 sts of back, 39 sts of sleeve, 29 sts of last front = 185 sts (leave all border sts at raglan edges unworked). Shape raglans as foll: *Work to 3 sts before raglan edge, work 2 hdc tog, 2 hdc, 2 hdc tog*. Work * to * 3 more times across row = 8 dec. Rep these dec on every row 18 times so that there are always 2 sts between raglan dec until last 2 dec rows. After the 14th dec row, work neck shaping as foll: At each neck edge of every row, dec 5 sts once, dec 2 sts once, dec 1 st 3 times. Fasten off.

Finishing

Block pieces to indicated measurements. Sew raglan seams. Sew sleeve seams. With knitting needles and black, pick up 5 sts from left front holder and inc 1 st at center edge. Work in 1/1 ribbing until border fits to neck. Dec the center edge st and place rem sts on holder. Work same border on right front, making buttonholes when piece measures 4-1/2 (7-1/2, 10-3/4, 14, 17-1/4, 20-1/4, 23-1/2) in. - 11 (19, 27, 35, 43, 51, 59) cm. Work buttonholes same as on lower ribbing. With knitting needles and black, pick up 75 sts from around neck and work 1/2 in. (1.5 cm) in 1/1 ribbing. Work last buttonhole. Work until ribbing measures 1-1/4 in. (3 cm), bind off loosely. Sew on front borders and sew on buttons.

(continued on page 50)

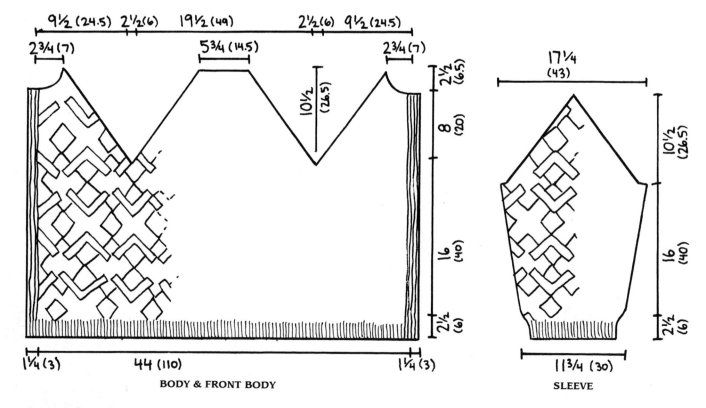

BODY & FRONT BODY   **SLEEVE**

Soft Mohair Cardigan

(continued from page 46)

Worsted Cardigan

(continued from page 44)

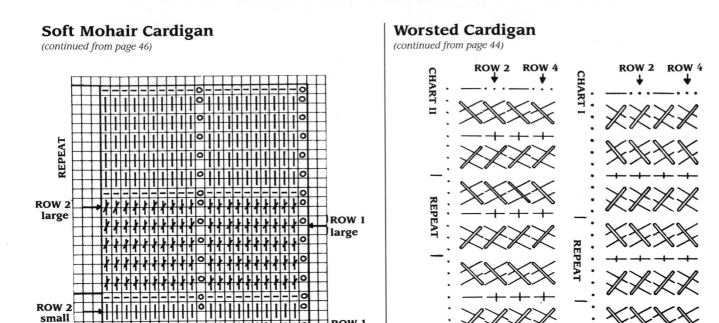

CHART FOR CROCHETED JACKET

Key to Chart

- ⊥ = 1 dc in yellow
- ⊬ = 1 dc in pink
- ⊟ = 1 sc in gray
- ⊡ = ch 1

Key to Chart

- ▪ = ch 1
- ⊞ = back relief dc on odd rows, front relief dc on even rows
- ⫾ = dc
- ⏻ = tr

Mohair Jacquard Cardigan

(continued from page 48)

Key to Chart

- ⊠ = black
- ⊔ = sea green
- ▪ = rose
- □ = ecru
- ▼ = cognac
- ⊙ = gray

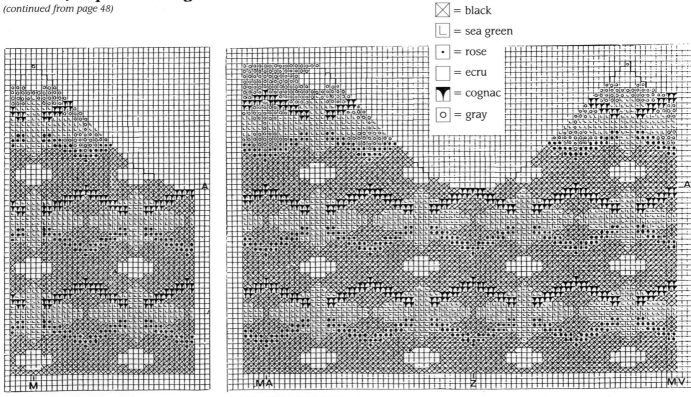

HALF SLEEVE

HALF BACK & FRONT

Striped Cardigan

(photo on preceding page)

Level: Challenging

Size
❖ Woman's Medium, bust 33-35 in. — (84-89) cm
❖ Finished bust measurements: 44 in. (110 cm)
❖ Length: 28-1/4 in. (71 cm)
❖ Sleeve seam: 16 in. (40 cm)

Materials
❖ Mohair worsted weight yarn (approx. 110 yds per 50 g skein) 6 skeins color black, 4 skeins color white
❖ 8 buttons
❖ Crochet hook U.S. size J/10 (Metric size 6) or size needed to obtain gauge
❖ Knitting needles U.S. size 8 (Metric size 5)
To save time, take time to check gauge!

Gauge
11 hdc and 8 rows = 4 in. (10 cm)

Stitches
Chain (ch), single crochet (sc), double crochet (dc), treble crochet (tr).
Zebra st: Follow the chart. Odd numbered rows are shown. Work even rows as foll: 1 sc in each sc, 1 dc in each dc and 1 tr in each tr. For the first sc, ch 1; for first dc, ch 3; for the first tr, ch 4. The border sts are worked the same as the adjacent sts and are not shown on chart. When changing colors, work the last loop of the last st with the color of the next st. Hold the unused yarn against the wrong side of work. When inserting hook, work around the unused yarn so that the new sts hold it against the work.
1/1 ribbing: Row 1: *K1, p1*. Rep * to * across. Row 2 and all foll rows: Work sts as established in previous row.

Note: See "Stitches and Techniques" for detailed instructions on stitches and shapings.

Left Front
With knitting needles and black, cast on 44 sts and work 2 in. (5 cm) in 1/1 ribbing. Bind off the first 38 sts and place rem 6 sts on a holder. With crochet hook, continue in zebra pat, dec 8 sts = 30 sts. Work as foll: Row 1: 1 border st, foll chart from A to B = 4 tr, 3 dc, 10 sc, 2 dc, 3 tr, 3 dc, 3 sc, 1 border st. Continue in zebra pat foll chart. Work until piece measures 16-3/4 in. (42.5 cm), including the ribbing. For sleeve: At right edge, inc 3 sts once, inc 4 sts once, inc 10 sts twice, inc 13 sts once. Continue by foll chart over these 70 sts until piece measures 8 in. (20 cm) from beg of sleeve = 16 rows. At neck edge, dec 8 sts for neck. At neck edge of every 2nd row, dec 3 sts once, dec 2 sts once. Work rem 57 sts until piece measures 11 in. (28.5 cm) = 23 rows from beg of sleeve. End with right side of work row = 53 rows. Ch 28 at neck edge for back neck. Fasten off.

Right Front
With knitting needles and black, cast on 44 sts and work 3/4 in. (2 cm) in 1/1 ribbing. Make 1 buttonhole: Bind off 4th and 5th sts. On the foll row, cast on 2 sts over bound off sts. Work in ribbing until border measures 2 in. (5 cm), end on wrong side row. Leave first 6 sts on holder, bind off 38 sts in ribbing. With crochet hook and black, work in zebra pat, dec 8 sts on first row = 30 sts. Work as foll: Row 1: 1 border st, work foll chart from point C to D, 1 border st. Continue to correspond to left front, working inc at left edge.

Back
With crochet hook and black, work the wrong side row over 57 sts of right front, work the 28 ch of back neck and the 57 sts of left front = 142 sts. Foll the chart from the top down, rev shapings. After the last sleeve dec, you will have 62 sts. Work these sts for the back to the same length as front, end on first row of chart. Fasten off.

Finishing
Block pieces to indicated measurements. With knitting needles and black, pick up 84 sts from lower edge of back and work 2 in. (5 cm) in 1/1 ribbing. Bind off loosely. With knitting needles and black, pick up 40 sts from lower edge of sleeve and work 1-1/2 in. (4 cm) in 1/1 ribbing. Bind off loosely. Sew side and sleeve seams. With knitting needles and black, pick up 6 sts from left front holder, inc 1 st at center edge and work in garter st (knit all rows) until piece fits to neck. Alternate white and black to match zebra pat on fronts. Place sts on holder. Work same border on right front, making buttonholes when piece measures 4 (7, 10-1/4, 13-1/2, 16-3/4, 20) in. - 10 (18, 26, 34, 42, 50) cm from beg as on lower ribbing. With knitting needles and black, pick up and knit 65 sts around neck (including sts on holders) and work 1/2 in. (1.5 cm) in 1/1 ribbing. Make last buttonhole above previous ones. Work in ribbing until neckband measures 1-1/4 in. (3 cm), bind off loosely. Sew on buttons.

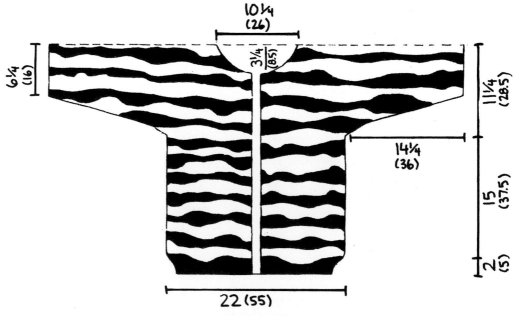

FRONT & BACK

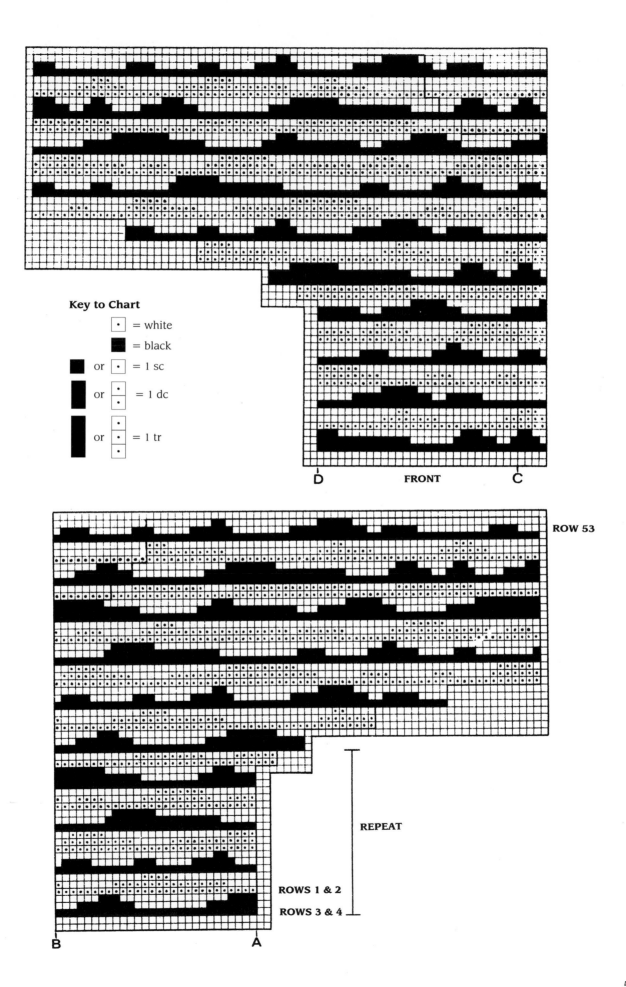

Key to Chart

$\boxed{\cdot}$	= white
■	= black

or $\boxed{\cdot}$ = 1 sc

or $\boxed{\genfrac{}{}{0pt}{}{\cdot}{\cdot}}$ = 1 dc

or $\boxed{\genfrac{}{}{0pt}{}{\cdot}{\genfrac{}{}{0pt}{}{\cdot}{\cdot}}}$ = 1 tr

D   **FRONT**   C

ROW 53

REPEAT

ROWS 1 & 2

ROWS 3 & 4

B   A

SUMMER WEAR

T-Shirt Top

Level: Easy

Size
❖ Woman's Small (Medium, Large, X Large), bust 30-32 (33-35, 36-38, 39-42) in. — 76-81.5 (84-89, 91.5-97, 99-107) cm
❖ Finished bust measurements: 39 (41-1/2, 44, 46) in. — 90 (104, 110, 116) cm, length: 19-1/2 (20, 20-1/4, 21-1/4) in. — 49 (50, 51, 53) cm
❖ Sleeve seam: 2-3/4 in. (7 cm)

Materials
❖ Mayflower Cotton 8 (approx. 186 yds per 50 g skein) 6 (6, 7, 7) skeins color white
❖ Crochet hook U.S. size B/1 (Metric size 2.5) or size needed to obtain gauge
❖ Knitting needles U.S. size 2 (Metric size 2.5)
To save time, take time to check gauge!

Gauge
25 dc and 11-1/2 rows = 4 in. (10 cm). 14 open squares and 11-1/2 rows = 4 in. (10 cm)

Stitches
Chain (ch), single crochet (sc), double crochet (dc), treble crochet (tr).
2 dc worked tog: Work the first dc until 2 loops rem on the hook, work the 2nd dc until 3 loops rem on hook, yo, draw through 3 loops on hook.
Filet crochet: 1 open square = 1 dc, ch 1, 1 dc. 1 filled square = 3 dc; the last dc of 1 square is the first dc of the foll square.
Bobble: Work 2 dc tog in an open square, then work 1 ch around the ch of the previous row.
Beg each row with ch 3 = the first dc. For a row beg with an open square, beg with ch 4.
1/1 ribbing: Row 1: *K1, p1*. Rep * to * across.
Row 2 and all foll rows: Work sts as established in previous row.

Note: See "Stitches and Techniques" for detailed instructions on stitches and shapings.

Back
With crochet hook, ch 139 (147, 155, 163) + ch 4 for first open square. Row 1: 1 dc in

the 7th ch from the hook, *ch 1, skip 1 ch, 1 dc in the foll ch*, rep * to * = 69 (73, 77, 81) open squares. Row 2: Ch 4, 1 dc in the foll dc, *ch 1, 1 dc in the foll dc*, rep * to *, end with 1 dc in the 3rd st of the turning ch. Work this row 1 (2, 3, 4) times. Beg chart 1, beg first row with A (B, C, D). Work 31 rows of chart = 5 bobble rows. After chart is complete, work in open squares. At the same time, when piece measures 8-3/4 9, 9-1/4, 9-1/2) in. - 22 (22.5, 23, 24) cm = 25 (26, 27, 28) rows, inc 1 open square at each edge of every row 5 times. (Note: At beg of row, inc 1 square as foll: ch 5, then work the first dc of the row in the last dc of the previous row. At the end of the row: ch 1, 1 tr under the last dc.) After you have inc 5 open squares at each end, beg next row with ch 10 + ch 4 to turn for the first open square. With a separate strand, ch 10 and join to the last dc of the previous row. Work in open squares across all sts and ch sts = 89 (93, 97, 101) open squares. Work the 5th bobble row, then work in open squares until piece measures 13-1/4 (13-3/4, 14, 15) in. - 33.5 (34.5, 35.5, 37.5) cm. The sleeve end will measure 3(3-1/4, 3-1/4, 3-1/2) in. - 7.5 (8, 8.5, 9.5) cm. Continue with chart 2. The points of the filled squares are worked above the bobbles. Beg with point A (B, C, D) and end with A (B, C, D).

After the last row of chart, work 1 row of open squares as foll: Ch 4, skip 1 dc, 1 dc in the foll st, *ch 1, skip 1, 1 dc in the foll dc*, rep * to * across. Over the first and last 28 (29, 30, 31) open squares, work 1 row of open squares for shoulder. Fasten off.

Front
Work same as back.

Finishing
Block pieces to indicated measurements. With knitting needles, pick up and knit 98 (104, 110, 116) sts along lower edge of each piece and work 2 in. (5 cm) in 1/1 ribbing. Bind off loosely. Sew shoulder, side and sleeve seams. Around the neck, work 1 row of sc: 1 sc in each dc and 1 sc around each ch. Fasten off.

Key to Chart
● = 1 bobble
☐ = open square
⊠ = filled square

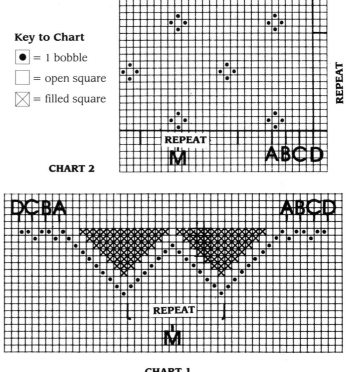

CHART 2

CHART 1

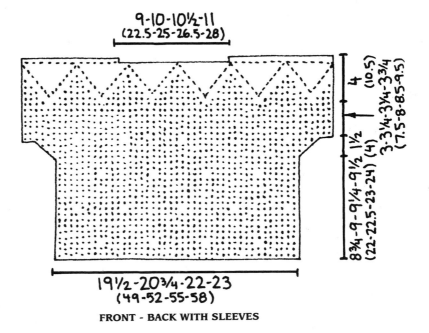

9-10-10½-11
(22.5-25-26.5-28)

4 (10.5)

3-3¼-3¼-3¾ (7.5-8-8.5-9.5)

8¾-9-9¼-9½ (22-22.5-23-24) 1½ (4)

19½-20¾-22-23 (49-52-55-58)

FRONT - BACK WITH SLEEVES

Filet Sun Top

Level: Intermediate

Size

❖ Woman's Small (Medium, Large, X Large), bust 30-32 (33-35, 36-38, 39-42) in. — 76-81.5 (84-89, 91.5-97, 99-107) cm

❖ Finished bust measurements: 35 (37-1/2, 40, 42-1/2) in. — 88 (94, 100, 106) cm

❖ Length to armhole: 13 (13-1/2, 14, 14-3/4) in. — 33 (34, 35, 37) cm

Materials

❖ Pearl cotton (approx. 320 yds per 50 g skein) 3 (4, 4, 4) skeins color white

❖ Crochet hook U.S. size B/1 (Metric size 2.5) or size needed to obtain gauge

❖ Knitting needles size U.S. size 2 (Metric size 2)

To save time, take time to check gauge!

Gauge

27 dc and 15 rows = 4 in. (10 cm). 31 sts in pat st (ch 1, 1 dc) = 4 in. (10 cm)

Stitches

Chain (ch), slip st (sl), single crochet (sc), double crochet (dc).

1/1 ribbing: Row 1: *K1, p1*. Rep * to * across.

Row 2 and all foll rows: Work sts as established in previous row.

Note: See "Stitches and Techniques" for detailed instructions on stitches and shapings.

Back

The top is worked from top down. With crochet hook, ch 119 (127, 135, 143) + ch 3 to turn. Continue by foll chart, beg with A (B, C, D). Row 1: 1 dc in the 5th ch from the hook, 1 dc in each of the foll 13 (17, 21, 25) ch, *ch 1, skip 1 ch, 1 dc in each of the foll 29 ch*, rep * to *, end with ch 1, skip 1 ch, 1 dc in each of the foll 15 (19, 23, 27) sts. Row 2: Ch 3, 1 dc in each of the foll 13 (17, 21, 25) sts, ch 1, skip 1 dc, *1 dc in the foll ch, ch 1, skip 1 dc, 1 dc in each of the foll 27 dc, ch 1, skip 1 dc*, rep * to *, end with 1 dc in the foll st, ch 1, skip 1 dc, 1 dc of each of the foll 13 (17, 21, 25) dc, 1 dc in the 3rd ch of the turning ch. Continue in this way, foll chart. After the chart is completed,

rep the last 2 rows of the chart until piece measures 12 (12-1/4, 12-3/4, 13-1/2) in. - 30 (31, 32, 34) cm. Fasten off.

Front

Work same as back.

Finishing

Block pieces to indicated measurements. With knitting needles, pick up and knit 120 (126, 132, 138) sts of each piece and work 1-1/4 in. (3 cm) in 1/1 ribbing. Bind off loosely. Sew side seams. Along the top edge, work 2 rows as foll: Row 1: 1 dc in 1 dc, *ch 1, skip 1 st, 1 dc in the foll st*, rep * to *, end with ch 1, sl 1 in the 3rd ch from the first dc. Row 2: Ch 1, 1 sc in each dc and 1 sc in each ch. End row with a sl st. Fasten off. For straps, make 4 chains 10-12 in. - 25-30 cm long. Work in sc working first sc in 3rd ch from hook. Fasten off. Sew side seams. Sew on straps.

Key to Chart

• = ch 1

| = 1 dc

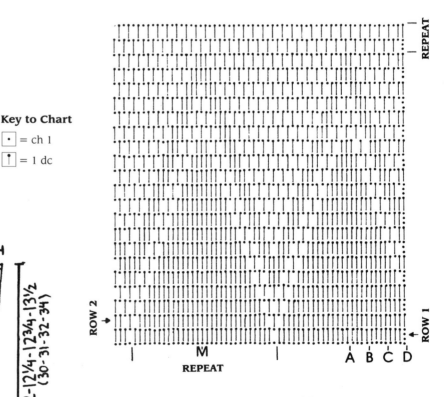

CHART FOR TOP

17½-18¾-20-21¼
(44-47-50-53)

DIRECTION OF WORK

12-12¼-12¾-13½
(30-31-32-34)

15¼-16¼-17¼-18½
(38.5-41-43.5-46)

FRONT - BACK

Long Filet Top

Level: Easy

Size
❖ Woman's Small (Medium, Large), bust 30-32 (33-35, 36-38) in. — 76-81.5 (84-89, 91.5-97) cm
❖ Finished bust measurements: 40-1/2 (44, 48) in. — 102 (110, 120) cm, length: 27-1/2 (28-1/2, 30) in. — 69 (72, 75) cm
❖ Sleeve seam: 2-1/4 in. (5.5 cm)

Materials
❖ Mayflower Helarsgarn (approx. 88 yds per 50 g skein) 9 (10, 10) skeins color white
❖ Crochet hook U.S. size E/4 (Metric size 3.5) or size needed to obtain gauge
To save time, take time to check gauge!

Gauge
7 squares and 7 rows = 4 in. (10 cm).

Stitches
Chain (ch), single crochet (sc) double crochet (dc)

Note: See "Stitches and Techniques" for detailed instructions on stitches and shapings.

Back
Ch 114 (123, 132) and work in filet st. Row 1: 1 dc in the 9th ch from the hook, *ch 2, skip 2 ch, 1 dc in the foll ch*, rep * to * = 36 (39, 42) open squares. Row 2 and all foll rows: Ch 5 for the first open square, 1 dc in the foll dc, *ch 2, 1 dc in the foll dc*, rep * to * across. Work until piece measures 16-3/4 (17-1/4, 18) in.-42 (43.5, 45) cm. At each edge of foll row, inc 4 open squares by ch 17, working first dc in the 9th ch from the hook, rep * to * across = 44 (47, 50) squares. Work until piece measures 27-1/2 (28-1/2, 30) in. - 69 (72, 75) cm from beg. Fasten off.

Front
Work same as back.

Finishing
Block pieces to indicated measurements. Sew side and sleeve seams. Lay the 2 pieces right sides tog. For shoulder seam: Beg at armhole edge, work 1 sc in the first square of both pieces, then *ch 2, 1 sc in the foll square*, rep * to * over 12 (13, 14) squares. Fasten off. Work 2nd shoulder in the same way, leaving center 20 (21, 22) squares open for neck.

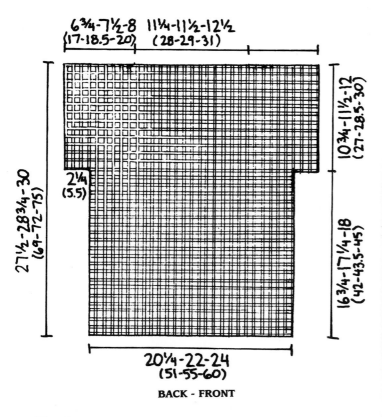

6¾-7½-8 (17-18.5-20) 11¼-11½-12½ (28-29-31)

10¾-11½-12 (27-28.5-30)

27½-28¾-30 (69-72-75)

2¼ (5.5)

16¾-17¼-18 (42-43.5-45)

20¼-22-24 (51-55-60)

BACK - FRONT

Floral Motif Top

Level: Challenging

Size
❖ Woman's Small/ Medium (Large/ X Large), bust 30-35 (36-42) in. — 75-89 (91.5-107) cm
❖ Finished bust measurements: 43 (46) in. — 108 (116) cm
❖ Length: 21-1/2 in. (64 cm)
❖ Sleeve seam: 4 (4-1/4) in. — 10 (11) cm

Materials
❖ Novelty sport weight cotton yarn (approx. 150 yds per 50 g skein) 7 skeins color orange
❖ Crochet hook U.S. size B/1 (Metric size 2.5) or size needed to obtain gauge
❖ Knitting needles U.S. size 2 (Metric size 2.5)
To save time, take time to check gauge!

Gauge
28 dc and 16 rows in pat st = 4 in. (10 cm). 1 repeat of web pat = 1 3/4 in. (4.5 cm) and 2 in. (5 cm)

Stitches
Chain (ch), single crochet (sc), double crochet (dc), treble (tr).
1/1 ribbing: Row 1: *K1, p1*. Rep * to * across.
Row 2 and all foll rows: Work sts as established in previous row.
Note: The top is worked sideways, beg at sleeve end. Work the first row of sc of the pat st in the front loop of the underlying st. When working the dc row of web st, work through both loops of underlying rows. Work pat st and web st foll chart. All rows are shown on chart.

Note: See "Stitches and Techniques" for detailed instructions on stitches and shapings.

Back
With crochet hook, ch 77 + ch 3 to turn (counts as first dc). Work on ch sts foll chart: Row 1: 1 dc in the 5th ch from the hook, 1 dc in each of the foll 2 ch, *ch 1, skip 1 ch, 1 dc in each of the foll 3 ch*, rep * to *, end last rep with ch 1, skip 1

ch, 1 dc in each of the foll 4 ch = 19 groups of 3 dc, with ch 1 between groups and 1 border st at each edge. Row 2: Ch 1, 1 sc in each st (worked in the front loop), end with 1 sc in the 3rd ch from the beg of previous row. Now beg the 7 rows of web pat. Row 3: Ch 3, *1 dc in the foll sc, ch 1, skip 1 sc*, rep * to *, end with 1 dc in each of the last 2 sc. Row 4: Ch 3, *1 dc in the foll dc, ch 1, 1 dc in the foll dc, ch 4, 1 tr in each of the foll 4 dc, ch 4*, rep * to *, end row with 1 dc in the foll dc, ch 1, 1 dc in each of the foll 2 sts = 6 web motifs. Continue by foll chart. After last row of web pat, work in pat st. At beg of 6th (8th) row of pat st = 15th (16th) row from beg, inc 18 motifs as foll: Ch 72 + ch 3 to turn, work 1 dc in the 5th ch from the hook, 1 dc in each of the foll 2 ch, *ch 1, skip 1 ch, 1 dc in each of the foll 3 ch*, rep * to * across. Join to sleeve sts with 1 ch, skip the border st (= 1 sc), 1 dc in each of the foll 3 sc, ch 1, etc. = 37 motifs. Continue over all sts for a total of 13 (15) rows of pat st. Work *7 rows of web st, 13 (15) rows of pat st*, work * to * twice more, then work 7 rows of web pat and 8 rows of pat st. The piece will measure 21-1/2 (23) in. - 54 (58) cm from side seam edge. At end of foll row, leave last 72 sts unworked. Work rem sts for 5 (7) rows of pat st and 7 rows of web st and 2 rows of pat st. Fasten off.

Front
Work same as back until 7th (9th) row of pat st after the 2nd rep of web pat. On the foll row at left edge, leave the last 24 sts unworked. Continue on the rem 31 motifs until the 6th row of pat st after the 4th web pat. Make a ch of 25. Work 1 sc in the 2nd ch from hook, 1 sc in foll 23 sts, join to front sts at upper edge and work 1 sc in each of the sts of the front. Complete front as on back.

Finishing
Block pieces to indicated measurements. With knitting needles, pick up and knit 120 (130) sts along lower edge of front and work 3/4 in. (2 cm) of 1/1 ribbing. Bind off. Work same border on back. Sew shoulder seams. With knitting needles, pick up and knit 130 sts along

each sleeve end and work 1/2 in. (1.5 cm) of 1/1 ribbing. Bind off. With knitting needles, pick up and knit 70 sts along long sides of front neck edge and work 1/2 in. (1.5 cm) of 1/1 ribbing. Bind off. Work same border along back neck edge. Work same border along sides of front neck, picking up and knitting 24 sts. Overlap the long neckbands over the short and sew in place. Sew side and sleeve seams.

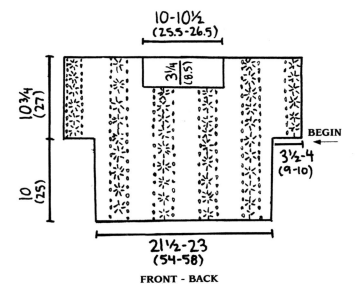

10-10½ (25.5-26.5)

10¾ (27)

3¾ (8.5)

10 (25)

BEGIN

3½-4 (9-10)

21½-23 (54-58)

FRONT - BACK

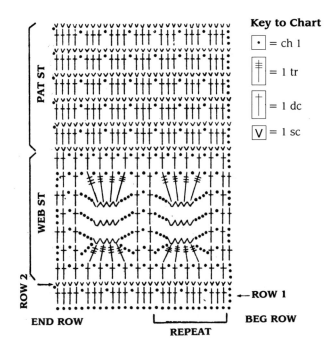

PAT ST

WEB ST

ROW 2

ROW 1

END ROW

BEG ROW

REPEAT

Key to Chart
· = ch 1

‡ = 1 tr

† = 1 dc

V = 1 sc

Lace Motif Pullover

Level: Challenging

Size

❖ Woman's Small (Medium, Large), bust 30-32 (33-35, 36-38) in. — 76-81.5 (84-89, 91.5-97) cm
❖ Finished bust measurements: 38-1/2 (43, 48) in. — 96 (108, 120) cm, length: 24 in. (60 cm)
❖ Sleeve seam: 17-1/2 in. (44 cm)

Materials

❖ Mercerized fingering weight yarn (approx. 186 yds per 50 g skein) 12 (13, 14) skeins color white
❖ Crochet hook U.S. size B/1 (Metric size 2.5) or size needed to obtain gauge
❖ Knitting needles U.S. size 3 (Metric size 2.5)
To save time, take time to check gauge!

Gauge

1 filled motif, 1 open motif, 1 filled motif and 1 open motif = 4-3/4 in. (12 cm)

Stitches

Chain (ch), single crochet (sc), double crochet (dc), treble crochet (tr), Front Relief dc: Work 1 dc in the front of the post by inserting hook from front to back, right to left. Yo before inserting hook around post. Back Relief dc: Work 1 dc in the back of the post by inserting hook from right to left from back to front. Yo before inserting hook around post.
Pattern st: Work by foll chart. Beg on a chain base (Multiple of 14 ch + ch 1).
Row 1: Ch 3, 1 dc in the 4th ch from hook, *ch 2, skip 2 ch, 2 sc, ch 2, skip 2 ch, work in the foll st: 1 dc, ch 1, 1 dc*, rep * to *. Row 2: Ch 3, 1 dc in the v-motif, *ch 2, 1 sc in the ch 2 arc, ch 1, skip 2 sc + ch 2 (in the foll rows, work 2 relief dc instead of 2 sc), in the foll v-motif, work 2 tr, 2 dc, ch 1, 2 dc, 2 tr, ch 1, skip 2 ch + 2 sc (or 2 relief dc in foll rows), 1 sc in the ch 2 arc, ch 2, work in the v-motif: 1 dc, ch 1, 1 dc*, rep * to *. Row 3: Ch 3, 1 dc in the v-motif, *ch 2, 1 sc in the

ch 2 arc, ch 2, skip 1 sc + ch 1, work around the dc of the v-motif: 2 relief dc in front of the work, 2 relief dc in back of work; in ch space work: 1 dc, ch 1, 1 dc; 2 relief dc in back of work and 2 relief dc in front of work, ch 2, skip 1 ch + 1 sc, 1 sc in the ch 2 arc, ch 2, in the v-motif: 1 dc, ch 1, 1 dc*, rep * to *. Row 4: Ch 3, 1 dc in the v-motif, *ch 2, 1 sc in the ch 2 arc, ch 2, skip 1 sc + ch 2, work in the v-motif: 2 back relief dc, 3 front relief dc; in the center ch: 1 dc, ch 1, 1 dc; 3 front relief dc and 2 back relief dc, ch 2, skip ch 2 + 1 sc, 1 sc in the ch 2 arc, ch 2, work in the v-motif 1 dc, ch 1, 1 dc*, rep * to *. Row 5: Ch 3, 1 dc in the v-motif, *ch 2, skip 2 ch, 1 sc, ch 2, 2 front relief dc, ch 2, skip 4 dc, in the center ch: work 1 dc, ch 1, 1 dc; ch 2, skip 4 dc, 2 front relief dc, ch 2, skip 2 ch, 1 sc, ch 2, work in the v-motif: 1 dc, ch 1, 1 dc*, rep * to *. Rows 6 to 9: Work by foll chart. Open and filled v-motifs alternate. Rep rows 2 to 9.
1/1 ribbing: Row 1: *K1, p1*. Rep * to * across.
Row 2 and all foll rows: Work sts as established in previous row.

Note: See "Stitches and Techniques" for detailed instructions on stitches and shapings.

Back

Ch 113 (127, 141) + ch 3 = first dc. Row 1: Work in pat st: 1 dc in the 4th ch from the hook, *ch 2, skip 2 ch, 2 sc, ch 2, skip 2 ch, in the foll st: 1 dc, ch 1, 1 dc*, rep from * to * 15 (17, 19) times = 17 (19, 21) v-motifs including v-motif at beg. Work by foll chart. The first row is worked as foll: 1/2 open motif, *1 filled motif, 1 open motif*, work * to * 6 (7, 8) times, 1 filled motif, 1/2 open motif. Work 17 rows of motif - 20 in. (51 cm) from beg. On the 18th row, leave the center 7 (7, 9) motifs unworked. Work each side separately. At each neck edge, leave 1 motif unworked foll chart. Fasten off. Piece will measure 21-1/2 in. (54 cm) from beg. Work the other side to correspond.

Sleeves

Ch 71 + ch 3 = first dc. Row 1: Work in pat st: 1 dc in the 4th ch from hook, *ch 2, skip 2

ch, 2 sc, ch 2, skip 2 ch, in the foll st: 1 dc, ch 1, 1 dc*, rep * to * 9 times = 11 v-motifs. Continue by foll chart. The first row is worked as foll: 1/2 open motif, *1 filled motif, 1 open motif*, rep * to * 9 times = 11 motifs. After the first row, inc 1 st at each edge alternately every 2nd and 3rd row 14 times. Work these sts in pat st, alternating 1 open motif with 1 filled motif. Work a total of 13 motif rows. The last row is worked as foll: 1/2 open motif, *1 filled motif, 1 open motif*, rep * to * 6 times, 1 filled motif, 1/2 open motif. The length is 15-1/4 in. (39 cm). Fasten off.

Finishing

Block pieces to indicated measurements. With knitting needles, pick up and knit 100 (110, 120) sts along lower edge of back and work 2-1/2 in. (6 cm) in 1/1 ribbing. Bind off loosely. Work same border on front. With knitting needles, pick up and knit 46 sts along lower edge of each sleeve and work 2 in. (5 cm) in 1/1 ribbing. Bind off loosely. Sew shoulder seams. Sew sleeves to armholes, matching center of sleeve with shoulder seams. Sew side and sleeve seams. Around the neck, work 1 row in sc. Work 2 sc in each ch 2 and 1 sc in each relief dc, 1 sc in the v-motif (skip the 2 dc of the v-motifs.) Fasten off.

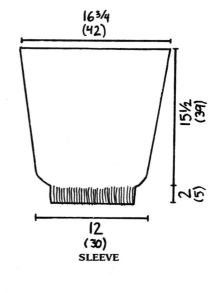

SLEEVE

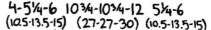
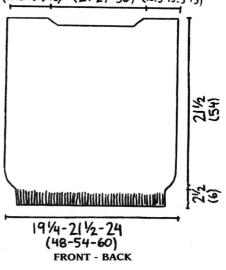

FRONT - BACK

(chart on following page)

Finger Weight Top

Level: Challenging

Size

❖ Woman's Small (Medium, Large), bust 30-32 (33-35, 36-38) in. — 76-81.5 (84-89, 91.5-97) cm
❖ Finished bust measurements: 39-1/2 (44, 48) in. — 99 (110, 120) cm
❖ Length: 24 in. (60 cm)

Materials

❖ Mercerized fingering weight yarn (approx. 220 yds per 50 g skein) 10 (10, 11) skeins color blue
❖ Steel crochet hook U.S. size 6 (Metric size 1.75) or size needed to obtain gauge
❖ Knitting needles U.S. size 1 (Metric size 2).
To save time, take time to check gauge!

Gauge

1 filled motif, 1 open motif, 1 filled motif and 1 open motif = 4-1/4 in. (11 cm)

Stitches

Chain (ch), single crochet (sc), double crochet (dc), treble crochet (tr).
Front relief dc: Work 1 dc in the front of the post by inserting hook from front to back, right to left. Yo before inserting hook in st.
Back relief dc: Work 1 dc in the back of the post by inserting hook from right to left from back to front. Yo before inserting hook in st.
Pattern st: Work by foll chart. Beg on a chain base (Multiple of 14 ch + ch 1).
Row 1: Ch 3, 1 dc in the 4th ch from hook, *ch 2, skip 2 ch, 2 sc, ch 2, skip 2 ch, work in the foll st: 1 dc, ch 1, 1 dc*, rep * to *.
Row 2: Ch 3, 1 dc in the v-motif, *ch 2, 1 sc in the ch 2 arc, ch 1, skip 2 sc + ch 2 (in the foll rows, work 2 relief dc instead of 2 sc), in the foll v-motif, work 2 tr, 2 dc, ch 1, 2 dc, 2 tr, ch 1, skip 2 ch + 2 sc (or 2 relief dc in foll rows), 1 sc in the ch 2 arc, ch 2, work in the v-motif: 1 dc, ch 1, 1 dc*, rep * to *.
Row 3: Ch 3, 1 dc in the v-

motif, *ch 2, 1 sc in the ch 2 arc, ch 2, skip 1 sc + ch 1, work around the dc of the v-motif: 2 relief dc in front of the work, 2 relief dc in back of work, work in ch space: 1 dc, ch 1, 1 dc; 2 relief dc in back of work and 2 relief dc in front of work, ch 2, skip 1 ch + 1 sc, 1 sc in the ch 2 arc, ch 2, in the v-motif: 1 dc, ch 1, 1 dc*, rep * to *.
Row 4: Ch 3, 1 dc in the v-motif, *ch 2, 1 sc in the ch 2 arc, ch 2, skip 1 sc + ch 2, work in the v-motif: 2 back relief dc, 3 front relief dc, in the center ch: 1 dc, ch 1, 1 dc; 3 front relief dc and 2 back relief dc, ch 2, skip ch 2 + 1 sc, 1 sc in the ch 2 arc, ch 2, work in the v-motif: 1 dc, ch 1, 1 dc*, rep * to *. Row 5: Ch 3, 1 dc in the v-motif, *ch 2, skip 2 ch, 1 sc, ch 2, 2 front relief dc, ch 2, skip 4 dc, in the center ch: work 1 dc, ch 1, 1 dc; ch 2, skip 4 dc, 2 front relief dc, ch 2, skip 2 ch, 1 sc, ch 2, work in the v-motif: 1 dc, ch 1, 1 dc*, rep * to *.
Rows 6 to 9: work by foll chart. Open and filled v-motifs alternate. Rep rows 2 to 9.
1/1 ribbing: Row 1: *K1, p1*. Rep * to * across.
Row 2 and all foll rows: Work sts as established in previous row.

Note: See "Stitches and Techniques" for detailed instructions on stitches and shapings.

Back

Ch 127 (141, 155) + ch 3 = first dc. Row 1: Work in pat st: 1 dc in the 4th ch from the hook, *ch 2, skip 2 ch, 2 sc, ch 2, skip 2 ch, work in the foll st: 1 dc, ch 1, 1 dc*, rep * to * 17 (19, 21) times = 19 (21, 23) v-motifs including the v-motif at the beg. Continue by foll chart. The first row is worked as foll: 1/2 open motif, *1 filled motif, 1 open motif *, rep * to * 8 (9, 10) times, 1 filled motif, 1/2 open motif. Work for a total of 19 rows and piece will measure 20-3/4 in. (52 cm) from beg. On the 20th row, leave the center 11 (13, 13) motifs unworked for neck. Work each half separately, dec 1 motif at neck edge as shown on chart. Fasten off, on the 20th row, the piece will measure 22 in. (55 cm) from beg. Work 2nd shoulder to correspond.

Front

Work the same as back.

Finishing

Block pieces to indicated measurements. With knitting needles, pick up and knit 126 (140, 154) sts along lower edge of back and work 2 in. (5 cm) in 1/1 ribbing. Bind off loosely. Work same border on front. Sew shoulder seams. Along the top 8 motifs of each side seam, work 1 row of 132 sc. Pick up 1

sc from each sc and 2 sc from each row. Fasten off. With knitting needles, pick up 1 st from each sc and work 1-1/2 in (4 cm) of 1/1 ribbing. Bind off loosely. Sew side and armhole band seams. Around the neck, work 1 round in sc. On the first round, work 2 sc in each ch 2 and 1 sc in each relief dc and 1 sc in each v-motif (the 2 dc of each v-motif are unworked). Work 2 rounds of sc. Fasten off.

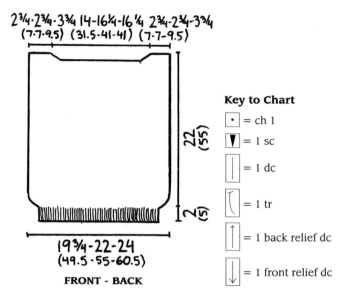

2¾·2¾·3¾ 14-16¼-16¼ 2¾·2¾·3¾
(7·7·9.5) (31.5·41·41) (7·7·9.5)

22 (55)

2 (5)

19¾-22-24
(49.5-55-60.5)

FRONT - BACK

Key to Chart

·	= ch 1
▼	= 1 sc
│	= 1 dc
⌡	= 1 tr
↑	= 1 back relief dc
↓	= 1 front relief dc

SHOULDER

DEC FOR NECK

ROW 2

ROW 1

REPEAT

Salmon Pullover

Level: Challenging

Size

❖ Woman's Small (Medium, Large), bust 30-32 (33-35, 36-38) in. — 76-81.5 (84-89, 91.5-97) cm

❖ Finished bust measurements: 42-1/2 (46, 49) in. — 107 (115, 123) cm, length: 22-3/4 in. (57 cm)

❖ Sleeve seam: 16-1/2 in. (42 cm).

Materials

❖ Sport weight yarn (50 g skein) 10 (11, 12) skeins color light salmon.

❖ Crochet hook U.S. size B/1 (Metric size 2.5) or size needed to obtain gauge

❖ Knitting needles U.S. size 2 (Metric size 2.5).

To save time, take time to check gauge!

Gauge

23 dc and 10 1/2 rows = 4 in. (10 cm).

Stitches

Chain (ch), single crochet (sc), double crochet (dc).

2 dc tog: Work dc in the first dc until there are 2 loops, work 2nd dc in the next st, until 3 loops are on hook, yo and draw through all loops.

Pat st: Work by foll chart, beg all rows with ch 3 = first dc of the row.

1/1 ribbing: Row 1: *K1, p1*. Rep * to * across.

Row 2 and all foll rows: Work sts as established in previous row.

Note: See "Stitches and Techniques" for detailed instructions on stitches and shapings.

Back

With crochet hook, ch 123 (133, 143). Work by foll chart, beg with point A (B, C). Motifs are centered as shown on chart. Work 36 rows of chart. At the center of every row, work ch 1 between the 2 diamonds. For the V-neck, divide work in half. Dec by foll chart, dec 3 diamonds over 14 rows. Work 6 rows even. Work 56 rows from beg, fasten off.

Work other side to correspond.

Front

Work same as back, omitting V-neck shapings. Fasten off on row 56.

Sleeves

With crochet hook, ch 63 + ch 4 (= first dc + ch 1). Work by foll chart, beg first row with point C and end with point C. At each edge of 2nd row, inc 1 st once. Then at each edge of every row, inc 1 st 30 (31, 32) times. Work inc sts in pat st = 123 (125, 127) sts until piece measures 15 in. (38 cm). Fasten off.

Finishing

Block pieces to indicated measurements. With knitting needles, pick up and knit 100 (104, 108) sts along lower edge of back and work 1-1/2 in. (4 cm) in 1/1 ribbing. Bind off loosely. Work same border along lower edge of front. Work same border along sleeve ends over 48 (50, 52) sts. Sew shoulder seams. Sew sleeves to arm-holes, matching center of sleeve with shoulder seams. Sew side and sleeve seams. Around neck work 2 rows of sc as foll: Row 1: Beg at 1 shoulder seam: Work 1 sc in each sc along back neck edge, along the straight edges of V-neck work 2 sc per row. On dec rows, work 3 sc per row, work 1 sc in the center ch. Row 2: Work 1 sc in each sc, skip the sc at the center front and work 2 sc at each edge of center front. Fasten off.

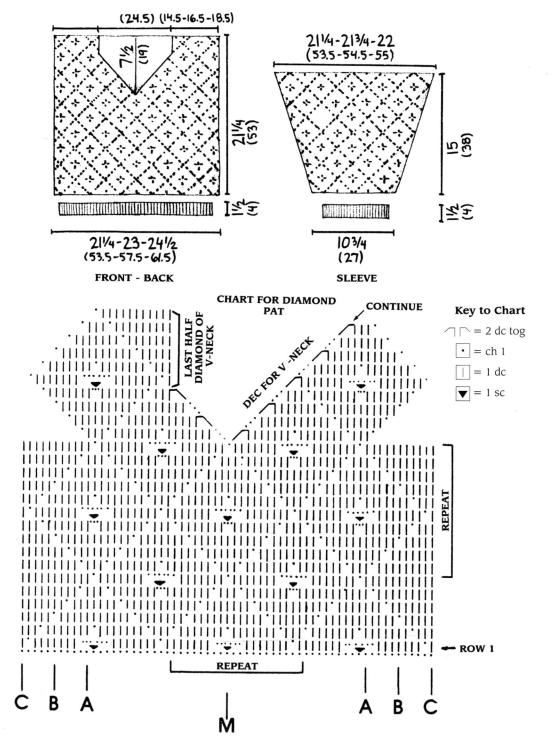

FRONT - BACK

SLEEVE

CHART FOR DIAMOND PAT

Key to Chart

⌐⌐ = 2 dc tog

|•| = ch 1

|| = 1 dc

▼ = 1 sc

Filet Motif Top

Level: Intermediate

Size

❖ Woman's Large, bust 36-38 in. — (91.5-97 cm)
❖ Finished bust measurements: 52 in. (131 cm), length: 22 in. (55 cm)
❖ Sleeve seam: 4-3/4 in. (12 cm)

Materials

❖ Mayflower Cotton 12 (approx. 285 yds per 50 g skein) 7 skeins color white.
❖ Steel crochet hook U.S. size 7 (Metric size 1.5) or size needed to obtain gauge.
To save time, take time to check gauge!

Gauge

11 squares and 14 rows = 4 in. (10 cm)

Stitches

Chain (ch), single crochet (sc), double crochet (dc)
Filet st: work by foll chart. One open square = 1 dc, ch 2, 1 dc. A filled square = 4 dc. The first dc is the last dc of the previous square.

Note: See "Stitches and Techniques" for detailed instructions on stitches and shapings.

Back

Ch 219 + ch 1 as first sc. Row 1: 1 sc in the 3rd ch from the hook, 1 sc in each of the foll ch sts. Work in sc until piece measures 3/4 in. (2 cm). Ch 1 to turn at beg of each row.
Continue as foll: Row 1: Ch 3 for first dc (= 1 border st), 1 dc in the foll sc, ** *ch 2, skip 2, 1 dc in the foll sc*, work * to * twice, 1 dc in each of the foll 12 sc, ch 2, skip 2, 1 dc in the foll 10 sc, *ch 2, skip 2, 1 dc in the foll sc*, work * to * 7 times, 1 dc in each of the foll 3 sc, *ch 2, skip 2, 1 dc in the foll sc*, work * to * 7 times, 1 dc in each of the foll 9 sc, ch 2, skip 2, 1 dc in each of the foll 13 sc, *ch 2, skip 2, 1 dc in the foll sc*, work * to * 3 times**, rep from ** to ** once, end with 1 dc in the last sc = 1 border st (72 squares + 2 border sts).
Continue by foll chart. Work rep

twice. Beg each row with ch 3 for first dc. Work 72 rows (2 repeats). After 40 rows, inc for sleeves as foll: Row 41: Work across row, ch 43 at end of row. Row 42: 1 dc in the 5th ch, *ch 2, skip 2, 1 dc*, work * to * 12 times, ch 2, skip 2, 1 dc in the foll dc, continue by foll chart. At end of row, skip the border st, ch 43. Row 43: 1 dc in the 5th

ch from hook, *ch 2, skip 2, 1 dc in the foll ch*, work * to * 12 times, ch 2, skip 2, 1 dc in the foll dc, continue by foll chart, end row with 13 open squares, 1 border st. Work 13 open squares at each edge. Work to 72nd row. Work 3/4 in. (2 cm) in sc. Beg each row with ch 1 = 1 border st. Piece will measure 22 in. (55.5 cm). Fasten off.

Front

Work front same as back.

Finishing

Block pieces to indicated measurements. Sew shoulder seams over 11-1/2 in. (29 cm), leaving center open for neck. Sew side and sleeve seams.

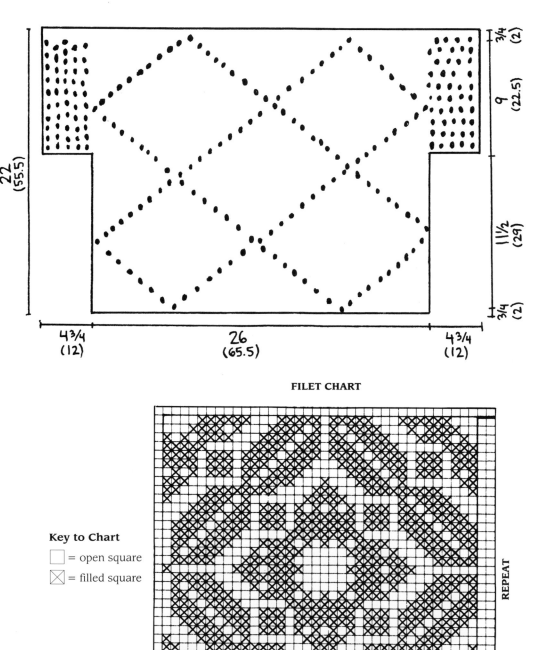

FRONT - BACK WITH SLEEVES

FILET CHART

Key to Chart

☐ = open square
☒ = filled square

Teal Relief Top

Level: Intermediate

Size
❖ Woman's Small (Medium, Large), bust 30-32 (33-35, 36-38) in. — 76-81.5 (84-89, 91.5-97) cm
❖ Finished bust measurements: 41-1/2 (44-1/2, 48) in. — 104 (112, 120) cm
❖ Length: 23-1/2 in. (59 cm)
❖ Sleeve seam: 17-1/2 in. (43 cm)

Materials
❖ Scheepjeswol Voluma (approx. 209 yds per 50 g skein) 14 (15, 16) skeins color teal
❖ Crochet hooks U.S. sizes C/2 and E/4 (Metric sizes 3 and 3.5) or size needed to obtain gauge To save time, take time to check gauge!

Gauge
20 dc and 13 rows in relief pat using larger size hook = 4 in. (10 cm)

Stitches
Chain (ch), slip st (sl), single crochet (sc), half double crochet (hdc), double crochet (dc). Relief dc: Worked around post of underlying dc. Front Relief dc: Work around post of dc of previous row. Work around front post, inserting hook from right to left, working yo before inserting hook. Back Relief dc: Work around back post, inserting hook from right to left, working yo before inserting hook.
Border pat: Work first row in dc, beg with ch 3. Alternate 1 front relief dc with 1 back relief dc. On the foll row, work back relief dc over front relief dc and vice versa.

Note: See "Stitches and Techniques" for detailed instructions on stitches and shapings.

Back
Ch 106 (114, 122) with larger size hook. Row 1: Ch 3 = first dc, 1 dc in the 5th ch from the hook. Work 1 dc in each ch = 106 (114, 122) dc. Continue by foll chart with 1 border st at each edge. Border sts are not

shown on chart. Beg with point A (B, C). Beg wrong side row with C. Row 1 of chart: Right side, ch 2, 104 (112, 120) relief dc, 1 hdc. Continue by foll chart for 20-1/4 in. (51 cm). Now work 1-1/4 in. (3 cm) in border pat, beg with 1 front relief dc, 1 back relief dc. Fasten off.

Front
Work same as back.

Sleeves
Ch 64 (66 ,68) with larger size hook. Row 1: Ch 3 = first dc, 1 dc in the 5th ch from hook, 1 dc in each ch = 64 (66 ,68) dc. Continue by foll chart. Beg at point D (B, E). Row 1 of chart: right side of work, ch 2, 62 (64,

66) relief dc, 1 hdc. Continue by foll chart. At each edge alternately every 2nd and 3rd row, inc 1 st 16 times = 96 (98, 100) relief dc + 1 border st at each edge. When piece measures 16 in. (40 cm) from beg, fasten off.

Finishing
Block pieces to indicated measurements. Join shoulder seams with 1 row of sc worked on the outside with smaller size hook over 5-1/4 (6, 6-1/2) in. - 13.5 (15, 16.5) cm. Fasten off. Sew sleeves to armholes, matching center of sleeve with shoulder seams. Sew side and sleeve seam. Along lower edge of each sleeve with smaller

size hook, work 32 (34, 36) sc around lower edge and slip st to join. Then work in border pat for 1-1/4 in. (3 cm). Fasten off. Around lower edge of body with smaller size hook, work 170 (184, 198) sc, sl st to join. Work 2 in. (5 cm) in border pat. Fasten off.

Key to Chart
☐ = 1 front relief dc on the right side of work, 1 back relief dc on the wrong side of work

☒ = 1 back relief dc on the right side of work, 1 front relief dc on the wrong side of work.

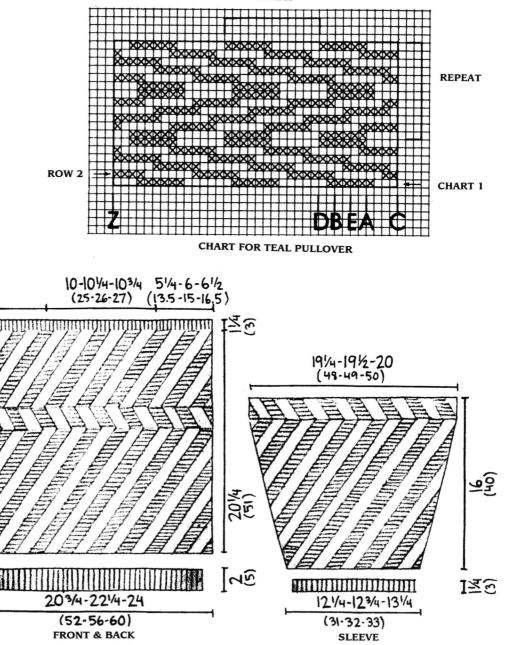

CHART FOR TEAL PULLOVER

FRONT & BACK

SLEEVE

Sport Stripes Top

Level: Intermediate

Size
❖ Woman's Small (Medium, Large), bust 30-32 (33-35, 36-38) in. — 76-81.5 (84-89, 91.5-97) cm
❖ Finished bust measurements: 46 (48-1/2, 50-1/2) — 115 (121, 127) cm, length: 20 (20-3/4, 21-1/2) in. — 50 (52, 54) cm
❖ Sleeve seam: 2-1/4 in. (5.5 cm)

Materials
❖ Sport weight cotton novelty yarn (approx. 150 yds per 50 g skein): 2 skeins each color black, light yellow, light blue, and light pink.
❖ Crochet hook U.S. size C/2 (Metric size 3) or size needed to obtain gauge.
To save time, take time to check gauge!

Gauge
27 sts and 28 rows in pat st = 4 in. (10 cm).

Stitches
Chain (ch), slip st (sl), single crochet (sc).
Pat st: Multiple of 15 + 2 (10, 4) ch and 1 ch for the beg of row.
Row 1: Light yellow, 1 sc in the 2nd ch from the hook, 1 sc in each of the foll 4 (8, 5) ch, *ch 7, skip 7 ch, 1 sc in the foll 8 ch*, rep * to *, end last rep with 1 sc in each of the last 5 (9, 6) ch. Rows 2 and 3: Light yellow, ch 1, 1 sc in each sc, ch 7 between groups of sc. Row 4: Black, ch 1, 1 sc in each sc. Between the groups of sc, ch 3, 1 sc around the underlying ch 7 arc, ch 3. Rows 5, 6, and 7: Light pink: ch 1, 1 sc in each sc, ch 7 between groups of sc. Rep rows 4 to 7, in the foll colors: light blue, light yellow, and light pink with a black row between them. When changing colors, work the last loop of the last st with the color of the next st.

Note: See "Stitches and Techniques" for detailed instructions on stitches and shapings.

Back
With black, ch 122 (130, 139) + ch 1 to turn. Continue in pat st. Work until piece measures 10-1/4 in. (26 cm) from beg. Inc 15 sts at each edge = 152 (160, 169) sts. Work in pat st until piece measures 8-3/4 (9-1/2, 10-1/4) in. - 22 (24, 26) cm from the beg of sleeve. End on the 4th row. Fasten off.

Front
Work same as back until piece measures 7 (8, 8-3/4) in. - 18 (20, 22) cm from the beg of sleeves. End on 4th row. Leave the center 52 (52, 51) sts unworked. Work each side separately. Work 50 (54, 59) sts until piece measures 8-3/4 (9-1/2, 10-1/4) in. - 22 (24, 26) cm from beg of sleeve. End on 4th row. Fasten off. Work 2nd side to correspond.

Side Panels
Worked from side to side. With black, ch 85 + ch 1 for the beg of row. Row 1: Light pink, 1 sc in the 2nd ch from the hook, 1 sc in each of the foll 8 ch, ch 7, skip 7 ch, 1 sc in each of the foll 8 ch, etc, end with 1 sc in each of the last 9 ch. Work until piece measures 5-1/4 in. (13 cm). End on 4th row. Fasten off. Make a 2nd piece.

Finishing
Block pieces to indicated measurements. Sew shoulder seams. Sew side panels to side seams of back and front. Around neck and each sleeve, with black work 1 row as foll: *Ch 1, 1 sc*, work * to * around, sl st to join to beg of round. Fasten off. Along lower edge of body, work as foll : Row 1: With black, *ch 1, 1 work in sc along back, front and side panels, sl st to join in the first ch. Row 2: Light blue, ch 1, 1 sc in each sc and end round with sl st in the first ch. Rows 3, 4, and 5: Like round 2, but work in black, light pink, and black. Fasten off.

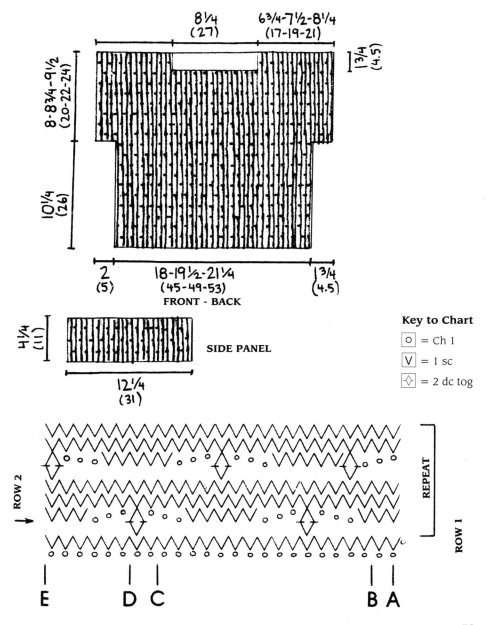

Novelty Yarn Top

Level: Intermediate

Size

❖ Woman's Small (Medium, Large), bust 30-32 (33-35, 36-38) in. — 76-81.5 (84-89, 91.5-97) cm

❖ Finished bust measurements: 44-1/2 (47-1/2, 51) in. — 112 (120, 128) cm, length: 19-1/4 (20, 20-3/4) in. — 48 (50, 52) cm

❖ Sleeve seam: 2 in. (5 cm)

Materials

❖ Sport weight cotton novelty yarn (approx. 150 yds per 50 g skein): 3 skeins color black, 2 skeins each color light yellow, light blue, and light green

❖ Crochet hook U.S. size C/2 (Metric size 3) or size needed to obtain gauge

To save time, take time to check gauge!

Gauge

27 sts and 24 rows in pat st = 4 in. (10 cm).

Stitches

Chain (ch), slip st (sl), single crochet (sc), double crochet (dc).

2 dc tog: work 1 dc in the underlying st until 2 loops rem on hook, work 1 dc in the same st until 3 loops rem on hook, yo and draw through all loops on hook.

Pat st: Multiple of 12 + 1 or 12 + 7. Work in pat st foll chart. Beg each sc row with ch 1, work the first sc in the first st. On each row with 2 dc tog, beg with ch 3, 1 dc in the first st. Work 2 rows of sc alternating light green, light yellow, or light blue. Work rows with 2 dc tog in black. When changing colors, work the last loop of the last st with the color of the next st.

Note: See "Stitches and Techniques" for detailed instructions on stitches and shapings.

Back

Worked sideways, beg at lower edge of 1 sleeve. With light green, ch 55 (61, 67) + ch 1 for the beg of row. Work in pat st foll chart, beg with A to B, then rep B to C, end with C to D (E, D). Row 1: With light green, 1 sc in the 2nd ch from hook, 1 sc in each of the foll ch. Work by foll chart until piece measures 2 in. (5 cm). With right side facing, ch 72 and join to the body. Work over 127 (133, 139) sts in pat st until piece measures 18 (19-1/2, 21-1/4) in. - 45 (49, 53) cm, measured at right edge. Leave 72 sts at right edge unworked and work 2 in. (5 cm) over rem 55 (61, 67) sts for the 2nd sleeve. End with 2 rows of light blue, green, or yellow. Fasten off.

Front

Work same as back until piece measures 4-3/4 (5-1/2, 6-1/4) in. - 12 (14, 16) cm measured at right edge. Leave 12 sts unworked at left edge for neck. Work rem 115 (121 ,127) sts until piece measures 13-1/4 (14, 14-3/4) in. - 33 (35, 37) cm. Inc 12 sts at left edge on foll row. Work 127 (133, 139) sts as on back. Fasten off.

Side Panels

With light pink, ch 31 + ch 1 to turn for first row. Work in pat st foll chart. Work from point A to B, then work B to C twice, end with C to D. Work until piece measures 12-1/4 in. (31 cm). End with 2 rows light blue, green or yellow. Fasten off. Make a 2nd piece.

Finishing

Block pieces to indicated measurements. Sew shoulder seams. Sew side panels to side seams of back and front and 2 in. (5 cm) from lower edge of sleeves. Around neck and each sleeve, work 1 row of sc as foll with black: ch 1, sc around, end with 1 sl st in first ch. Fasten off. Along the lower edge of body, work as foll: Row 1: With black, ch 1, sc around lower edge of back and front and side panels. Slip st to first ch. Row 2: With black, ch 1, 1 sc in each sc, sl st to join in first ch. Rows 3 to 5: Like row 2, alternating black, light green, and black. Fasten off.

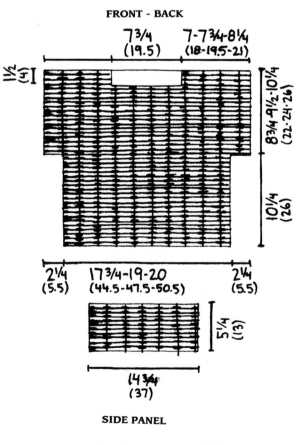

FRONT - BACK

7 3/4 (19.5) 7-7 3/4-8 1/4 (18-19.5-21)

8 3/4-9 1/2-10 1/4 (22-24-26)

10 1/4 (26)

1 1/2 (4)

2 1/4 (5.5) 17 3/4-19-20 (44.5-47.5-50.5) 2 1/4 (5.5)

5 1/4 (13)

14 3/4 (37)

SIDE PANEL

(Use chart from page 73.)

V-Motif Top

Level: Challenging

Size
❖ Woman's Small (Medium, Large), bust 30-32 (33-35, 36-38) in. — 76-81.5 (84-85.5, 91.5-97) cm
❖ Finished bust measurements: 38 (42, 46) in. — 95 (105, 115) cm, length: 19-3/4 (20-3/4, 21) in. — 49.5 (51, 52.5) cm
❖ Sleeve seam: 12-3/4 in. — (32 cm)

Materials
❖ Novelty sport weight cotton yarn (approx. 150 yds per 50 g skein) 8 (8, 9) skeins color navy
❖ Crochet hook U.S. size B/1 (Metric size 2.5) or size needed to obtain gauge
❖ Knitting needles U.S. size 2 (Metric size 2.5)
To save time, take time to check gauge!

Gauge
8 dc groups and 13 rows in pat st = 4 in. (10 cm)

Stitches
Chain (ch), single crochet (sc), double crochet (dc).
Pat st: Worked over multiple of 3 + 2 and ch 3 at beg of row.
Row 1: 1 dc in the 4th ch from the hook, skip 1 ch, *3 dc in the foll ch, skip 2 ch*, rep * to *, end with 3 dc in the foll ch, skip 1 ch, 1 dc in the last ch.
Row 2: Ch 3, 1 dc in the last dc of the previous row, *3 dc between the foll 2 dc groups*, rep * to *, end with 3 dc after the last dc group, 1 dc in the top st of the turning ch at the beg of the row. Edge sts are not shown on chart. Always rep the 2nd row. Inc 1 dc group at beg of row: Beg with ch 4, 3 dc in the last dc of the previous row. Continue in pat st. Inc 2 dc groups at the beg of row: Beg row with ch 7, 3 dc in the 5th ch from hook, skip 2 ch, 3 dc between the last dc of the last dc group of the last row. Continue in pat st. Inc 3 dc groups at the beg of row: Beg row with ch 10, 3 dc in the 5th ch from the hook, skip 2 ch, 3 dc in the foll ch, skip 2 ch, 3 dc between the last dc of the last dc group of the previ-

ous row. Continue in pat st.
Eyelet st: Continue by foll chart.
1/1 ribbing: Row 1: *K1, p1*. Rep * to * across.
Row 2 and all foll rows: Work sts as established in previous row.

Note: See "Stitches and Techniques" for detailed instructions on stitches and shapings.

Back
With crochet hook, ch 116 (128, 140) + ch 3 to turn (counts as first dc). Work in pat st = 38 (42, 46) dc groups, with 1 border st at each edge. Work until piece measures 5-1/4 (6,

6-1/2) in. - 13.5 (15, 16.5) cm - 18 (20, 22) rows. Beg eyelet point by centering chart. Work the first row in the ch between the 2 middle dc groups. At the same time, beg the sleeve incs after the 18th (20th, 22nd) row. At beg of every row, inc 1 dc group 12 times, inc 2 dc groups 12 times, inc 3 dc groups 4 times. After the last inc, you will have 24 inc dc groups at each edge = 46 (48, 50) rows. Piece will measure 14 (14-3/4, 15-3/4) in. - 35.5 (37, 38.5) cm. Continue in eyelet pat with pat st at each edge for a total of 62 (64, 66) rows - 18-3/4 (19-1/2, 20-1/2) in. - 47.5 (49, 50.5) cm. Fasten off.

Front
Work same as back.

Finishing
Block pieces to indicated measurements. With knitting needles, pick up and knit 78 (86, 94) sts along lower edge of back and work 3/4 in. (2 cm) of 1/1 ribbing. Bind off. Work same border on front. Sew shoulder and top of sleeve seams, leaving center 22 in. (55 cm) open. With knitting needles, pick up and knit 66 sts along lower edge of each sleeve and work 3/4 in. (2 cm) of 1/1 ribbing. Bind off. Sew side and sleeve seams.

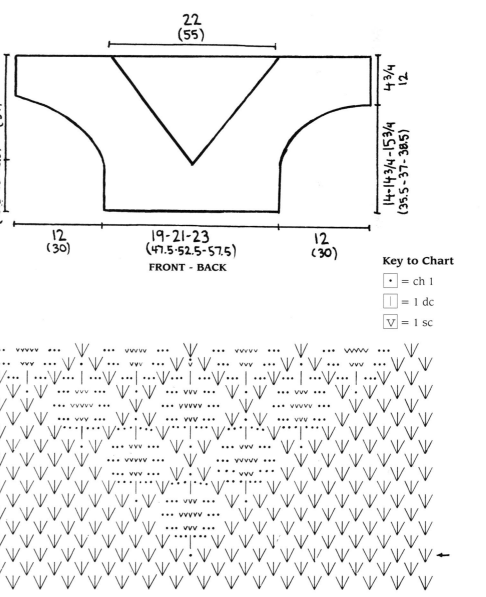

Key to Chart

- ⋅ = ch 1
- | = 1 dc
- V = 1 sc

22 (55)

13½ (34)

5¼-6-6½ (13.5-15-16.5)

4¾ (12)

14-14¾-15¾ (35.5-37-38.5)

12 (30)

19-21-23 (47.5-52.5-57.5)

12 (30)

FRONT - BACK

CENTER FRONT/CENTER BACK

EYELET STITCH

Pullover Vest

Level: Intermediate

Size

❖ Woman's Small (Medium, Large, X Large), bust 30-32 (33-35, 36-38, 39-42) in. — 76-81.5 (84-89, 91.5-97, 99-107) cm
❖ Finished bust measurements: 38-1/2 (41-1/2, 45, 48) in. — 97 (104, 113, 120) cm
❖ Length: 23-1/2 (24-1/2, 25, 25-1/2) in. — 59 (61, 62.5, 64) cm
❖ Sleeve seam: 16-1/2 (16-1/2, 17-1/4, 17-1/4) in. — 42 (42, 43, 43) cm

Materials

❖ Sport weight novelty cotton yarn (approx. 150 yds per 50 g skein) 11 (12, 13, 14) skeins color ecru
❖ Crochet hook U.S. size C/2 (Metric size 3)
❖ Knitting needles U.S. size 2 (Metric size 2.5) or size needed to obtain gauge
To save time, take time to check gauge!

Gauge

9 motifs (1 motif = 1 hdc, ch 1 and 1 hdc) and 12 rows = 4 in. (10 cm)

Stitches

Chain (ch), slip st (sl), single crochet (sc), half double crochet (hdc).
Pat st: Row 1: 1 sc, *ch 1, 1 sc*, rep * to *.
Row 2: Ch 2 = 1 border st, *1 hdc, ch 1, 1 hdc in the ch*, rep * to * across row, end with 1 hdc = 1 border st. Always rep row 2.
1/1 ribbing: Row 1: *K1, p1*. Rep * to * across.
Row 2 and all foll rows: Work sts as established in previous row.

Note: See "Stitches and Techniques" for detailed instructions on stitches and shapings.

Back

With knitting needles, cast on 90 (96, 104, 110) sts and work 2-1/2 in. (6 cm) in 1/1 ribbing. Bind off loosely. In the bound off row, with crochet hook work 1 sc, *ch 1, 1 sc*, rep * to * 44 (47, 51, 54) times, end with 1 sc. Work in pat st. When piece measures 14-1/4 in. (36 cm), shape raglans. Dec 1 motif at each edge of foll row. At each edge of every row, dec 1/2 motif 27 (29, 31, 33) times. (Slip over the dec motifs at the beg of the row and leave the dec motifs at the end of the row unworked.) = 14 (15, 17, 18) whole motifs with 1/2 motif + 1 border st at each edge. Raglan will measure 9-1/4 (10, 10-1/2, 11) in. - 23 (25, 26.5, 28) cm, fasten off.

Front

Work same as back until piece measures 13 in. (32.5 cm). Divide work into 2 parts and work separately. Work the first 22 (23-1/2, 25-1/2, 27) motifs. At neck edge of every 2nd row, dec 1/2 motif 11 (11, 12, 13) times. At neck edge of every row, dec 1/2 motif 7 (8, 9, 9) times. At the same time, when piece measures 14-1/4 in. - (36 cm), shape raglans as on back until 24 (26, 28, 30) 1/2 motifs have been decreased at raglan edges. The raglan will measure 8 (11, 11-1/2, 12) in. - 20.5 (22.5, 24, 25.5) cm. Fasten off. Work the other side to correspond, rev shapings.

Left Sleeve

With knitting needles, cast on 48 (50, 52, 54) sts and work 2-1/2 in. (6 cm) in 1/1 ribbing. Bind off loosely. On bound off row, with crochet hook work 1 sc, then *ch 1, 1 sc*, work * to * 26 (28, 29, 30) times. Work in pat st = 26 (28, 29, 30) motifs with 1 border st at each edge. Inc 1/2 motif at each edge every 1-1/4 in. (3 cm) 10 times = 36 (38, 39, 40) motifs. Piece will measure 16-3/4 (16-3/4, 17-1/4, 17-1/4) in. - 42 (42, 43, 43) cm. On the foll row, dec 1 motif at each edge. Work same as back raglan dec on right edge. Work same as front raglan dec on left edge, then at left edge of every row, dec 2-1/2 motifs once, dec 3 (3, 2-1/2, 2) motifs twice. Fasten off.

RightSleeve

Work same as left sleeve, rev raglan shapings.

Neckband

With knitting needles, cast on 165 (169, 173, 177) sts and work 1-1/4 in. (3 cm) in 1/1 ribbing. At the same time, at each edge of every row, inc 1 st. Bind off by knitting all sts.

Finishing

Block pieces to indicated measurements. Sew sleeve and side seams. Sew in raglan seams, with the short side of the sleeves at the front. Sew neckband to neck edge with inc edge at center front. Sew center seam.

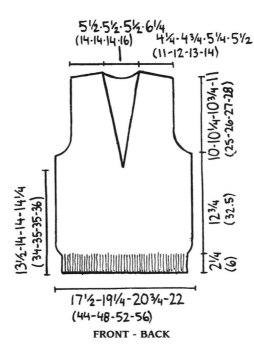

5½·5½·5½·6¼
(14·14·14·16)
4¼·4¾·5¼·5½
(11-12-13-14)
10-10¼-10¾-11
(25-26-27-28)
13½-14-14-14¼
(34-35-35-36)
12¾
(32.5)
2¼
(6)
17½-19¼-20¾-22
(44-48-52-56)

FRONT - BACK

Shell Top

Level: Intermediate

Size

❖ Woman's Small (Medium, Large), bust 30-32 (33-35, 36-38) in. — 76-81.5 (84-89, 91.5-97) cm
❖ Finished bust measurements: 43 (45-1/2,48) in. — 108 (114, 120) cm, length: 24-1/4 in. (60 cm)

Materials

❖ Sport weight yarn (approx. 230 yds per 50 g skein) 8 (8, 9) skeins color aqua
❖ Crochet hook U.S. size E/4 (Metric size 3.5) or size needed to obtain gauge
❖ Knitting needles U.S. size 6 (Metric size 4)
To save time, take time to check gauge!

Gauge

15 dc and 12 rows in pat st = 4 in. (10 cm).

Stitches

Chain (ch), single crochet (sc), double crochet (dc)
Bobble: *yo, insert hook in the front loop of st, yo, draw through loop*, rep * to * 3 times, yo, draw through 9 loops on hook.
Pat st: Rows 1 and 2: Sc. Row 3: Ch 3 = 1 border st, 1 dc in the foll st, *1 dc in each of the foll 4 sts (work in front loops), 1 dc in each of the foll 4 sts (work in both loops)*, rep * to *, end with 1 dc in the last 2 sts. Row 4: Ch 1 = 1 border st, 1 sc in the foll st, *1 sc in each of the foll 4 sts, 1 bobble in each of the foll 4 sts of previous row*, rep * to *, end with 1 sc in each of the last 2 sts. Row 5: Like row 3. Row 6: Like row 4. Row 7: Ch 3 = 1 border st, 1 dc in the foll st, *1 dc in each of the foll 4 sts (work in both loops), 1 dc in each of the foll 4 sts (work in front loops)*, rep * to *, end with 1 dc in each of the last 2 sts. Row 8: Ch 1 = 1 border st, 1 sc in the foll st, *1 bobble in each of the foll 4 sts of the previous row, 1 sc in each of the foll 4 sts*, rep * to *, end with 1 sc in the last 2 sts. Row 9: Like row 7. Row 10: Like row 8. Rep rows 3 to 10.
Note: For size medium work

8th row instead of the 4th row and the 4th row instead of the 8th row.
1/1 ribbing: Row 1: *K1, p1*. Rep * to * across.
Row 2 and all foll rows: Work sts as established in previous row.

Note: See "Stitches and Techniques" for detailed instructions on stitches and shapings.

Back

With knitting needles and double strand, cast on 84 (88, 92) sts and work 2 in. (5 cm) in 1/1 ribbing. Bind off loosely. With crochet hook and single strand, work in pat st until piece measures 21-3/4 in. (54 cm). Leave center 22 (24, 26) sts unworked. Work each side separately. At neck edge of every row, dec 3 sts once, dec 2 sts once, dec 1 st twice = 24 (25, 26) sts on shoulder. Work

until piece measures 24-1/4 in. (60 cm) = 66 rows. Fasten off.

Front

Work small and large same as back. For medium, work row 7 after row 2.

Finishing

Block pieces to indicated measurements. With knitting needles and double strand, pick up and knit 64 (66, 68) sts around front neck and work 1-1/4 in. (3 cm) in 1/1 ribbing. Bind off loosely. Work same border on back neck. Sew shoulder and neckband seam. Mark armholes 8 (8-1/4, 8-3/4) in. - 20(21,22) cm from shoulder seams. With knitting needles and double strand, pick up and knit 78 (82, 86) sts from side seam between markers and work 1-1/4 in. (3 cm) in 1/1 ribbing. Bind off loosely. Sew side and armhole border seams.

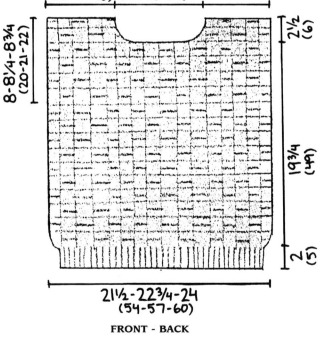

6¼-6½-7 8¾-9¼-9½
(16-17-18) (22-23-24)

8-8¼-8¾
(20-21-22)

2½
(6)

19¾
(49)

2
(5)

21½-22¾-24
(54-57-60)

FRONT - BACK

CHILDREN'S WEAR

Yellow Bobbles Pullover

Level: Intermediate

Size
❖ Child's size 2 (4, 6) years, chest 21 (23, 25) in. — 52.5 (57.5, 62.5) cm
❖ Finished chest measurements: 24 (25, 27) in. — 60 (64, 68) cm
❖ Length: 13 (13-3/4, 14-1/2) in. — 33 (35, 37) cm
❖ Sleeve seam: 9-1/2(10-1/2, 11-3/4) in. — 24 (27, 30) cm

Materials
❖ Scheepjeswol Voluma (approx. 209 yds per 50 g skein) 2 (3, 3) skeins color light blue and 1 skein color yellow
❖ 4 buttons
❖ Crochet hook U.S. size F/5 (Metric size 4) or size needed to obtain gauge
❖ Knitting needles U.S. size 3 (Metric size 3)
To save time, take time to check gauge!

Gauge
12 sc and 15 rows = 4 in. (10 cm)

Stitches
Chain (ch), single crochet (sc)
Bobbles: Insert hook lengthwise 1 row below foll sc and draw through loop, yo, insert hook in the same st again and draw through another loop, yo and draw through both loops.
1/1 ribbing: Row 1: *K1, p1*. Rep * to * across.
Row 2 and all foll rows: Work sts as established in previous row.

Note: See "Stitches and Techniques" for detailed instructions on stitches and shapings.

Back
With knitting needles and light blue, cast on 42 (44, 46) sts and work 2 in. (5 cm) in 1/1 ribbing. Bind off loosely. With crochet hook, join light blue to edge st and work 36 (38, 41) sc in the bound off edge. Turn and beg each row with ch 1. Work 2 rows of sc. Bobble row: Join yellow yarn to the last st of the last row. Work 4 sc with light

blue, hold the unused yarn against the wrong side of work. When inserting hook, work around the unused yarn so that the new sts hold it against the back of the work. Work the last loop of the last st with yellow and make a bobble and work the last loop of the bobble with light blue, *4 sc with light blue, make 1 bobble with yellow*, rep * to * to the last st. With light blue, work 1 sc. Work 5 rows of sc with light blue. Foll bobble row: With light blue, work 2 sc, then 1 bobble with yellow, *4 sc with light blue, 1 bobble with yellow*, rep from * to *. Work 5 rows of light blue in sc. Rep these 12 rows. After each row of yellow bobbles, break off the yellow yarn. The piece is 12 (12-1/2, 13-1/2) in.- 30 (32, 34) cm wide and 13 (13-3/4, 14-1/2) in. - 33 (35, 37) cm from beg. Fasten off.

Front
Work same as back until piece measures 11-3/4 (12-1/2, 13-1/4) in. - 30 (32, 34) cm from beg. Leave the center 8 (8, 9) sc unworked. Work each side separately. At each neck edge of every row, dec 1 sc twice = 12 (13, 14) sc on each shoulder. Work until piece measures same as back. Fasten off.

Sleeves
With knitting needles and light blue, cast on 30 (32, 34) sts and work 2 in. (5 cm) in 1/1 ribbing. Bind off loosely. With crochet hook, work 28 (30, 32) sc in bound off sts. Continue as on back until piece measures 6 (7, 8-1/4) in. - 15 (18, 21) cm above ribbing. At each edge of every 2nd row, inc 1 sc 3 times. Work even until piece measures 7-1/2 (8-1/2, 9-3/4) in. - 19 (22, 25) cm above ribbing. Fasten off.

Finishing
Block pieces to indicated measurements. Sew right shoulder seam. Sew left shoulder seam for 3/4 in. (2 cm) from side edge. With knitting needles and light blue, pick up 48 (50, 52) sts around neck and work 1-1/2 in. (4 cm) in 1/1 ribbing. Bind off loosely. Fold neckband in half to inside and slip st in place. Along front edge of left shoulder, make 4 button loops and sew on 4 buttons to correspond on back shoulder edge. Sew sleeves to armholes, matching center of sleeve with shoulder seams. Sew side and sleeve seams.

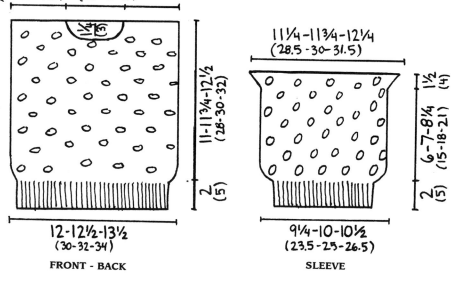

4-4¼-4½ (10-11-11.5) 4-4-4½ (10-10-11)

11-11¾-12½ (28-30-32)

2 (5)

12-12½-13½ (30-32-34)

FRONT - BACK

11¼-11¾-12¼ (28.5-30-31.5)

1½ (4)

6-7-8¼ (15-18-21)

2 (5)

9¼-10-10½ (23.5-25-26.5)

SLEEVE

Toddler Pullover

Level: Intermediate

Size
❖ Child's size 2 (4, 6) years, chest 21 (23, 25) in. — 52.5 (58.5, 63.5) cm
❖ Finished chest measurements: 24 (25-1/2, 27) in. — 60 (64, 68) cm
❖ Length: 12-1/4 (13-1/2, 15) in. — 31 (34,3 8) cm
❖ Sleeve seam: 9-1/2 (11-1/4, 12-1/4) in. — 24 (28.5, 31) cm

Materials
❖ Sport weight yarn (approx. 165 yds per 50 g skein) 3 (3, 4) skeins each color white and gray
❖ Tapestry wool: color light green, green, red, and pink
❖ 2 buttons
Crochet hook U.S. size E/4 (Metric size 3.5) or size needed to obtain gauge
❖ Knitting needles U.S. sizes 3 and 4 (Metric sizes 3 and 3.5)
To save time, take time to check gauge!

Gauge
21 sts and 17 rows in pat st = 4 in. (10 cm)

Stitches
Chain (ch), single crochet (sc), half double crochet (hdc)
Relief dc: Worked on a row of sc. Insert hook in the back of the post right to left, yo, then work dc.
Pat st: Multiple of 4 + 2 + ch 1 to turn.
Row 1: With gray, 1 sc in each ch, beg with the 2nd ch from the hook.
Row 2: With gray, ch 2 to turn, 1 hdc in each sc. Work the last loop with white.
Row 3: With white, ch 1 to turn, *1 sc in each of the foll 3 hdc, insert hook in the back loop of the hdc, 1 relief dc around the foll hdc of the previous row*, rep * to *, end with 2 sc.
Row 4: With white, ch 2 to turn, 1 hdc in each st, beg with the first sc. Work the last loop with gray.
Row 5: With gray, ch 1 to turn, 1 sc in the first hdc (back loop), *1 relief dc in the foll sc of the previous row, 1 sc in each of the foll 3 hdc*, rep * to *, end with 4 sc.
Row 6: With gray, work like row 4.
Rep rows 3 to 6.
1/1 ribbing: Row 1: *K1, p1*. Rep * to * across.
Row 2 and all foll rows: Work sts as established in previous row.

Note: See "Stitches and Techniques" for detailed instructions on stitches and shapings.

Back
Work body and sleeves separately to the yoke. Work yoke sts over all pieces. With crochet hook and gray, ch 67 (71, 75). Work in pat st over 66 (70, 74) sts until piece measures 6 (7, 8) in. - 15.5 (17.5, 20) cm, end with 6th row of pat st. Shape raglans: At each edge of every row, dec 4 sts once, dec 1 st 3 times = 52 (56, 60) sts. Work until piece measures 7-3/4 (8-3/4, 9-3/4) in. - 20 (22, 24.5) cm, end on 6th row of pat st. Fasten off.

Front
Work same as back.

Sleeves
With crochet hook and gray, ch 43 (47, 51). Work in pat st over 42 (46, 50) sts. At each edge of every 5th (6th, 7th) row, inc 1 st 5 times = 52 (56, 60) sts. Piece will measure 8 (9-3/4, 10-3/4) in. - 20 (24.5, 27) cm, end with same row as back. At each edge of every row, dec 4 sts once, dec 1 st 3 times = 38 (42, 46) sts. End with same row as back. Fasten off.

Yoke
With larger size knitting needles and gray, pick up back loop of 172 (188, 204) sts from back, front and sleeves. Inc 15 sts around first row as foll: 50 (54, 58) sts from back and inc 4 sts (sl the first and last sts of each piece), 36 (40, 44) sts from left sleeve, inc 3 sts, 50 (54, 58) sts from front, inc 5 sts, 36 (40, 44) sts from right sleeve, inc 3 sts = 187 (203, 219) sts and work 10 rows in 1/1 ribbing, working back and forth. Row 11: Work 4 sts, *sl 1, k2 tog, psso, work 5 sts*, work * to * 24 (24, 26) times, end with sl 1, k2 tog, psso, work 4 sts = 141 (153, 165) sts. Continue in 1/1 ribbing in white for 5 (6, 7) rows. Row 6

(continued on page 86)

(7, 8): Work 3 sts, *sl 1, k3 tog, psso, work 3 sts*, work * to * 23 (25, 27) times = 95 (103, 111) sts. Work 5 (6, 7) rows. Row 12 (14, 16): With white, k2 tog, *sl 1, k2 tog, psso, work 5 sts*, work * to * 11 (12, 13) times, end with sl 1, k2 tog, psso, work 2 sts = 71 (77, 83) sts. Work 5 (7, 9) rows. With smaller size needles, work in 1/1 ribbing as foll: 10 rows in white, 2 rows in gray, 2 rows in white, 2 rows in gray, 2 rows in white, 1 row in gray. Bind off in gray.

Finishing

Block pieces to indicated measurements. Trace the motifs on tissue paper and pin to front above gray section of yoke. Embroider the stems in stem st and flowers and leaves in ch st through the paper. In each flower make a French knot. Use the photo as a guide for colors. Trim away tissue paper. With smaller size knitting needles and white, pick up and knit 76 (80, 84) sts from back and front and work in 1/1 ribbing as foll: 3 rows in white, 2 rows in gray, 2 rows in white, 2 rows in gray, 2 rows in white, 2 rows in gray and 1 row in white. Bind off in white. With smaller size knitting needles and white, pick up and knit 42 (46, 50) sts along each sleeve end and work 1-1/2 in. (4 cm) in 1/1 ribbing. Bind off in ribbing in white. Fold the striped part of the neckband in half to outside and sew ends closed. Sew raglan seams, leaving top 2-3/4 in. (7 cm) open on left front seam. Work 1 row of sc along raglan seams, make 2 loops 4 ch sts long for button clasps. Fasten off. Sew side and sleeve seams. Sew on buttons.

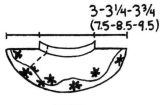

YOKE

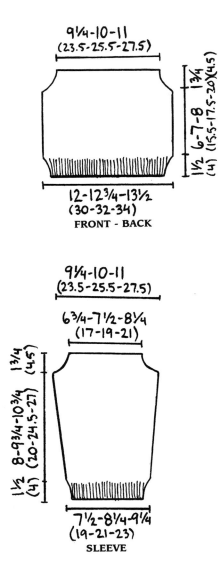

9¼-10-11
(23.5-25.5-27.5)

1¾ (4.5)

6-7-8 (15.5-17.5-20)

1½ (4)

12-12¾-13½
(30-32-34)

FRONT - BACK

9¼-10-11
(23.5-25.5-27.5)

6¾-7½-8¼
(17-19-21)

1¾ (4.5)

8-9¾-10¾ (20-24.5-27)

1½ (4)

7½-8¼-9¼
(19-21-23)

SLEEVE

CENTER FRONT

Level: Intermediate

Size

❖ Child's size 2 (4, 6) years, chest 21 (23, 25) in. — 52.5 (58.5, 63.5) cm
❖ Finished chest measurements: 22-3/4 (25-1/4, 27-1/4) in. — 57 (63, 68) cm
❖ Length: 13 (14-1/2, 16-1/4) in. — 33 (37, 41) cm
❖ Sleeve seam: 8-1/2 (10-1/4, 11-3/4) in. — 22 (26, 30) cm

Materials

❖ Sport weight yarn (approx. 165 yds per 50 g skein) 3 (3, 4) skeins each color white and gray
❖ Tapestry wool: color light green, green, red and pink
❖ 5 buttons
❖ Crochet hook U.S. size E/4 (Metric size 3.5) or size needed to obtain gauge
❖ Knitting needles U.S. size 3 (Metric size 3)
To save time, take time to check gauge!

Gauge

22 sts and 20 rows in pat st = 4 in. (10 cm). 1 motif is 2 hdc and 2 rows.

Stitches

Chain (ch), single crochet (sc), half double crochet (hdc)
Pat st: Worked on an odd number of sts + ch 1 to turn.
Row 1: With white, 1 sc in 2nd ch from the hook, *ch 1, skip 1 ch, 1 sc in the foll ch*, rep * to *.
Row 2: With white, ch 1 to turn, *2 hdc in the foll ch, skip 1 sc*, rep * to *, 1 hdc in the last sc. Work the last loop with gray.
Row 3: With gray, ch 1 to turn, 1 sc between the first hdc and 1 motif, *ch 1, skip 1 motif = 2 hdc, 1 sc between the motifs*, rep * to *, end with 1 sc between 1 motif and the last hdc.
Row 4: With gray, like row 2. Work the last loop with white.
Row 5: With white, like row 3. Rep rows 2 to 5.
When changing colors, work the last loop of the last st with

the color of the next st.
1/1 ribbing: Row 1: *K1, p1*.
Rep * to * across.
Row 2 and all foll rows: Work sts as established in previous row.

Note: See "Stitches and Techniques" for detailed instructions on stitches and shapings.

Body
With crochet hook and white, ch 126 (138, 150). Work in pat st over 62 (68, 74) motifs with 1 hdc at each edge as border sts. Work until piece measures 5-1/2(6-3/4 ,8) in. - 14 (17, 20) cm, end with 4th (2nd, 4th) row of pat st = gray. Divide work into 3 pieces. Work the first 15 (17, 18) motifs for the right front. Inc 1 st at armhole edge and work in pat st for 4 (6, 4) rows. The last row is the 4th row of pat st. Work 12 rows in white and continue in gray until armhole measures 4-1/4 (4-3/4, 5-1/4) in. - 11 (12, 13) cm. Shape neck: At right edge of every 2nd row, dec 8 (8, 10) sts once, dec 2 sts 2 (3, 3) times = 6 (7, 8) motifs. Work rem 9 (10, 10) motifs + 2 border sts. Continue until armhole measures 6 (6-1/4, 6-3/4) in.-15 (16, 17) cm. Fasten off. Work left front over last 15 (17, 18) motifs rev shapings of right front. Fasten off. Work center 32 (34, 38) motifs in pat st. Inc 1 st at each edge for border sts. Work in same colors and same length as front. Fasten off.

Sleeves
With crochet hook and white, ch 48 (50 ,52). Work in pat st over 23 (24, 25) motifs + 2 border sts. At each edge alternately every 2nd and 4th row, inc 1 st 10 (11, 12) times = 33 (35, 37) motifs + 2 border sts. Piece will measure 7 (8-3/4,10-1/4) in. - 18 (22, 26) cm. End with 4th row of pat st. Fasten off.

Finishing
Block pieces to indicated measurements. Trace the motifs on tissue paper and pin to white bands of body. Embroider the stems in stem st and flowers and leaves in ch st through the paper. In each flower make a French knot. Use the photo as a guide for colors. Trim away tissue paper. With knitting needles and gray, pick up and knit 137 (149, 163) sts from lower edge of body and work in 1/1 ribbing as foll: Alternating 2

rows in gray, 2 rows in white for 1 1/2 in.-(4 cm), ending with 2 rows of gray. Bind off in gray. With knitting needles and gray, pick up and knit 42 (44, 46) sts along each sleeve end and work 1-1/2 in. (4 cm) in striped 1/1 ribbing as on body, ending with 2 rows of gray. Bind off in ribbing in gray. With knitting needles and gray, pick up and knit 69 (77, 85) sts along neck and work in 1/1 ribbing as foll: 2 rows of gray, 2 rows of white and 2 rows in gray. Bind off on the 2nd row of gray. With knitting needles and gray, pick up and knit 94 (102, 110) sts along left front edge and work 6 rows in 1/1 ribbing. Bind off. On right front, work the same band. On the 3rd row, make 5 buttonholes as foll: Right side facing, work 4 sts, *work 2 tog, yo, work 19 (21, 23) sts*, rep * to * 3 times, end by working 2 sts tog, yo, work 4 sts. Sew sleeve seams. Sew sleeves to armholes. Sew on buttons.

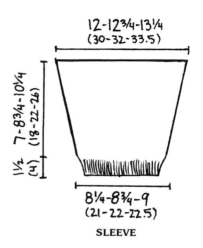

12-12¾-13¼
(30-32-33.5)

7-8¾-10¼
(18-22-26)

1½
(4)

8¼-8¾-9
(21-22-22.5)

SLEEVE

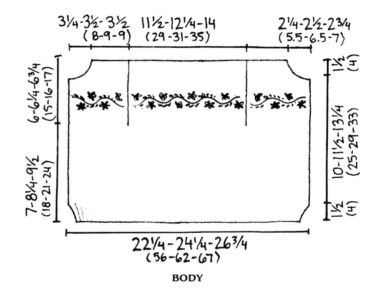

3¼-3½-3½
(8-9-9)   11½-12¼-14
(29-31-35)   2¼-2½-2¾
(5.5-6.5-7)

6-6¼-6¾
(15-16-17)

1½
(4)

7-8¼-9½
(18-21-24)

10-11½-13¼
(25-29-33)

1½
(4)

22¼-24¼-26¾
(56-62-67)

BODY

Boy's Cable Pullover

Level: Challenging

Size
❖ Child's size 6 (8, 10) years, chest: 25 (27, 28-1/2) in. — 63.5 (69, 72.5) cm
❖ Finished chest measurements: 29-1/2 (31, 32-1/2) in. — 74 (78, 82) cm
❖ Length: 19-1/4 (20-3/4, 22) in. — 48 (51, 55) cm
❖ Sleeve seam: 14 (14-3/4, 15-1/2) in. — 35 (37, 39) cm

Materials
❖ Sport weight yarn (approx. 130 yds per 50 g skein) 9 (10, 11) skeins color orange
❖ Crochet hook U.S. size C/2 (Metric size 3) or size needed to obtain gauge
❖ Knitting needles U.S. size 3 (Metric size 3)
To save time, take time to check gauge!

Gauge
20 hdc and 17 rows = 4 in. (10 cm)

Stitches
Chain (ch), slip st (sl), half double crochet (hdc).
3 relief tr tog: Work 1 tr in the vertical post of the hdc, inserting hook front to back and back to front. Work until there are 2 loops left on the hook, work in the same manner in the same hdc in the foll tr until 3 loops rem on hook, work the 3rd tr in the same manner in the same hdc until 4 loops are left on the hook, work tr.
Cable:
Row 1: Right side facing, work 3 relief tr tog in the foll hdc in the previous row, 1 hdc in same hdc, work 3 relief tr in the same hdc like the first 3 relief tr tog. Row 2: Hdc, working through all sts worked together in the previous row. Beg each row with ch 2 which counts as the first hdc.

Note: See "Stitches and Techniques" for detailed instructions on stitches and shapings.

Back
With crochet hook, ch 77 (81, 85) + ch 2 to turn = first hdc. Work in hdc until piece mea-sures 9-1/4 (10-1/4, 11-1/2) in. - 23 (26, 29) cm. Inc 7 sts at each edge of every row 3 (0, 0) times, inc 8 sts 5 (6, 1) time, inc 9 sts 0 (2, 7) times = 199 (213, 227) sts. At the same time, with the first inc, beg the cable pat. Work 1 cable at the center. At each edge of cable on every 2nd row, work 1 addi-tional cable with 3 sts between them 15 times = 1 cable, 3 hdc, 1 cable, 3 hdc, 1 cable, etc. Work until piece measures 16 (17-1/4, 18-1/2) in. - 40 (43, 46) cm from beg. Leave center 21 (23, 25) sts unworked. Work each side separately. (Each cable counts as 1 st.) At neck edge, dec 4 sts once. Work until piece measures 16-3/4 (18, 19-1/2) in. - 42 (45, 49) cm. Fasten off. Work 2nd half to correspond.

Front
Work front same as back until piece measures 15 -1/2 (16-3/4, 18) in. - 39 (42, 45) cm from beg. Leave center 13 (15, 17) sts unworked. Work each side separately. At neck edge of every 2nd row, dec 4 sts twice. Fasten off when piece mea-sures 16-3/4 (18, 19-1/2) in. - 42 (45, 49) cm from beg.

Finishing
Block pieces to indicated mea-surements. Sew 1 shoulder and sleeve seam. With knitting nee-dles, pick up and knit 104 (114, 124) sts around neck and work 2-3/4 in. (7 cm) in 1/1 ribbing. Bind off loosely. Sew 2nd shoulder, sleeve and neckband seam. Fold neckband in half to inside and sl st in place. With knitting needles, pick up and knit 1 st from every ch st along lower edge of body and work 2-1/2 in. (6 cm) in 1/1 ribbing. Bind off loosely. Sew sleeves to armholes, matching center of sleeve with shoulder seams. Sew side and sleeve seams. Fold sleeve cuffs in half to outside and sl st in place.

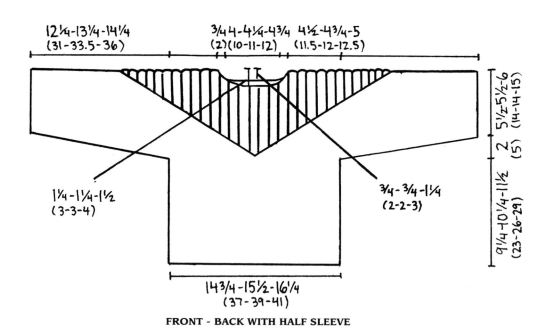

12¼-13¼-14¼ (31-33.5-36) 3/4-4-4¼-4¾ (2)(10-11-12) 4½-4¾-5 (11.5-12-12.5)

5½-5½-6 (14-14-15)

2 (5)

9¼-10¼-11½ (23-26-29)

1¼-1¼-1½ (3-3-4)

3/4-3/4-1¼ (2-2-3)

14¾-15½-16¼ (37-39-41)

FRONT - BACK WITH HALF SLEEVE

Diagonal Stripe Top

Level: Intermediate

Size

❖ Child's size 5 (7, 9) years, chest 24 (26, 27-3/4) in. — 60 (65, 69.5) cm
❖ Finished chest measurements: 29 (32, 34-1/2) in. — 74 (81, 88) cm
❖ Length: 18-3/4 (19-3/4, 20-3/4) in. — 47.5 (50.5, 53.5) cm

Materials

❖ Mayflower Cotton 10 (approx. 235 yds per 50 g skein) 5 (5, 6) skeins color white
❖ Crepe cotton in the following colors: turquoise, yellow, orange, green, and red
❖ Crochet hook U.S. size B/1 (Metric size 2.5 mm) or size needed to obtain gauge
❖ Knitting needles U.S. size 2 (Metric size 2.5 mm)
To save time, take time to check gauge!

Gauge

31 st and 14 rows = 4 in. (10 cm) in pat st. 1 pat rep of 11 sts = 1-1/4 in. (3.5 cm)

Stitches

Chain (ch), single crochet (sc), double crochet (dc).
Pat st: Alternately work 5 dc, ch 1, 1 dc, ch 2, 1 dc, ch 1. Shift the motif by 1 dc to the right on every row. Foll the chart. Beg and end every row with a border st (Ch 3 to turn at beg of row and end each row with 1 dc around the ch 3 to turn).
Row 1: Ch 3 to turn (= 1 border st), *1 dc in each of the foll 5 sts, ch 1, skip 1 st, 1 dc in the foll st, ch 2, skip 2, 1 dc in the foll st, ch 1, skip 1*, rep * to * across, end with 1 dc in each of the last 5 sts, 1 dc in the ch 3 (= 1 border st).
Row 2: Ch 3 to turn, ch 1, skip 1, 1 dc in each of the foll 5 sts, ch 1, skip 1, 1 dc in the foll st, ch 2, skip 2 dc, 1 dc in the foll st, ch 1, skip 1, etc., ending row with 4 dc, 1 dc in the ch 3 of the previous row.
Row 3: Ch 3, 3 dc, ch 1, 1 dc, ch 2, 1 dc, ch 1, etc. Continue by foll chart. (Chart doesn't show border sts.)

1/1 ribbing: Row 1: *K1, p1*. Rep * to * across.
Row 2 and all foll rows: Work sts as established in previous row.

Note: See "Stitches and Techniques" for detailed instructions on stitches and shapings.

Front

With crochet hook and Cotton 10, ch 118 (129, 140). Work 1 row of sc, beg with the 3rd ch from the hook. Continue in pat st = 117 (128, 139) sts with 1 border st at each edge. Work by foll chart until piece measures 10-1/4 (11, 11-3/4) in. - 26 (28, 30) cm. Inc 1 st at each edge of the foll 5 rows. At end of next 2 rows, inc 13 (14, 15) sts. Work inc sts in pat st. Work until sleeve measures 5 (5-1/2, 6) in. - 13 (14, 15) cm. Leave the center 61 (62, 65) sts unworked. Work each shoulder separately. Work even until sleeve measures 6 (6-1/4, 6-1/2) in. - 15 (16, 17) cm. Fasten off.

Back

Work same as front, but shift diagonal stripes to the left.

Color Bands

With crochet hook and crepe cotton, ch 5. In the 4th and 5th ch from the hook, work 1 dc. Ch 3 to turn and work 2 dc.

Continue in this way, beg with ch 3 and working 2 dc on each row. Work until piece measures the same as the width of the body and sleeves and shoulders. Fasten off. Make a piece in yellow, green, red, orange, and turquoise.

Finishing

Along the lower edge of back and front, with knitting needles and Cotton 10, pick up 1 st from every st, dec 5 (7, 9) sts evenly spaced across row and work 1-1/4 in. (3 cm) in 1/1 ribbing. Bind off loosely. Work same border along each neck edge 3/4 in. (2 cm) wide. Bind off loosely. Sew sides of front and back neckband. Sew shoulder seams. With crochet hook and Cotton 10, work 1 row of sc along lower edge of cap sleeves. Fasten off. With knitting needles and Cotton 10, pick up 1 st from each sc and work 3/4 in. (2 cm) of 1/1 ribbing. Bind off loosely. Thread the color bands through the eyelets of pat st using photo as a guide for color placement. Tack ends at shoulder seams and top of ribbing. Sew side and sleeve seams.

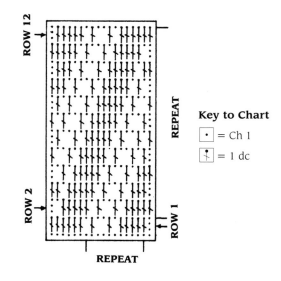

ROW 12
ROW 2
ROW 1
REPEAT
REPEAT

Key to Chart

• = Ch 1

= 1 dc

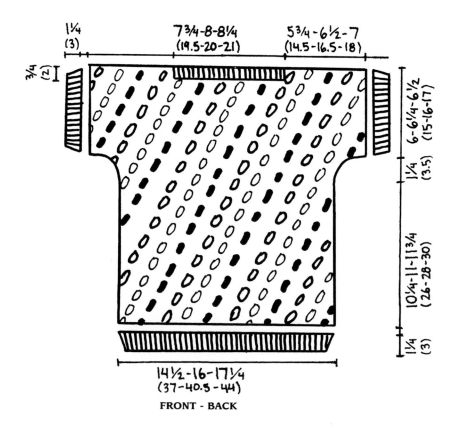

1¼ (3)
¾ (2)
7¾-8-8¼ (19.5-20-21)
5¾-6½-7 (14.5-16.5-18)
6-6¼-6½ (15-16-17)
1¼ (3.5)
10¼-11-11¾ (26-28-30)
1¼ (3)
14½-16-17¼ (37-40.5-44)

FRONT - BACK

Horizontal Stripe Top

Level: Easy

Size
❖ Child's size 5 (7, 9) years, chest 24 (26, 27-3/4) in. — 60 (65, 69.5) cm
❖ Finished chest measurements: 30-1/2 (33, 34) in. — 78 (84, 86) cm
❖ Length: 16-3/4 (18-1/2, 20-1/4) in. — 42.5 (47, 51.5) cm
❖ Sleeve seam: 6-1/4 in. (16 cm)

Materials
❖ Mayflower Cotton 10 (approx. 235 yds per 50 g skein) 5 (6, 6) skeins color white
❖ Crepe cotton in the following colors: turquoise, yellow, orange, green, and red
Crochet hook U.S. size B/1 (Metric size 2.5 mm) or size needed to obtain gauge
❖ Knitting needles U.S. size 2 (Metric size 2.5 mm)
To save time, take time to check gauge!

Gauge
28 st and 13 rows = 4 in. (10 cm). 1 pat over 6 rows = 1-3/4 in. (4.5 cm)

Stitches
Chain (ch), single crochet (sc), double crochet (dc), treble crochet (tr).
Pat st:
Row 1: Work in dc. Beg row with ch 3 to turn (= 1 border st), end each row with 1 extra dc.
Rows 2 and 3: Like row 1.
Row 4: Ch 3, *1 dc in the foll st, ch 1, skip 1 dc*, rep * to * across, end with 1 dc in the foll st and 1 dc in the ch (= 1 border st).
Row 5: Ch 3, *1 tr in the foll dc, ch 1*, rep * to *, end with 1 tr and 1 tr in the turning ch (= 1 border st).
Row 6: Ch 3, *1 dc in the foll tr, ch 1*, rep * to *, end with 1 dc in the foll tr and 1 dc in the ch (= 1 border st).
Always rep these 6 rows.
1/1 ribbing: Row 1: *K1, p1*. Rep * to * across.
Row 2 and all foll rows: Work sts as established in previous row.

Note: See "Stitches and Techniques" for detailed instructions on stitches and shapings.

Back
With crochet hook and Cotton 10, ch 112 (118, 124). Work 1 row of sc, beg with the 3rd ch from the hook. Continue in pat st = 109 (115, 121) dc with 1 border st at each edge. Work 6 rows of pat st 8 (9, 10) times, end with 2 rows of dc = 14-3/4 (16-1/2, 18-1/4) in. - 37.5 (42, 46.5) cm. Fasten off.

Front
Work same as back until piece measures 14-3/4 (16-1/2, 18-1/4) in. - 37.5 (42, 46.5) cm. Leave the center 7-1/2 (8, 8-1/4) in. - 19 (20, 21) cm unworked = 55 (57, 59) sts and work each shoulder separately. Work the 1st, 3rd, 5th and 6th rows of pat st, end with first row. Fasten off. The 5th row is the shoulder seam.

Sleeves
With crochet hook and Cotton 10, ch 86 (90, 94). Work 1 row of sc, beg with ch 3 to turn = 85 (89, 93) sc. Continue in pat st, working the 6 rows 3 times total. *At each edge of 1st and 2nd rows, inc 1 st. Do not inc on 3rd row.* Work * to * 3 times total = 12 inc sts at each edge = 109 (113, 117) sts. Fasten off.

Color Bands
With crochet hook and crepe cotton, ch 5. In the 4th and 5th ch from the hook, work 1 dc. Ch 3 to turn and work 2 dc. Continue in this way, always beg with ch 3 and working 2 dc on each row. Work until piece measures the same as the width of the body and sleeves and shoulders. Fasten off. Make pieces in yellow, green, red, orange, and turquoise. See photo.

Finishing
Along the lower edge of back and front, with knitting needles and Cotton 10, pick up and knit 1 st from every st and work 1-1/4 in. (3 cm) in 1/1 ribbing. Bind off loosely. Work same border on each sleeve, but 3/4 in. (2 cm) wide. Fold shoulder sections at 5th row and sew ends to top of back. With knitting needles and Cotton 10, pick up 1 st from every st along front neck edge and work in 1/1 ribbing to height of shoulder line. Bind off loosely. Sew ends in place. Work same border along back neck edge. Sew sleeves to side seams, matching center of sleeve with shoulder seams. Sew side and sleeve seams. Thread the color bands through the eyelet rows of pat st (5th row) using photo as a guide for color placement. Sew ends in place.

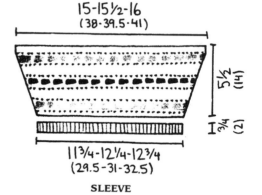

15-15½-16
(38-39.5-41)

5½
(14)

¾
(2)

11¾-12¼-12¾
(29.5-31-32.5)

SLEEVE

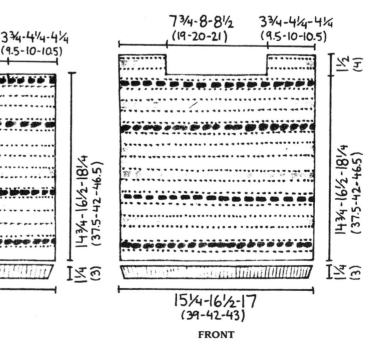

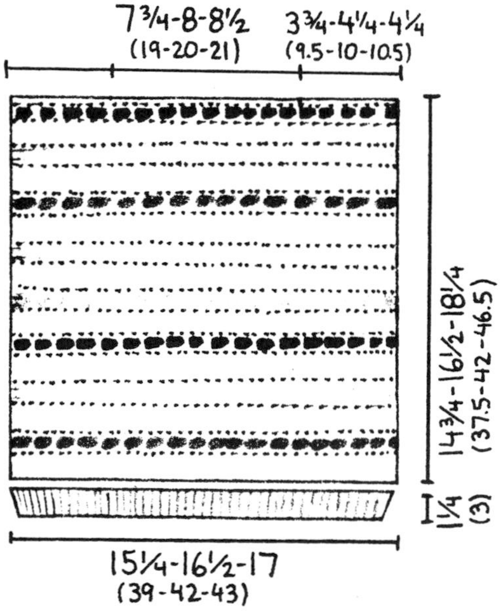

7¾-8-8½
(19-20-21)

3¾-4¼-4¼
(9.5-10-10.5)

14¾-16½-18¼
(37.5-42-46.5)

¼
(3)

15¼-16½-17
(39-42-43)

BACK

7¾-8-8½
(19-20-21)

3¾-4¼-4¼
(9.5-10-10.5)

1½
(4)

14¾-16½-18¼
(37.5-42-46.5)

1¼
(3)

15¼-16½-17
(39-42-43)

FRONT

Bright Winter Jacket

Level: Challenging

Size

❖ Child's size 6 (8, 10) years, chest 25 (27, 28-1/2) in. — 63.5 (69, 72.5) cm

❖ Finished chest measurements: 31 (32-1/2, 34-1/2) in. — 78 (82, 86) cm

❖ Length: 18-3/4 (19-3/4, 21) in. — 47 (50, 53) cm

❖ Sleeve seam: 14-3/4 (15, 15-1/2) in. — 37 (38, 39) cm

Materials

❖ Bulky weight yarn (approx. 83 yds per 50 g skein) 18 (20, 22) skeins color yellow

❖ 4 buttons

❖ Crochet hook U.S. size G/6 (Metric size 4.5) or size needed to obtain gauge

To save time, take time to check gauge!

Gauge

15 dc and 13 rows = 4 in. (10 cm)

Stitches

Chain (ch), slip st (sl), single crochet (sc), half double crochet (hdc), double crochet (dc). Relief dc: Worked in the front post of the previous row by inserting hook right to left. Yo hook before inserting hook. Relief hdc: Work same as relief dc, but work hdc instead of dc.

Note: See "Stitches and Techniques" for detailed instructions on stitches and shapings.

Back

Work the pieces from side to side.

Ch 52 (55, 58). Work the first hdc in the 4th ch from the hook = 1 border st. Work as foll: 1 border st, 10 hdc, 38 (41, 44) dc, 1 hdc as border st. Foll row: Ch 2 for border st, 38 (41, 44) relief dc, 10 hdc, 1 sc for border st. Foll row: Ch 1 for border st, 10 relief hdc, 38 (41, 44) relief dc, 1 hdc for border st. Always rep these 2 rows. At end of the 5th row, inc 22 (24, 26) sts as foll: ch 24 (26, 28), work first dc in the 4th ch from hook, work 1 dc in each ch, work to end of row. Work next

row as foll: Ch 1 for border st, 10 relief hdc, 60 (65, 70) relief dc, 1 hdc as border st. Work until piece measures 13-1/4 (14, 14-3/4) in. - 33 (35, 37) cm. Shape armholes, leave 22 (24, 26) sts unworked at left edge. Work 5 rows on rem sts. Fasten off.

Right Front

Work same as back until piece measures 3-1/4 in. (8 cm), shape pocket opening as foll: Right side facing, ch 1 for border st, 10 relief hdc, 7 (8, 9) relief dc, skip 16 (17, 18) dc, ch 16 (17, 18), work to end of row. On foll row, work in relief dc over the ch sts. Continue in relief dc until piece measures 3-1/2 in. (9 cm), measured at shoulder edge. Dec 1 st at neck edge 9 (10, 11) times. (Work dec after the border st, work dec by working 2 sts tog.) After the last dec, work 1 row. Fasten off.

Left Front

Beg at center edge. Ch 65 (69, 73), work first dc in the 4th ch from hook = 1 border st. Work next row as foll: 1 border st, 51 (55, 59) dc, 10 hdc, 1 sc in the last st = 1 border st. On foll row: Ch 1 for border st, 10 relief hdc, 50 (54, 58) relief dc, work 2 relief dc in the foll st, work 1 dc in last st for border st. Foll row: Ch 3 for border st, work 2 relief dc in foll dc, work to end of row. Work these 2 rows until 9 (10, 11) dc have been increased. Continue left front by rev shapings of right front. For pocket opening, work as foll: 1 border st, 37 (40, 43) relief dc, skip 16 (17, 18) dc, ch 16 (17, 18), 7 (8, 9) relief dc, 10 relief hdc, 1 border st. Fasten off.

Sleeves

Beg at upper edge of side of sleeve. Ch 16 (18, 20), work 1 row of dc, working first dc in the 4th ch from hook. At end of this row, ch 14 to inc 12 dc. Turn and work 1 dc in the 4th ch from hook. Inc 12 sts at this edge on every row 4 times. Work in relief dc in the ch sts = 60 (62, 64) dc with 1 border st at each edge. Along the lower edge, work first 10 sts in relief hdc, work rem sts in relief dc. Work until piece measures 9-1/2 (10-1/4, 11) in. - 24 (26, 28) cm, measured at upper edge. Dec 12 sts at lower edge every row 4 times. After the

last dec, work 1 row across rem sts. Fasten off.

Collar

Ch 44 (46, 48), beg in the 4th ch from hook. Work 1 row of dc and continue in relief dc. Inc 1 st at each edge of every 2nd row 3 times by working 2 relief dc in the dc next to the border sts. When collar measures 5-1/4 in. (13 cm), fasten off.

Finishing

Block pieces to indicated measurements. Sew shoulder, side and sleeve seams, leaving the

top 1-1/4 in. (3 cm) of sleeves unsewn. Sew sleeves to armholes, matching center of sleeve with shoulder seams and sewing top of sleeve to armhole. Sew center front seam to 4-3/4 in. (12 cm) from neck edge. Evenly space 4 button loops along this edge. (For each button loop, make a ch loop.) Sew on buttons. For pockets, work 1 row of dc along pocket opening edges. Along back opening edge, work in dc to desired length of pocket. Fasten off. Sew in place.

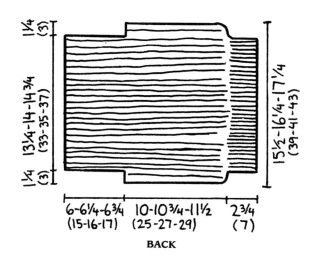

BACK

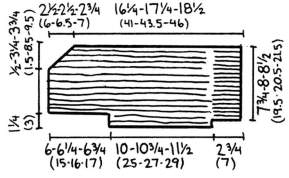

RIGHT FRONT

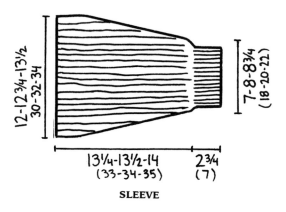

SLEEVE

Pink Pullover

Level: Intermediate

Size
❖ Child's size 2 (4) years, chest 21 (23) in. — 52.5 (57.5) cm
❖ Finished chest measurements: 25-1/2 (27) in. — 64 (68) cm
❖ Length: 12-3/4 (14) in. — 32 (35) cm
❖ Sleeve seam: 9-1/4 (10-1/4) in. — 23 (26) cm

Materials
❖ Mayflower Cotton 8 (approx. 186 yds per 50 g skein) 5 skeins color pink
❖ 6 buttons
❖ Crochet hook U.S. size C/2 (Metric size 3) or size needed to obtain gauge
❖ Knitting needles U.S. size 2 (Metric size 2.5)
To save time, take time to check gauge!

Gauge
5 shells and 16 rows (8 shells) = 4 in. (10 cm)

Stitches
Chain (ch), single crochet (sc), double crochet (dc)
1/1 ribbing: Row 1: *K1, p1*. Rep * to * across.
Row 2 and all foll rows: Work sts as established in previous row.

Note: See "Stitches and Techniques" for detailed instructions on stitches and shapings.

Back
With crochet hook, ch 80 (85) + ch 1 to turn. Continue by foll chart as foll: Row 1: 1 sc at beg of row, *ch 2, skip 2 ch, 1 sc in each of the foll 3 ch*, rep * to *, end last rep with 1 sc in each of the foll 2 ch. Row 2: Ch 1, 1 sc in the sc, *work 5 dc (= 1 shell) around the ch 2, 1 sc in the center of the foll 3 sc*, rep * to *. Continue by foll chart. Rep the 2nd to the 5th row. When piece measures 11 (12-1/4) in. - 28 (31) cm, work 5 shells at each edge separately for 4 rows = 2 rows of shells. Leave center sts unworked. Fasten off.

Front
Work same as back until piece measures 10-3/4 (12) in.- 27 (30) cm. Work 5 shells at each edge separately for 6 rows = 3 rows of shells. Fasten off.

Sleeves
With crochet hook, ch 40 (45) + ch 1 for the beg of the row. Work by foll chart. At each edge of every 9th and 10th (10th and 11th) rows, inc 1/2 shell 3 times = 14 (15) shells. Piece will measure 8-1/4 (9-1/2) in. - 14 (15) cm. Fasten off.

Finishing
Block pieces to indicated measurements. With knitting needles, pick up and knit 60 (64) sts along lower edge of front and back and work 3/4 in. (2 cm) in 1/1 ribbing. Bind off loosely. With knitting needles, pick up and knit 30 (32) sts along lower edge of sleeve and work 3/4 in. (2 cm) in 1/1 ribbing. Bind off loosely. Overlap the last 2 shell rows of front shoulders over the last 2 shell rows of back and tack the armhole edge. Sew sleeves to armholes, matching center of sleeve with shoulder seams. Sew side and sleeve seams. Sew on buttons to correspond to openings in shell pat.

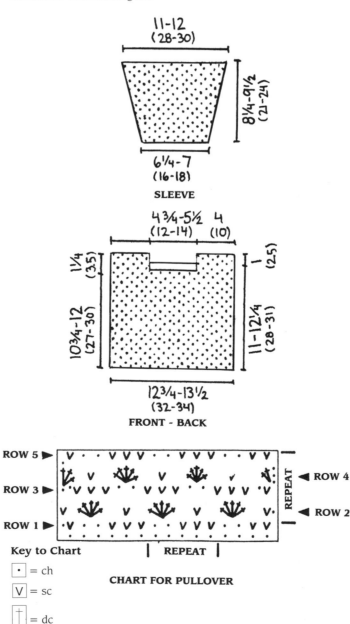

11-12 (28-30)
8¼-9½ (21-24)
6¼-7 (16-18)
SLEEVE

4¾-5½ (12-14) 4 (10)
1¼ (3.5)
1 (2.5)
10¾-12 (27-30)
11-12¼ (28-31)
12¾-13½ (32-34)
FRONT - BACK

ROW 5 ►
◄ ROW 4
ROW 3 ►
◄ ROW 2
ROW 1 ►
REPEAT

Key to Chart
REPEAT

• = ch
V = sc
† = dc

CHART FOR PULLOVER

Holiday Spirit Cardigan

Level: Intermediate

Size

❖ Child's size 4 (6, 8) years, chest 23 (25, 27) in. — 58.5 (63.5, 69) cm

❖ Finished chest measurements: 30-1/4 (32, 33-1/2) in. — 76 (80, 84) cm

❖ Length: 13-3/4 (15-1/2, 17-1/2) in. — 35 (39, 44) cm

❖ Sleeve seam: 10 (11, 12-3/4) in. — 25 (28, 32) cm

Materials

❖ Sport weight yarn (approx. 150 yds per 50 g skein) 1 (1, 2) skeins color red, 1 skein color white, 3 (3, 4) skeins color bright green, 2 (2, 3) skeins color dark green

❖ 4 red buttons, 3 white buttons

❖ Crochet hook U.S. size E/4 (Metric size 3.5) or size needed to obtain gauge

❖ Knitting needles U.S. size 4 (Metric size 3.5)

To save time, take time to check gauge!

Gauge

16-1/2 hdc and 12 rows = 4 in. (10 cm)

Stitches

Chain (ch), single crochet (sc), half double crochet (hdc) 1/1 ribbing: Row 1: *K1, p1*. Rep * to * across.
Row 2 and all foll rows: Work sts as established in previous row.

Note: See "Stitches and Techniques" for detailed instructions on stitches and shapings.

When changing colors, work the last loop of the last st with the color of the next st. Hold the unused yarn against the back of work. When inserting hook, work around the unused yarn so that the new sts hold it against the work.

Body

With crochet hook and bright green, ch 122 (128, 134) + ch 2 = 1 hdc. Beg each row with ch 2 = 1 hdc. Row 1: 1 hdc in the 4th ch from the hook, 1 hdc in each of the foll 120 (126, 132) ch. Work in hdc over 122 (128, 134) sts for 7 (11, 16) rows of bright green, 1 row of red and 2 rows of dark green. Over the foll 8 rows of bright green, work large mushroom motifs as foll: Row 1 for size small and large: 4 (5) hdc with green, *3 hdc with white, 7 hdc with green*, work * to * 11 (12) times, 3 hdc with white, 5 (6) hdc with green. Row 1 for size medium: 5 hdc with green, *3 hdc with white, 7 hdc with green*, work * to * twice, 3 hdc with white, 9 hdc with green, *3 hdc with white, 7 hdc with green*, work * to * 5 times, 3 hdc with white, 9 hdc with green, *3 hdc with white, 7 hdc with green*, work * to * twice, 3 hdc with white, 6 hdc with green. Continue working mushrooms motifs by foll chart = 12 (12, 13) motifs. Work the last loop of one color with the foll color. After these 8 rows, work 1 row of red and 1 row of dark green = 20 (24, 29) rows - 6-1/2 (8, 9-1/2) in. - 16.5 (20, 24) cm from beg. Beg armholes: Work the first 26 (28, 29) hdc to a length of 5-1/4 (5-1/2, 6) in. - 13.5 (14, 15) cm. At neck edge of every 2nd row, dec 6 (7, 8) sts once, dec 1 st once. Work 1 row over rem 19 (20, 20) sts. The armhole will measure 6-1/4 (6-1/2, 7) in. - 16 (16.5, 17.5) cm. Fasten off. Work 2nd front to correspond. For the back, work the center 56 (58, 62) hdc, (leave 7 hdc unworked at each edge for armholes). Work to same length as fronts. Fasten off.

Sleeves

With crochet hook and dark green(dark green, bright green), ch 44 (46, 48) + ch 2 to turn = first dc. Row 1: 1 hdc in the 4th ch from the hook, 1 hdc in each of the foll 42 (44, 46) ch = 44 (46, 48) hdc. Continue in hdc, work 0 (0, 4) rows of bright green, 1 (4, 4) rows of dark green, *4 rows of bright green, 4 rows of dark green*, rep * to * 3 times, 4 rows of bright green and 1 row of dark green = 10 (10-3/4, 12-1/4) in. - 25 (27, 30.5) cm from beg. On the center 2 rows of every 4 row stripe, work small mushroom motifs centering chart. At the same time, at each edge of every 5th row, inc 1 hdc 5 (5, 6) times - 54 (56, 60) sts. Fasten off.

Finishing

Block pieces to indicated measurements. Sew shoulder seams. Sew sleeves to armholes, matching center of sleeve with shoulder seams. Sew sleeve seams. With knitting needles and bright green, pick up and knit 121 (127, 133) sts along lower edge and work 1 in. (2.5 cm) in 1/1 ribbing. Bind off loosely. With knitting needles and red, pick up and knit 38 (40, 42) sts along each sleeve end and work 1 row in stockinette st in red, 1-1/4 (1, 1-1/4) in. - 3 (2.5, 3) cm in 1/1 ribbing. Bind off loosely. With knitting needles and dark green, cast on 85 (89, 91) sts. Change to red and continue for 1-1/2 in. (4 cm) in 1/1 ribbing. Bind off loosely. Along the front edge of collar and front edge, with bright green or red (matching color of collar and front), work 1 row of sc as foll: Alternately work 1 or 2 sc per row, with 1 sc in each corner. Change to bright green, work 1 row of sc along front edge. Fasten off. Along left front, work 3 rows of sc with bright green. Along right front, on the first of these 3 rows, make 7 buttonholes evenly spaced. For each buttonhole, ch 2 and skip 2 sts of previous row. On foll row, work in sc in these ch sts. Fasten off on 3rd row. Sew on collar so edges meet front bands. Sew on buttons, alternating white and red buttons.

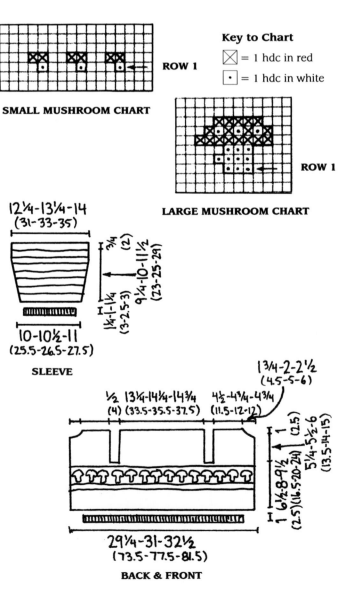

Key to Chart

⊠ = 1 hdc in red

• = 1 hdc in white

ROW 1

SMALL MUSHROOM CHART

ROW 1

LARGE MUSHROOM CHART

12¼-13¼-14
(31-33-35)

¾ (2)

9¼-10-11½
(23-25-29)

1¼-1-1¼
(3-2.5-3)

10-10½-11
(25.5-26.5-27.5)

SLEEVE

1¾-2-2½
(4.5-5-6)

½ 13¼-14¼-14¾
(4) (33.5-35.5-37.5)

4½-4¾-4¾
(11.5-12-12)

5¼-5½-6
(13.5-14-15)

1 (2.5)

6½-8-9½
(16.5-20-24)

29¼-31-32½
(73.5-77.5-81.5)

BACK & FRONT

House Motif Cardigan

Level: Intermediate

Size
❖ Baby's size 3-6 (9-12) months, chest 19-20 (21-22) in. — 47.5-50 (52.5-55) cm
❖ Finished chest measurements: 21 (22-1/4) in. — 53 (56.5) cm
❖ Length: 9-1/4 (10) in. — 23 (25) cm
❖ Sleeve seam: 8 (8-1/2) in. — 20 (21.5) cm

Materials
❖ Sport weight yarn (approx. 150 yds per 50 g skein) 2 skeins each color green and light blue, 1 skein each color red and white
❖ 6 red buttons
❖ Crochet hook U.S. size C/2 (Metric size 3) or size needed to obtain gauge
❖ Knitting needles U.S. size 3 (Metric size 3)
To save time, take time to check gauge!

Gauge
18 hdc and 13 rows = 4 in. (10 cm)

Stitches
Chain (ch), single crochet (sc), half double crochet (hdc)
1/1 ribbing: Row 1: *K1, p1*. Rep * to * across.
Row 2 and all foll rows: Work sts as established in previous row.
Note: The body is worked in 1 piece in hdc. Beg each row with ch 2. The houses are worked by foll chart. When changing colors, work the last loop of the last st with the color of the next st. Hold the unused yarn against the wrong side of work. When inserting hook, work around the unused yarn so that the new sts hold it against the work.

Note: See "Stitches and Techniques" for detailed instructions on stitches and shapings.

Body
With crochet hook and green, ch 90 (97) + ch 2 (= 1 hdc). Beg in the 4th ch and work 3 (5) rows with green. Beg working the house motifs as foll: 3 sts in green, *7 sts in white,

(continued on page 102)

4 (5) sts green*, rep * to * 6 times more, end with 7 sts white, 3 sts green. Work the house motifs by foll chart. After the 3rd row of house motif, work the background in light blue. After 13 (15) rows, piece will measure 4 (4-1/2) in. - 10 (11.5) cm from beg. Divide the work in 3 pieces as foll: Work 17 (19) sts for the first front, skip 9 sts for 1 armhole, 38 (41) sts for the back, skip 9 sts for the 2nd armhole, 17 (19) sts for the 2nd front. Now work on 1 front: Work 7(8) rows. Then at neck edge of every row, dec 5 (6) sts once, dec 2 sts once, dec 1 st once. Work rem 9 (10) sts for 3 rows. Fasten off. The armhole is 13 (14) rows high = 4 (4-1/4) in. - 10 (10.5) cm. Work the 2nd front to correspond, rev shapings. Work 11 (12) rows in light blue across the back. On the foll row, leave the center 14 (15) sts unworked. Working each shoulder separately, work 1 row across 12 (13) sts on each shoulder, dec 3 sts at neck edge. Fasten off. Work 2nd shoulder to correspond.

Sleeves

With crochet hook and green, ch 35 (39) + ch 2 to turn (= 1 hdc). Row 1: 1 hdc in the 4th ch from hook, 1 hdc in each of the foll ch sts = 35 (39) hdc. Work 7 (9) rows with green. Work house motifs by foll chart. Work first row as foll: 3 (4) sts in green, *7 sts in white, 4 (5) sts in green*, rep * to * once, end with 7 sts in white, 3 (4) sts in green. After the 3rd row, work background sts in light blue. After the last row of chart, work 18 (20) rows in light blue. Piece will measure 5-1/2 (6) in. - 14 (15.5) cm. Mark edges for armhole. Work 4 rows as foll: Row 1: Hdc in green. Row 2: Work in hdc, work 2 sts in light blue, then alternate 1 st in white, 1 st in light blue, end with 2 sts in light blue. Row 3: Hdc in red. Row 4: Sc in light blue. Fasten off.

Finishing

Block pieces to indicated measurements. With knitting needles and green, pick up and knit 90 (97) sts along lower edge of body. Work 1-1/4 in. (3 cm) in 1/1 ribbing, dec 1 (0) st on first row = 89 (97) sts. Bind off loosely. With knitting nee-dles and light blue, pick up and knit 28 (32) sts along lower edge of sleeve. Work 1-1/4 in. (3 cm) in 1/1 ribbing. Bind off loosely.

Sew shoulder seams. Sew sleeves to armholes, matching center of sleeve with shoulder seams and sewing top of sleeve at marker to armholes. Sew sleeve seams. With light blue, work 57 (61) sc around neck. Fasten off. With knitting needles and light blue, pick up and knit 1 st from every sc around neck and work in 1/1 ribbing as foll: 1 row of light blue (pick up row), 2 rows of red, 2 rows of light blue, 1 row in white, 8 rows in green. Place sts on a strand of yarn. Fold to inside and sew 1 st to each sc around neck. Front bands: (Make buttonholes on right for girls and left for boys.) Work 1 row of sc along each front edge, matching the colors of the front. Work 3 rows of sc in green. Fasten off. Work same border on other side, evenly spacing 6 buttonholes on the 2nd row of green. For each buttonhole, ch 2 and skip 2 sc. On foll row, work 2 sc in ch 2. Sew on buttons.

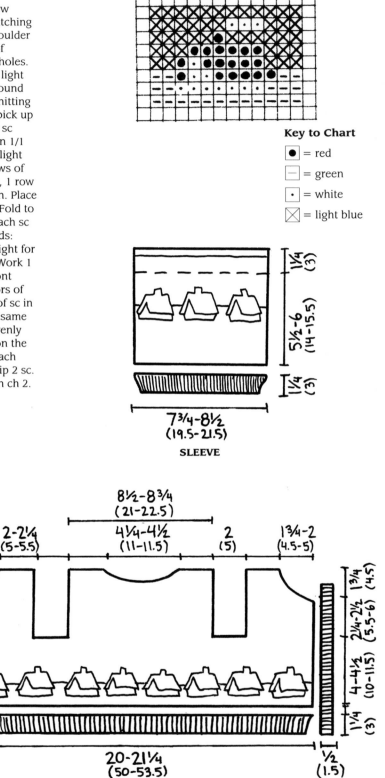

Key to Chart

● = red

─ = green

· = white

⊠ = light blue

SLEEVE

7¾-8½ (19.5-21.5)
1¼ (3)
5½-6 (14-15.5)
1¼ (3)

CARDIGAN **BACK AND FRONT**

8½-8¾ (21-22.5)
2-2¼ (5-5.5)
4¼-4½ (11-11.5)
2 (5)
1¾-2 (4.5-5)
4-4¼ (10-10.5)
1¾ (4.5)
2¼-2½ (5.5-6)
4-4½ (10-11.5)
4-4½ (10-11.5)
1¼ (3)
½ (1.5)
20-21¼ (50-53.5)
½ (1.5)

Filet Sun Top

Level: Intermediate

Note: Depending on the size and type of yarn used, this top can measure from 20 to 24-3/4 in. (50 to 62 cm). Because this kind of crochet will stretch, the finished measurements are about the same as the actual measurements of the child.

Size
❖ Child's size 6 years, chest 25 in. (62.5 cm)
❖ Finished chest measurement: 25-1/2 in. (63 cm)
❖ Length: 8-1/4 in. (21 cm)

Materials
❖ Mayflower Cotton 8 (approx. 186 yds per 50 g skein) 2 skeins color white
❖ Crochet hook U.S. size B/1 (Metric size 2.5) or size needed to obtain gauge
To save time, take time to check gauge!

Gauge
9-1/2 open squares and 11 rows = 4 in. (10 cm)

Stitches
Chain (ch), slip st (sl), single crochet (sc), double crochet (dc)
Filet st: Work by foll chart. Beg ch 3 for the first dc. The last dc of 1 square equals the first dc of the foll square.

Note: See "Stitches and Techniques" for detailed instructions on stitches and shapings.

Back
Ch 63 + ch 3 for the first dc. Row 1: 1 dc in the 9th ch from hook, then work in open squares across = 30 open squares. Rows 2 and 3: Work in open squares. Row 4: 3 open squares, *1 filled square, 5 open squares*, rep * to *, end with 3 open squares after the last filled square. Row 5: 2 open squares, *1 filled square, 1 open square, then work flower motif, **ch 4, sl 1 in the 3rd ch from the hook, ch 1**, 1 sl st in the top edge of the left dc of the underlying filled square on the 4th row, work ** to **, sl 1 in the top edge of the right dc of the same under-lying filled square, work ** to **, sl 1 in the top edge of the left dc of the last filled square of the 5th row, work ** to **, sl 1 in the last dc of the 5th row so that you have 4 flower motifs around an open square. Work 1 filled square, 3 open squares*, rep * to * end with 2 open squares. Row 6: Like row 4. Row 7: Work in open squares. Continue by foll chart. When piece measures 8 in. (20 cm) from beg, fasten off. Work front same as back. Work straps by foll chart. Fasten off. Join to back by working 1 row of open squares between straps and back.

Finishing
Block pieces to indicated measurements. Sew side seams. Around the lower edge, work as foll: Beg at side seam, work 1 sc in 1 open square, *1 picot = ch 3, sl 1 in the 3rd ch from the hook, skip 1 open square, 2 sc in the foll open square*, rep * to *. Along front and back neck and armhole edges, work in picot as foll: Row 1: Work in sc, working 2 sc in 1 open square. Row 2: 1 sc, *1 picot, skip 2 sc*, rep * to *. Fasten off. Make a cord about 40 in. (100 cm) long and thread through 2nd row around lower edge. Make a knot at each end.

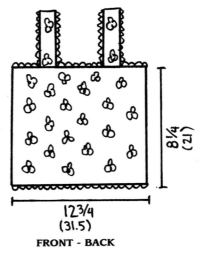

FRONT - BACK

12-3/4 (31.5)

8-1/4 (21)

SHOULDER STRAPS

← **BEGIN**

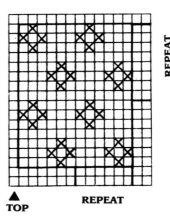

▲ **TOP**   **REPEAT**

REPEAT

Key to Chart
☐ = open square
☒ = filled square

Jacquard Top

Level: Intermediate

Size
❖ Child's size 4 (6, 8) years, chest 23 (25, 27) in. — 58.5 (63.5, 69) cm
❖ Finished chest measurements: 28 (30, 32) in. — 70 (75, 80) cm
❖ Length: 14 (15, 16-1/4) in. — 35 (38, 41) cm
❖ Sleeve seam: 10-1/4 (11, 12) in. — 26 (28, 30) cm

Materials
❖ Scheepjeswol Voluma (approx. 209 yds per 50 g skein) 2 (2, 3) skeins color orange/yellow, 2 (3, 3) skeins color blue
❖ 6 buttons
❖ Crochet hook U.S. size F/5 (Metric size 4) or size needed to obtain gauge
❖ Knitting needles U.S. size 4 (Metric size 3.5)
To save time, take time to check gauge!

Gauge
15 hdc and 10 rows = 4 in. (10 cm)

Stitches
Chain (ch), single crochet (sc), half double crochet (hdc)
Jacquard Pat: Work in hdc by foll chart. When changing colors, work the last loop of the last st with the color of the next st. Hold the unused yarn against the back of work. When inserting hook, work around the unused yarn so that the new sts hold it against the work.
1/1 ribbing: Row 1: *K1, p1*. Rep * to * across.
Row 2 and all foll rows: Work sts as established in previous row.

Note: See "Stitches and Techniques" for detailed instructions on stitches and shapings.

Back
With crochet hook and blue, ch 102 (110, 118) + ch 2 = first hdc. Row 1: 1 hdc in the 4th ch from the hook, 1 hdc in each of the 100 (108, 116) ch. Row 2: Right side facing: 2 hdc with blue, 2 hdc with orange/yellow, work *6 hdc with blue, 2 hdc with orange/yellow*, rep * to * 12 (13, 14) times, 2 hdc with blue. Continue by foll chart on 102 (110, 118) sts to a total length of 6-3/4 (7-1/2, 8-1/4) in. - 17 (19, 21) cm. Divide piece in 3 parts. Work first front over the the first 23 (25, 27) sts. When armhole measures 4-3/4 (5-1/4, 5-1/2) in. - 12 (13, 14) cm, shape neck. At neck edge of every row, dec 6 (7, 8) sts once, dec 1 st once. Work 1 row. Armhole will measure 6 (6-1/2, 6-3/4) in. - 15 (16, 17) cm. Fasten off. Work 2nd front by rev shapings. Work center 50 (54, 58) sts, leaving 3 sts unworked at each edge for armholes. Fasten off when armhole measures 6 (6-1/2, 6-3/4) in. - 15 (16, 17) cm.

Sleeves
With crochet hook and orange/yellow, ch 36 (38, 40) + ch 2 = first hdc. Row 1: 1 hdc in the 4th ch from the hook, 1 hdc in each of the 34 (36, 38) sts. Row 2: Right side facing, 5 (6, 7) hdc in orange/yellow, 2 hdc in blue, *6 hdc with orange/yellow, 2 hdc in blue*, rep * to * 3 times, 5 (6, 7) hdc in orange/yellow. Work in dots centering chart. Inc at each edge of every 4th (4th, 5th) row 5 times = 46 (48, 50) sts. When sleeve measures 9-1/4 (10, 10-3/4) in. - 23 (25, 27) cm, work 1 row of sc with blue. Fasten off.

Finishing
Block pieces to indicated measurements. Sew shoulder seams. With knitting needles and orange/yellow, pick up 32 (34, 36) sts along lower edge of each sleeve and work 1-1/4 in. (3 cm) in 1/1 ribbing. Bind off loosely. With knitting needles and blue, pick up and knit 101 (107, 115) sts along lower edge and work 1-1/4 in. (3 cm) in 1/1 ribbing. Bind off loosely. With crochet hook and blue, work 1 row of sc along each front edge, alternately working 1 and 2 sc in each hdc row. Work 2 rows on right front, neck, and left front, working 1 extra sc in each corner. On right front, make 6 buttonholes on the first row of sc as foll: *ch 2 , skip 2*, work * to * 6 times. On foll row, work 1 sc in each ch st. Fasten off. Sew on buttons. Sew sleeves to armholes, matching center of sleeve with shoulder seams. Sew side and sleeve seams.

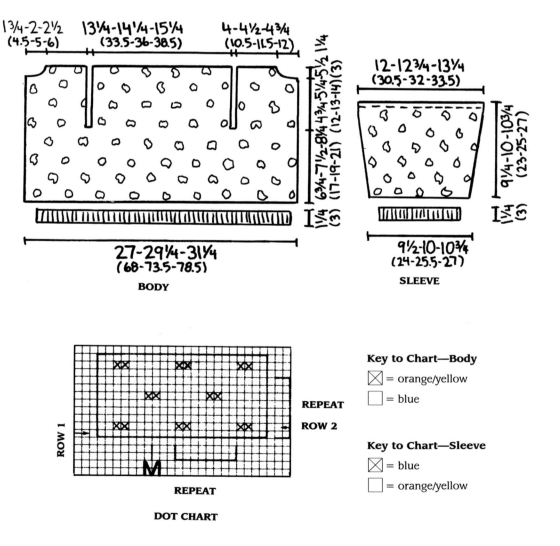

BODY

13¾-2-2½ (4.5-5-6)
13¼-14¼-15¼ (33.5-36-38.5)
4-4½-4¾ (10.5-11.5-12)
6¾-7½-8¼ (17-19-21)
4⅓-4½-5 / 1¼ (3)
4¾-5½-5½ / 1¼ (12-13-14) (3)
27-29¼-31¼ (68-73.5-78.5)

12-12¾-13¼ (30.5-32-33.5)
9¼-10-10¾ (23-25-27)
1¼ (3)
9½-10-10¾ (24-25.5-27)

SLEEVE

ROW 1
REPEAT
ROW 2
REPEAT

M

DOT CHART

Key to Chart—Body
⊠ = orange/yellow
☐ = blue

Key to Chart—Sleeve
⊠ = blue
☐ = orange/yellow

Geometric Cardigan

Level: Challenging

Size

❖ Child's size 6 (8, 10) years, chest 25 (27, 28-1/2) in. — 63.5 (69, 72.5) cm

❖ Finished chest measurements: 28 (30-3/4, 33-1/2) in. — 70 (77, 84) cm

❖ Length: 16-1/4 (18, 19-1/2) in. — 41 (45, 49) cm

❖ Sleeve seam: 12 (13-1/4, 14-1/4) in. — 30(33,36) cm

Materials

❖ Sport weight yarn (approx. 131 yds per 50 g skein) 2 (2, 3) skeins color blue, 2 skeins color black, 1 (2, 2) skeins color yellow, 2 (3, 3) skeins color red and 1 (2, 2) skeins color ecru

❖ Mohair yarn, 1 skein color green

❖ 4 snaps.

Crochet hook U.S. size E/4 (Metric size 3.5) or size needed to obtain gauge

To save time, take time to check gauge!

Gauge

16 sts = 4 in. (10 cm)

Stitches

Chain (ch), single crochet (sc), half double crochet (hdc), double crochet (dc).

Jacquard: A multiple of 12 sts with 1 border st at each edge. Work foll chart 2 in hdc. Work the last loop of the last st of 1 color with a strand of the foll color.

Block pat: A multiple of 6 sts with 1 border st at each edge. Foll chart 1 in sc.

Border pat: On chart 1, beg rows of sc with ch 1, end with 1 sc in ch 1 of previous row. On chart 2, beg with ch 2, end with hdc in the ch 2 at beg of previous row.

2 Color Block st: A multiple of 12 sts with 1 border st at each edge.

Row 1: Right side of work with red: Ch 1 = 1 border st, work in sc, end with 1 sc in the ch = 1 border st. Row 2: Wrong side of work with red: Ch 1 = 1 border st, work in sc, end with 1 sc in ch = 1 border st. Let strand hang. Row 3: Right side

of work, with yellow: Ch 1, *1 sc in the foll sc, 1 sc in the foll sc, but work 2 rows below, 1 sc in foll sc*, rep * to *, so that 2 sc are worked in the row between 2 sc that were worked 2 rows below. End with 1 sc in the ch = 1 border st. Break yarn. Turn to right side and with red, make 1 loop in the ch at the beg of previous row. Rows 4 and 5: With red, work in sc using the hanging thread. Row 6: With right side facing, join yellow yarn in the beg ch. Ch 1, *1 sc in the foll sc, 1 sc in the foll sc, but work 2 rows below, working in the yellow sc of the 3rd row, 1 sc in the foll sc*, rep * to *, end with 1 border st. Break yarn. Turn to right side with red thread and draw a loop through loop at beg of previous row. Rep the last 3 rows.

3 Color Block st: Multiple of 4 with 1 border st at each edge. Row 1: With blue, ch 1 = 1 border st, ch 2, *1 dc in each of the foll 2 sts, ch 2, skip 2*, rep * to *, end with 1 dc in each of the foll 2 dc, 1 dc in the ch of the border st = 1 border st. Row 2: With yellow, ch 1 = 1 border st, ch 2, *1 dc in each of the 2 skipped sts 2 rows below, working around the ch 2, ch 2*, rep * to *, end with 1 sc in the border st = first ch. Row 3: With red, ch 1, *ch 2, 1 dc in each of the 2 skipped dc 2 rows below*, rep * to *, end with 1 sc in the border st. Rep rows 2 and 3, alternating 1 row blue, 1 row yellow, and 1 row red.

Note: See "Stitches and Techniques" for detailed instructions on stitches and shapings.

Body

With black, ch 111 (123, 135). Work 4 rows in 2 color block pat. Work first sc in the 3rd ch from hook, so that there are 108 (120, 132) sc in pat with 1 border st at each edge. Work by foll chart 1. Border sts are not shown on chart. Work 15 rows in 2 color block st, 1 row of dc in green mohair, 1 row of sc in ecru and 1 row of sc in black. Continue in jacquard pat foll chart 2. Border sts are not shown on chart. Work first row on right side. Work until piece measures 10 (11, 12-1/4) in. - 25 (28, 31) cm. Now work in 3 parts: 27 (30, 33) sts for front,

54 (60, 66) sts for back, 27 (30, 33) sts for 2nd front. Work center sts for back in jacquard pat with 1 border st at each edge. When armhole measures 1-1/2 (2, 2-1/2) in. - 4 (5, 6) cm, work as foll: 1 row sc in black, 1 row sc in ecru, 1 row dc in green mohair. Work 15 rows in pat st, but substitute yellow for red and vice versa. Work 4 rows in 2 color block pat foll chart 1. Armhole measures 6-1/4 (6-3/4, 7) in. - 16 (17, 18) cm. Work until an even row of pat st is complete. Fasten off. Work right front sts the same until armhole measures 4 (4-1/4, 4-1/4) in. - 10 (11, 11) cm. At neck edge of every row, dec 3 sts 2 (3, 3) times, dec 2 sts 1 (0, 0) time, dec 1 st 3 (3, 4) times. Work rem 17 (19, 21) sts to same length as back and fasten off. Work left front by rev shapings of right front.

Sleeves

With black, ch 24 (27, 30), work 4 rows of 2 color block pat foll chart 1. Work the first sc in the 3rd ch from the hook, beg with 3 sc in ecru, end with 3 sc in ecru (black, ecru), 1 border st. Continue in 3 color block pat. Inc 15 (16, 17) sts evenly spaced across = 36 (40, 44) sts with 1 border st at each

edge. Inc 1 st at each edge of every 4th row 9 (10, 10) times. Work inc sts in pat st. After 8 rows work in 3 color block pat. Work the 9th row as foll: Ch 1, 1 sc in each of the 2 dc of the previous row, 1 dc in each of the 2 dc 2 rows below. Then work as foll: 1 row dc in green, 1 row in sc in ecru, 1 row sc in black, 11 rows of 3 color block pat (red, green mohair, and blue), then 1 row sc with black, 1 row sc in ecru, and 1 row dc in green mohair. Work in 3 color block pat in blue, ecru, and black. Work until sleeve measures 12 (13-3/4, 14-1/4) in. - 30 (33, 36) cm = 54 (60, 64) sts with 1 border st at each edge. Fasten off.

Finishing

Block pieces to indicated measurements. Sew shoulder seams. Along the front edges, work 4 rows in block pat over 66 (72, 78) sts. Fasten off. Work the same border around neck, working in block pattern, matching pat on back. Work 1 row of sc along upper edges of front bands and neckband. Fasten off. Sew sleeves to armholes, matching center of sleeve with shoulder seams. Sew side and sleeve seams. Attach snaps along fronts.

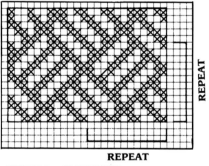

CHART 2 - JACQUARD

REPEAT

CHART 1 - BLOCK PAT

Key to Chart 1

⊠ = 1 sc in ecru

☐ = 1 sc in black

Key to Chart 2

☐ = 1 hdc in red

⊠ = 1 hdc in blue

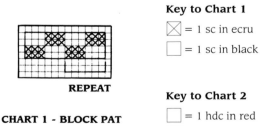

(continued on page 143)

Sailboats Pullover

Level: Intermediate

Size
❖ Child's size 18 months - 2 years, chest 20-21 in. (50-52.5 cm)
❖ Finished chest measurement: 24 in. (60 cm)
❖ Length: 12-3/4 in. (32 cm), sleeve seam: 10-1/4 in. (26 cm)

Materials
❖ Worsted weight yarn (approx. 99 yds per 50 g skein) 3 skeins each color dark blue and blue, 1 skein each color ecru and yellow
❖ 4 buttons
❖ Crochet hook U.S. size G/6 (Metric size 4.5) or size needed to obtain gauge
❖ Knitting needles U.S. size 4 (Metric size 3.5)
To save time, take time to check gauge!

Gauge
11 hdc and 9 rows = 4 in. (10 cm)

Stitches
Chain (ch), single crochet (sc), half double crochet (hdc)
Jacquard st: Foll chart in hdc. Beg each row with ch 2. When changing colors, work the last loop of the last st with the color of the next st. Use small bobbins of yarn for each section of color.
1/1 ribbing: Row 1: *K1, p1*. Rep * to * across.
Row 2 and all foll rows: Work sts as established in previous row.

Note: See "Stitches and Techniques" for detailed instructions on stitches and shapings.

Front
With crochet hook and dark blue, ch 33 + ch 2 = first st. Row 1: 1 hdc in the 4th ch from hook, 1 hdc in each of the foll 31 sts. Work 33 sts foll chart. On the 13th row, dec 3 sts at each edge. On the 24th row, leave the center 11 sts unworked. Work each side separately. With dark blue, work 1 row of sc across 1 shoulder, neck, 2nd shoulder, working 3 sc in each outer cor-

ner st and 3 sc tog in each inner corner st. On each shoulder, make 2 button loops evenly spaced. For each button loop, ch 2, skip 1 sc. Fasten off.

Back
Work same as front, but omit sailboat motifs and neck shaping. Work in striped pat throughout. End with 1 row of hdc and 1 row of sc in dark blue. Fasten off.

Sleeves
With crochet hook and dark blue, ch 30 + ch 2 = first st. Row 1: 1 hdc in the 4th ch from the hook, 1 hdc in each of the foll 28 ch. Work over 30 sts by foll chart. Fasten off.

Finishing
Block pieces to indicated measurements. With ecru, embroider 3 v sts at each edge of boats. With crochet hook, work 1 row of sc along armhole in blue or dark blue to correspond to sweater. Fasten off. Sew side seams. With knitting needles and dark blue, pick up 1 st from every ch st along lower edge and work 1-1/2 in. (4 cm) in 1/1 ribbing. Bind off loosely. With knitting needles and dark blue, pick up and knit 23 sts from each sleeve end and work 3-1/4 in. (8 cm) in 1/1 ribbing. Bind off loosely. Tack shoulders at armhole seams. Sew sleeves to side seams. Sew sleeve seams. Sew on buttons.

Sailboat Pullover

Level: Challenging

Size
❖ Child's size 2-3 years, chest 21-23 in. — (52.5-57.5 cm)
❖ Finished chest measurements: 26-1/2 in. (66 cm)
❖ Length: 13-3/4 in. (35 cm)
❖ Sleeve seam: 10-3/4 in. (27 cm)

Materials
❖ Worsted weight yarn (approx. 99 yds per 50 g skein) 3 skeins each color dark blue and blue, 1 skein each color ecru and yellow
❖ 6 buttons
❖ Crochet hook U.S. size G/6 (Metric size 4.5) or size needed to obtain gauge
❖ Knitting needles U.S. size 4 (Metric size 3.5)
To save time, take time to check gauge!

Gauge
11 hdc and 9 rows = 4 in. (10 cm)

Stitches
Chain (ch), single crochet (sc), half double crochet (hdc)
Jacquard st: Foll chart in hdc. Beg each row with ch 2. When changing colors, work the last loop of the last st with the color of the next st. Use small bobbins of yarn for each section of color.

1/1 ribbing: Row 1: *K1, p1*. Rep * to * across.
Row 2 and all foll rows: Work sts as established in previous row.

Note: See "Stitches and Techniques" for detailed instructions on stitches and shapings.

Front
With crochet hook and dark blue, ch 37 + ch 2 = first st. Row 1: 1 hdc in the 4th ch from hook, 1 hdc in each of the foll 35 sts. Work the 37 sts foll chart. Continue in dark blue, work 1 row of sc. Leave the center 13 sts unworked. Work 12 sc on each shoulder. With dark blue, work 1 row of sc across 1 shoulder, neck, 2nd shoulder, working 3 sc in outer corner st and 3 sc tog in each inner corner. On each shoulder, make 3 button loops evenly spaced. For each button loop, ch 2, skip 1 sc. Fasten off.

Back
Work same as front, but omit sailboat motif and neck shaping. Work striped pat throughout. End with 1 row of sc in dark blue. Fasten off.

Sleeves
With crochet hook and dark blue, ch 33 + ch 2 = first st. Row 1: 1 hdc in the 4th ch from the hook, 1 hdc in each of the foll 31 ch. Work 33 sts in stripes as foll: 5 rows in dark blue, 2 rows in blue, 2 rows in

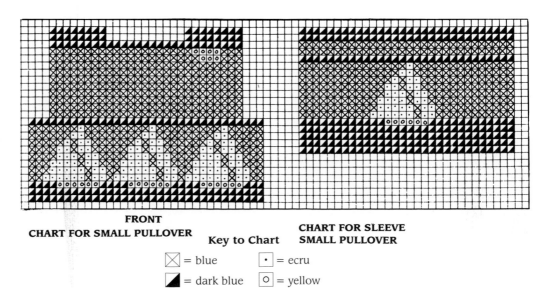

FRONT CHART FOR SMALL PULLOVER

Key to Chart

CHART FOR SLEEVE SMALL PULLOVER

⊠ = blue   • = ecru

◩ = dark blue   ○ = yellow

dark blue, 2 rows in blue, 2 rows in yellow, 2 rows in blue, 1 row in dark blue. Fasten off.

Finishing

Block pieces to indicated measurements. Tack the ends of the shoulder bands in place. Sew sleeves to armholes, matching center of sleeve with shoulder seams. With knitting needles and dark blue, pick up and knit 26 sts from lower edge of each sleeve and work 2-3/4 in. (7 cm) in 1/1 ribbing. Bind off loosely. Sew side and sleeve seams. With knitting needles and dark blue, pick up and knit 1 st from every ch st along lower edge and work 1-1/2 in. (4 cm) in 1/1 ribbing. Bind off loosely. Sew on buttons.

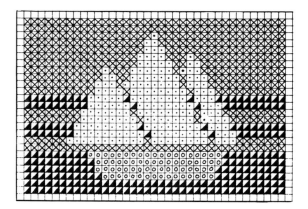

CHART FOR LARGE PULLOVER

Key to Chart

⊠ = blue

◣ = dark blue

· = ecru

○ = yellow

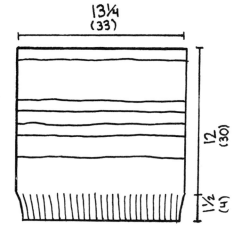

13¼ (33)

12 (30)

1½ (4)

BACK

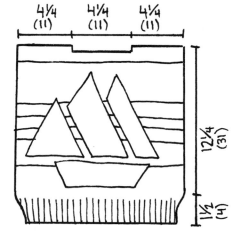

4¼ (11) 4¼ (11) 4¼ (11)

12¼ (31)

1½ (4)

FRONT

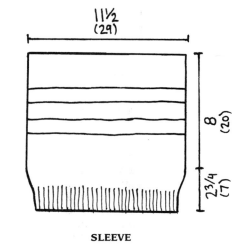

11½ (29)

8 (20)

2¾ (7)

SLEEVE

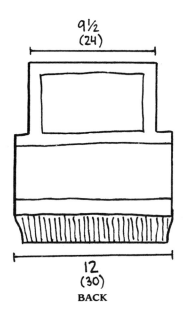

9½ (24)

12 (30)

BACK

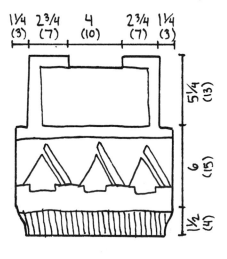

1¼ (3) 2¾ (7) 4 (10) 2¾ (7) 1¼ (3)

5¼ (13)

6 (15)

1½ (4)

FRONT

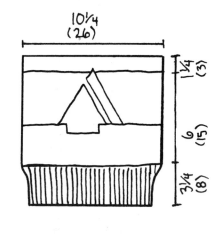

10¼ (26)

1¼ (3)

6 (15)

3¾ (8)

SLEEVE

Santa Jacket

Level: Challenging

Size
❖ Child's size 2 (4) years, chest 21 (23) in. — 52.5 (58.5) cm
❖ Finished chest measurements: 23-1/2 (25-1/2) in. — 59 (64) cm
❖ Length: 12-1/4 (14) in. — 31 (35) cm
❖ Sleeve seam: 8-3/4 (9-1/2) in. — 22 (24) cm (after folding cuff)

Materials
❖ Worsted weight yarn (approx. 93 yds per 50 g skein) 5 (6) skeins color dark blue, 1 skein each color red, yellow, pink, and white
❖ 4 (5) wooden buttons
❖ Crochet hook U.S. size E/4 (Metric size 3.5) or size needed to obtain gauge
To save time, take time to check gauge!

Gauge
17 hdc and 11-1/2 rows = 4 in. (10 cm)

Stitches
Chain (ch), single crochet (sc), half double crochet (hdc)
Shrimp st: Work same as sc, but work left to right instead of right to left.
Hold the unused yarn against the back of work. When inserting hook, work around the unused yarn so that the new sts hold it against the work. When changing colors, work the last loop of the last st with the color of the next st.

Note: See "Stitches and Techniques" for detailed instructions on stitches and shapings.

Body
With red, loosely ch 97 (105) sts. Row 1: Right side facing, ch 2 with blue = 1 hdc, *3 hdc with red, 1 hdc with blue*, rep * to * 23 (25) times = 97 (105) hdc and 24 (26) points on the lower edge. Continue by foll chart with the background in blue. Beg the motifs on 5th row as foll: Row 5: right side facing, 5 hdc in blue, 6 hdc in red, 2 hdc in blue, 6 hdc in red, 59 (67) hdc in blue, 6 hdc in red, 2 hdc in blue, 6 hdc in red, 5 hdc

in blue. Continue by foll chart for 21 (24) rows, then divide the work in 3 sections. Work the first 22 (24) hdc for front for 11 (13) rows. Dec 5 (6) hdc at neck edge. On foll row, dec 1 hdc at neck edge. Fasten off after the 14th (16th) row. Work 2nd front to correspond, rev shapings. Work center 45 (49) hdc for back, leaving 4 hdc unworked at each edge for armholes. Work 14 (16) rows of chart. Fasten off.

Sleeves
With red, ch 29 (33). Along the lower edge work the first 3 rows of chart to form 7 (8) points. Row 1: Right side facing, ch 2 in blue = 1 hdc, *3 hdc in red, 1 hdc in blue*, rep * to * 6 (7) times. After the 3rd row, work 23 (26) rows in blue. At each edge of every 3rd (4th) row 1 st 6 times = 41 (45) hdc. Row 30: Right side facing, 1 hdc with blue, *1 hdc with blue, 1 hdc with red, 2 hdc with blue*, rep * to * 9 (10) times = 10 (11) points. Work 2 rows in point motif = 10 (11)

in. - 25.5 (27.5) cm. Work 1 row of sc in red and 1 row in sc in blue. Fasten off. Fold the first 4 rows to outside for cuff.

Hood
Facing: With red, ch 69 (73) + ch 2 for the first hdc, working in the 4th ch from the hook = 69 (73) hdc. After the red row, work 2 rows in hdc with blue. Break yarn. Hood: Ch 69 (73) in red. Row 1: Ch 2 with blue = 1 hdc, *3 hdc with red, 1 hdc with blue*, rep * to * 16 (17) times. Work 2 rows of points foll chart = 17 (18) points. Continue in blue, laying the facing wrong side facing hood. Work next row in blue through both thicknesses. Work for a total length of 20 (21) rows. Fasten off.

Finishing
Embroider in stem stitch on the figures as foll: Work in blue on inner arms, yellow on lower edge of boots and sleeves, red for the nose and mouth. Block pieces to indicated measurements. Sew shoulder seams. Sew sleeves to armholes,

matching center of sleeve with shoulder seams. Sew sleeve seams. With red, work 1 row of shrimp stitch around lower edge of sleeve. Fasten off. Along center front and lower edges of body, work 1 row of sc in red: Along each front edge, work 1 sc in every row, 2 sc every 4th row, 3 sc in each corner. Work 1 sc in each st along lower edge. Work 1 more row of sc on wrong side of work, evenly spacing 4 (5) buttonholes on left front. For each buttonhole, ch 2, skip 2. Fasten off. Sew back seam of hood. Sew facing in place. Sew hood to neck edge. Work 1 row of shrimp stitch in red around hood, front, and lower edges. Work 2 sts in corners and work through both thicknesses of hood. Fasten off. Thread a cord through the facing of the hood. Make a yellow pompom and sew to top of hood. Sew on buttons. buttons. Sew sleeves to armholes, matching center of sleeve with shoulder seams. Sew side and sleeve seams.

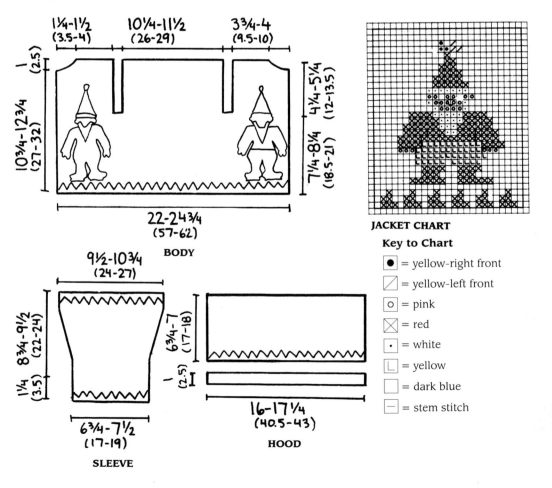

JACKET CHART

Key to Chart

● =	yellow-right front
⟋ =	yellow-left front
○ =	pink
⊠ =	red
· =	white
L =	yellow
=	dark blue
— =	stem stitch

BODY

SLEEVE

HOOD

Striped Pullovers

Level: Easy

Size

❖ Child's size 8 (10, 12) years, chest 27 (28-1/2, 30) in. — 69 (72.5, 75) cm
❖ Finished chest measurements: 37 (39, 41-1/2) in. — 92 (98, 104) cm
❖ Length: 21 (22, 23-1/4) in. — 52 (55, 58) cm
❖ Sleeve seam: 14-3/4 (15-3/4, 17) in. — 37 (40, 43) cm

Materials

❖ Mohair worsted weight yarn (approx. 130 yds per 50 g skein) 3 skeins each color yellow and blue, 1 skein each color turquoise and red
❖ Crochet hook U.S. size F/5 (Metric size 4) or size needed to obtain gauge
❖ Knitting needles U.S. size 4 (Metric size 3.5)
To save time, take time to check gauge!

Gauge

14 dc and 7 rows = 4 in. (10 cm)

Stitches

Chain (ch), double crochet (dc) When changing colors, work the last loop of the last st with the color of the next st.
1/1 ribbing: Row 1: *K1, p1*. Rep * to * across.
Row 2 and all foll rows: Work sts as established in previous row.

Note: See "Stitches and Techniques" for detailed instructions on stitches and shapings.

Back

With knitting needles and blue, cast on 65 (69, 73) sts and work 2-3/4 in. - (7 cm) in 1/1 ribbing. Bind off loosely. With crochet hook and yellow, work 1 dc in each bound off st and work as foll: 3 (4, 3) rows in yellow, *1 row turquoise, 1 row red, 2 rows yellow*, work * to * 3 (3, 4) times, ***1 row red, **2 rows blue, 2 rows yellow**, work ** to ** 3 times, end with 4 (5, 4) rows blue Piece will measure 21 (22, 23-1/4) in. - 52 (55, 58) cm. Fasten off.

Front

Work same as back.

Sleeves

With knitting needles and blue, cast on 40 (42, 42) sts and work 2-1/2 in. (6 cm) in 1/1 ribbing. Bind off. With crochet hook and yellow, work 1 dc in each bound off st. Work in stripe pat as on back from * to ***, but end with 1 row yellow instead of 2 rows yellow, then work 1 row red, 1 row blue, 1 row yellow, 1 row blue, 2 rows yellow and end with 2 (3, 2) rows blue. At the same time, at each edge every 1-1/2 in. (4 cm), inc 1 st 6 (7, 8) times = 52 (56, 58) dc. Sleeve will measure 14-3/4 (15-3/4, 17) in. - 37 (40, 43) cm. Fasten off.

Finishing

Block pieces to indicated measurements. Sew shoulder seams over 17 (18, 19) sts at each edge. Sew sleeves to armholes, matching center of sleeve with shoulder seam. Sew side and sleeve seams.

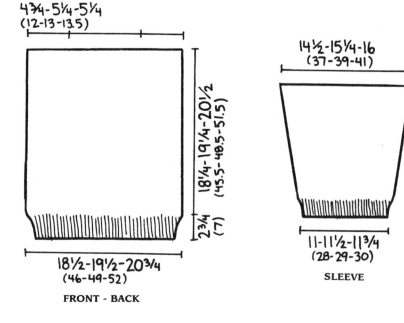

4¾-5¼-5¼
(12-13-13.5)

18¼-19¼-20½
(45.5-48.5-51.5)

2¾
(7)

18½-19½-20¾
(46-49-52)

FRONT - BACK

14½-15¼-16
(37-39-41)

12¼-13¼-14½
(31-34-37)

2½
(6)

11-11½-11¾
(28-29-30)

SLEEVE

Sweater, Hat, and Mittens

Level: Challenging

Size
❖ Child's size 4 (6, 8) years, chest 23 (25, 27) in. — 58.5 (63.5, 69) cm
❖ Finished chest measurements: 28 (30, 32) in. — 70 (75, 81) cm
❖ Length: 15-1/2 (16-3/4, 18) in. — 39 (42, 45) cm
❖ Sleeve seam: 13 (13-3/4, 14-1/2) in. — 33 (35, 37) cm
❖ Hat width: 17-1/2 in. (44 cm)

Materials
❖ Bulky weight yarn (approx. 75 yds per 50 g skein) 12 (13, 14) skeins color red
❖ 3 skeins color red for hat
❖ 1 skein color red for mittens
❖ 5 buttons.
❖ Crochet hook U.S. size F/5 (Metric size 4) or size needed to obtain gauge
❖ Knitting needles U.S. 3 (Metric size 3)
To save time, take time to check gauge!

Gauge
14 hdc and 12 rows = 4 in. (10 cm)

Stitches
Chain (ch), slip st (sl), single crochet (sc), half double crochet (hdc), double crochet (dc)
Pat stitch: Work on an odd number of sts.
Row 1: Ch 2 for the first hdc, continue in hdc.
Row 2: Ch 2, *1 dc in the front post of the underlying hdc, 1 hdc*, rep * to *.
Relief dc: Worked on a row of dc.
Row 1: Ch 2, work 1 front relief dc by inserting hook in front post of underlying st from right to left, 1 back relief dc by inserting hook in back post of underlying st from right to left*, rep * to *. On the foll row, work front relief sts over front relief sts and back relief sts over back relief sts of previous row.

Note: See "Stitches and Techniques" for detailed instructions on stitches and shapings.

Back
With crochet hook, ch 51 (55, 59), beg first hdc in the 4th ch from hook. Work in pat st for 12-1/4 (13-1/2, 14-3/4) in. - 31 (34, 37) cm. Leave the center 11 (13, 15) sts unworked. Work each side separately. At neck edge, dec 3 sts. Fasten off rem 16 (17, 18) sts when piece measures 13-1/2 (14-3/4, 16) in. - 34 (37, 40) cm.

Front
Work same as back, until piece measures 9-1/4 (10, 10-3/4) in. - 23 (25, 27) cm from beg. Work first 39 (41, 45) sts, turn and work wrong side of work row. Make 4 buttonholes at inner edge. Make the first buttonhole after the 2nd (4th, 6th) row. At inner edge, work 2 sts, ch 2, skip 2 sts. On the foll row, work the 2 ch sts in pat. Make a 2nd buttonhole after 3 rows. Work to a height of 11 (12-1/4, 13-1/2) in. - 28 (31, 34) cm. Fasten off. For 2nd part of piece, work over 19 (20, 21) sts. Turn and work wrong side row. At neck edge of every 2nd row, dec 1 st 3 times. Work to same height as back. Fasten off. Beg on right side, work over first part of sts. Dec 9 sts at neck edge and work in pat st. At neck edge of every 2nd row, dec 1 st 3 times. Work rem 6 sts to same height as first shoulder making 2 more buttonholes evenly spaced. Fasten off. For 2nd part of front, ch 6 and join to unworked sts at left side. Work in pat over all sts until piece measures 13-1/2 (14-3/4, 16) in. - 34 (37, 40) cm. Fasten off.

Sleeves
With crochet hook, ch 35 (37, 39). Work in pat st. Work the first row over 33 (35, 37) sts. Inc 1 st at each edge of every 6th row 5 times = 43 (45, 47) hdc. Work until piece measures 11 (12, 12-3/4) in. - 28 (30, 32) cm, fasten off.

Finishing
Block pieces to indicated measurements. Sew shoulder seams. Sew sleeves to armholes, matching center of sleeve with shoulder seams. Sew side and sleeve seams. With crochet hook, work 1 row of dc around lower edge of body, dec to 88 (94, 98) dc. Work in rounds of relief dc. Beg each round with ch 2. Sl st to join in the 2nd ch from the beg. Fasten off after 2 in. (5 cm). Work same border along lower edge of sleeves over 24 (26, 28) dc. Around the neck, work 1 row of sc, end with ch 6 for facing. Work in relief dc. After 1 row, make 1 more buttonhole above previous ones. Work 3 more rows. Fasten off. Sew on buttons.

Hat
With crochet hook, ch 63 and work 4 rows of 61 dc. Continue in pat st until piece measures 4-3/4 in. (12 cm). On the foll hdc row, dec 8 sts. Rep dec on foll hdc row. Work 2 rows of hdc, skipping 1 hdc every row. Break yarn and thread through rem sts. Sew back seam. Gather 3 rows below top to form a pompom. Along the lower edge, work 1 row of dc, inc to 70 dc. Work 2-1/2 in. (6 cm) in relief dc. Fasten off. Fold the border to outside. Along fold line, work 1 row of sc. Fasten off.

Mittens
Sizes: 1 to 2 (2 to 3, 3 to 4) years.
With knitting needles, cast on 30 (32, 34) sts and work 1-1/2 in. (4 cm) in 1/1 ribbing. Bind off loosely. With crochet hook, work 28 (28, 30) sc in bound off row as foll: Row 1: Sc, beg in 2nd ch from hook. Row 2: Ch 2 = 1 border st, *skip 1 sc, work 1 motif in the foll sc: 1 hdc and 1 sc*, rep * to *, end with 1 sc in the last st before the border st. Row 3: Ch 2, *work in sc of the motif: 1 hdc and 1 sc (skipping the hdc in the motif of previous row)*, rep * to *, end with 1 sc in the 2nd ch from the beg. Rep from row 3. You will have 13 (13, 14) motifs with 1 border st at each edge. Work 4 (6, 6) rows. Work thumb opening: 5 (5, 6) motifs, skip 2 motifs, ch 4, work end of row. Work 6 (8, 10) rows after thumb opening. On foll 2 rows, dec 3 motifs. Break yarn and thread yarn through rem sts. Sew side seams. Work 13 (14, 15) sc around thumb opening and work until piece measures 1-1/2 (2, 2-1/2) in. - 4 (5, 6) cm. Work 2 sc tog around. Break yarn. Thread through rem sts. Make a 2nd mitten by rev shapings. Make a cord 40 in. (100 cm) long and sew 1 end to each mitten.

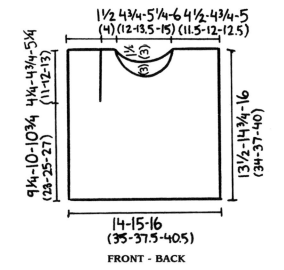

1½ 4¾-5¼-6 4½-4¾-5
(4) (12-13.5-15) (11.5-12-12.5)

4¼-4¾-5¼
(11-12-13)

9¼-10-10¾
(23-25-27)

13½-14¾-16
(34-37-40)

14-15-16
(35-37.5-40.5)

FRONT - BACK

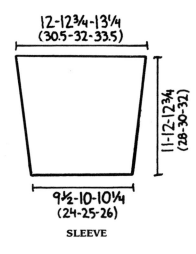

12-12¾-13¼
(30.5-32-33.5)

11-12-12¾
(28-30-32)

9½-10-10¼
(24-25-26)

SLEEVE

Blue Robe

Level: Intermediate

Size

❖ Child's size 2 (4, 6) years, chest 21 (23, 25) in. — 52.5 (58.5, 63.5) cm
❖ Finished chest measurements: 27-1/2 (29, 30-1/2) in. — 70 (74, 78) cm, with an overlap of 3 in. (7.5 cm)
❖ Length: 18-1/2 (20, 21-1/2) in. — 46 (50, 54) cm
❖ Sleeve seam: 9-1/2 (10-3/4, 12) in. — 24 (27, 30) cm

Materials

❖ Sport weight novelty cotton yarn (approx. 125 yds per 50 g skein) 8 (9, 10) skeins color turquoise and 1 skein color red
❖ Crochet hook U.S. size C/2 (Metric size 3) or size needed to obtain gauge
To save time, take time to check gauge!

Gauge

18 hdc and 14 rows = 4 in. (10 cm)

Stitches

Chain (ch), slip st (sl), single crochet (sc), half double crochet (hdc).
Shrimp Stitch: Work like sc, but work left to right instead of right to left.

Note: See "Stitches and Techniques" for detailed instructions on stitches and shapings.

Back

With turquoise, ch 65 (68, 72) + ch 2 = 1 border st. Work in hdc. Work the first hdc in the 4th ch from the hook = 63 (66, 70) hdc with 1 border st at each edge. Work until piece measures 18-1/2 (20, 21-1/2) in. - 46 (50, 54) cm. Fasten off.

Right Front

With turquoise, ch 47 (49, 51) + ch 2 = 1 border st. Work in hdc, working the first hdc in the 4th ch from the hook = 45 (47, 49) hdc with 1 border st at each edge. Work until piece measures 10-3/4 (12, 13-1/4) in. - 27 (30, 33) cm from beg. Mark the 9th st from the right edge. Dec 1 st every 1-3/4 (2, 2) in. - 4.5 (5, 5) cm by working the 9th and 10th sts tog 4 times. At the same time, when piece measures 14-1/4 (15-1/2, 16-3/4) in. - 36 (39, 42) cm from beg, shape shawl collar as foll: right side facing, work 1 border st, 8 hdc and 8 sc, turn with ch 1, skip 1 sc and work 8 sc and 7 hdc, 1 border st. After 4 in. (10 cm), work this short row once more. Work until piece measures 18-1/2 (20, 21-

1/2) in. - 46 (50, 54) cm measured along the side seam. At the side seam, leave 1 border st and 22 (24, 26) hdc unworked. Work over the rem 19 hdc + 2 border sts. Work 2 rows of hdc, then beg at center edge, work: 1 border st, 9 hdc, 10 sc, 1 border st, ch 1 to turn and work 9 sc and 10 hdc, 1 border st. Rep the last 4 rows once more. Continue in hdc until the shoulder is 2 in. (5 cm) high. Fasten off.

Left Front

Work same as right front, rev shapings.

Pockets

With turquoise, ch 20 + ch 2 = 1 border st. Work 4 in. (10 cm) in hdc with 1 border st at each edge. Fasten off.

Sleeves

With turquoise, ch 43 (47, 51) + ch 2 = 1 border st. Work in hdc with 1 border st at each edge. Work the first hdc in the 4th ch from the hook = 41 (45, 49) hdc with 2 border sts. Work until piece measures 8-1/4 (9-1/2, 10-3/4) in. - 21 (24, 27) cm. Work 4 rows more, inc 1 hdc at each edge of every row. When piece measures 9-1/2 (10-3/4, 12) in. - 24 (27, 30) cm, fasten off.

Finishing

Block pieces to indicated measurements. Sew shoulder seams and center back seam of collar. Sew edge of collar to back neck. Sew sleeves to armholes, matching center of sleeve with shoulder seams. Sew side and sleeve seams. With turquoise, work 1 row of sc around collar, front and lower edges of robe, then work 1 row of shrimp st in red. Fasten off. Work same border on sleeve ends. Around the edges of the pocket, work same border as on body. Fasten off. Sew on pockets to front 2 (2-3/4, 3-1/2) in. - 5 (7, 9) cm from lower edge and 1-1/4 in. (3 cm) from side seam. Make a cord 60 in. (150 cm) long in red. At side seams at waist height, make loops and thread cord through.

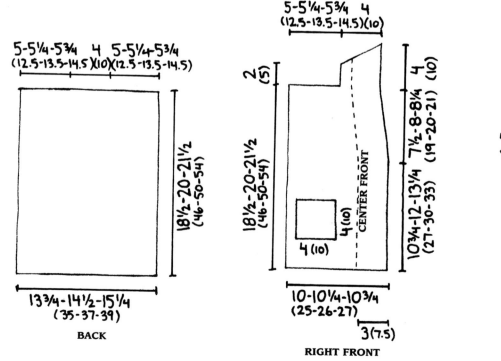

BACK

RIGHT FRONT

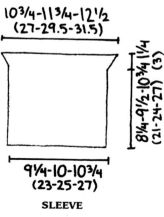

SLEEVE

Striped Robe

Level: Intermediate

Size
❖ Child's size 2 (4, 6) years, chest 21 (23, 25) in. — 52.5 (58.5, 63.5) cm
❖ Finished chest measurements: 28 (29-1/2, 31) in. — 70 (74, 78) cm, with an overlap of 3 in. (7.5 cm)
❖ Length: 18-3/4 (20-1/4, 22) in. — 47 (51, 55) cm
❖ Sleeve seam: 9-1/2 (10-3/4, 12) in. — 24 (27, 30) cm

Materials
❖ Sport weight novelty cotton yarn (approx. 125 yds per 50 g skein) 6 (7, 7) skeins color white, 2 skeins color red, 1 (2, 2) skeins each color yellow and turquoise
❖ Crochet hook U.S. size C/2 (Metric size 3) or size needed to obtain gauge
To save time, take time to check gauge!

Gauge
18 hdc and 16 rows in stripe pat = 4 in. (10 cm)

Stitches
Chain (ch), slip st (sl), single crochet (sc), half double crochet (hdc).

Stripe pat: White rows in hdc, alternating with color stripes in sc. Work stripes as foll: *2 rows white, 2 rows red, 2 rows white, 2 rows turquoise, 2 rows white, 2 rows red, 2 rows white, 2 rows yellow*, rep * to *. Beg each hdc row with ch 2 and end with 1 hdc in the turning ch of the previous row. Beg each sc row with ch 1 and work last sc in the turning ch of the previous row. Work the last loop of one color with a strand of next color. Break yarn at the end of a color stripe. Carry white yarn along the edge, from stripe to stripe. When changing colors, work the last loop of the last st with the color of the next st.

Note: See "Stitches and Techniques" for detailed instructions on stitches and shapings.

Back
With white, ch 65 (68, 72) + ch 2 = 1 border st. Work in stripe pat, working the first hdc in the 4th ch from the hook = 63 (66, 70) hdc with 1 border st at each edge. Work until piece measures 18-3/4 (20-1/4, 22) in. - 47 (51, 55) cm, end with 2 rows of white and 1 row of sc in the foll color of stripe pat. Fasten off.

Right Front
With white, ch 47 (49, 51) + ch 2. Work in stripe pat, working the first hdc in the 4th ch from the hook = 45 (47, 49) hdc with 1 border st at each edge. Work until piece measures 18-3/4 (20-1/4, 22) in. - 47 (51, 55) cm, end with 2 rows of white and 1 row of sc in the same color as back. Leave border st and 22 (24, 26) sts unworked. On the foll row, with white, work in hdc over the rem 23 sc and end this row with ch 11. Work in hdc, working the first hdc in the 4th ch of the hook = 32 hdc + 1 border st at each edge. Work in stripe pat, inc 1 st at left edge (shoulder edge) on every red stripe. Work until the hood measures 8-1/4 (8-3/4, 9-1/4) in. - 21 (22, 23) cm, end with 2 rows of white and 1 row of sc in next color of stripe pat. Fasten off.

Left Front
Work same as right front, rev shapings as foll: work until piece measures 18-3/4 (20-1/4, 22) in. - 47 (51, 55) cm, leaving last 22 (24, 26) sts + border st unworked on the 2nd row of sc. Ch 9 in white and join to 23 sc and work in white in hdc. On the foll row, with white, work in hdc - 32 hdc with 1 border st at each edge. Complete as on right front.

Sleeves
With white, ch 43 (47, 51) + ch 2. Work in hdc with 1 border st at each edge. Work the first hdc in the 4th ch from the hook = 41 (45, 49) hdc with 1 border st. Work in stripe pat until piece measures 8-1/4 (9-1/2, 10-3/4) in. - 21 (24, 27) cm, end with 2 rows in white. Continue in stripe pat. Work 6 more rows, inc 1 st at each edge of every row 4 times. End with 2 rows of sc in next color of stripe pat, fasten off.

Finishing
Block pieces to indicated measurements. Sew shoulder seams and center back seam of hood. Sew top of hood. Sew back of hood to back neck. Sew sleeves to armholes, matching center of sleeve with shoulder seams. Sew side and sleeve seams. Make a cord 60 in. (150 cm) long in white. At side seams at waist height, make loops and thread through cord.

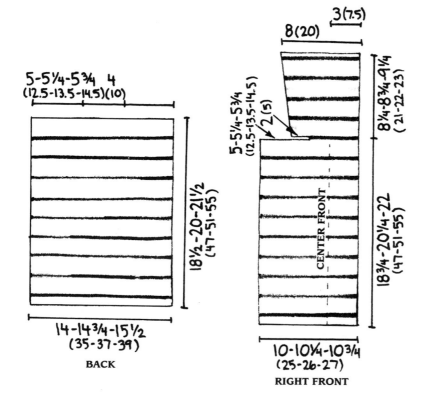

5-5¼-5¾ 4
(12.5-13.5-14.5)(10)

18½-20-21½
(47-51-55)

14-14¾-15½
(35-37-39)

BACK

8(20)   3(7.5)

5-5¼-5¾
(12.5-13.5-14.5)

2 (5)

8¼-8¾-9¼
(21-22-23)

CENTER FRONT

18¾-20¼-22
(47-51-55)

10-10¼-10¾
(25-26-27)

RIGHT FRONT

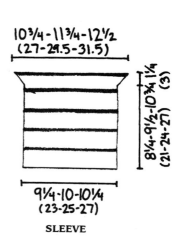

10¾-11¾-12½
(27-29.5-31.5)

8¼-9½-10¾ 1¼
(21-24-27) (3)

9¼-10-10¼
(23-25-27)

SLEEVE

Duck Motif Pullover

Level: Challenging

Size

❖ Child's size 1(3, 5) years, chest 20 (22, 23) in. — 50 (55, 57.5) cm

❖ Finished chest measurements: 24-1/2 (26, 27-1/2) in. — 62 (66, 70) cm

❖ Length: 11-3/4 (13-1/4, 14) in. — 30 (33.5, 36) cm

❖ Sleeve seam: 7-1/4 (8-1/4, 8-3/4) in. — 18.5 (20.5, 22.5) cm

Materials

❖ Worsted weight yarn (approx. 110 yds per 50 g skein) 1 skein each color white and dark blue, 2 skeins each color red and light blue, 1 (1, 2) skeins color turquoise

❖ 4 buttons

❖ Crochet hook U.S. size F/5 (Metric size 4) or size needed to obtain gauge

❖ Knitting needles U.S. size 4 (Metric size 3.5)

To save time, take time to check gauge!

Gauge

17 dc and 9 rows = 4 in. (10 cm)

Stitches

Chain (ch), single crochet (sc), double crochet (dc)

When changing colors, work the last loop of the last st with the color of the next st.

1/1 ribbing: Row 1: *K1, p1*. Rep * to * across.

Row 2 and all foll rows: Work sts as established in previous row.

Note: See "Stitches and Techniques" for detailed instructions on stitches and shapings.

Back

With knitting needles and red, cast on 50 (54, 58) sts and work 1-1/2 in. (4 cm) in 1/1 ribbing. Bind off in ribbing. With crochet hook and dark blue, work 52 (56, 60) dc along top of ribbing. Work in stripes and motif as foll: work stripe 1 foll chart, work 1 (2, 3) rows with light blue, work duck motif of stripe 2, centering motif. Work until piece measures 7-1/2 (7-3/4, 8) in. - 19 (20, 21) cm. Dec

5 sts at each edge for armholes. Work 1 (2, 3) rows with red, 1 (2, 3) rows with light blue. Work stripe 4 foll chart, but substitute red for white. Continue in dark blue until armhole measures 4-3/4 (5-1/2, 6) in. - 12 (14, 15.5) cm. Work the last row in dark blue as foll: 13 (14, 15) dc, ch 2, 16 (18, 20) sc = neck, ch 2, 13 (14, 15) dc. Fasten off.

Front

Work same as back until piece measures 10-1/4 (11-3/4, 13) in. - 26 (29.5, 32.5) cm. Leave the center 14 (16, 18) sts unworked. Work rem 13 (14, 15) dc at each edge to same length as back. With dark blue,

work 13 (14, 15) dc for 1 shoulder, work in sc along neck sts and 1 row in dc for 2nd shoulder. Fasten off.

Sleeves

With knitting needles and red, cast on 24 (28, 32) sts and work 2 in. (5 cm) in 1/1 ribbing. Bind off. With crochet hook and dark blue, work 28 (35, 40) dc in bound off row of ribbing. Then work 1 row in dark blue, 3 (4, 5) rows in light blue, 2 (3, 4) rows in dark blue, 1 row in turquoise, then work stripe 4 by foll chart, substituting red for white. Work 1 row in dark blue. At the same time, inc 1 st at each edge of every

2nd row 6 times = 40 (47, 52) sts. Work 3 rows in red. Fasten off on 3rd row of red.

Finishing

Block pieces to indicated measurements. Lap the top 1/4 in (1 cm) of the front shoulders over the back and sew in place. Tack armhole edges in place. Sew sleeves to armholes, matching center of sleeve with shoulder seams. Sew top 1-1/4 in. (3 cm) of sleeve to armhole edges. Sew side and sleeve seams. Make 2 button clasps on each front shoulder and sew on 2 buttons on each back shoulder to correspond.

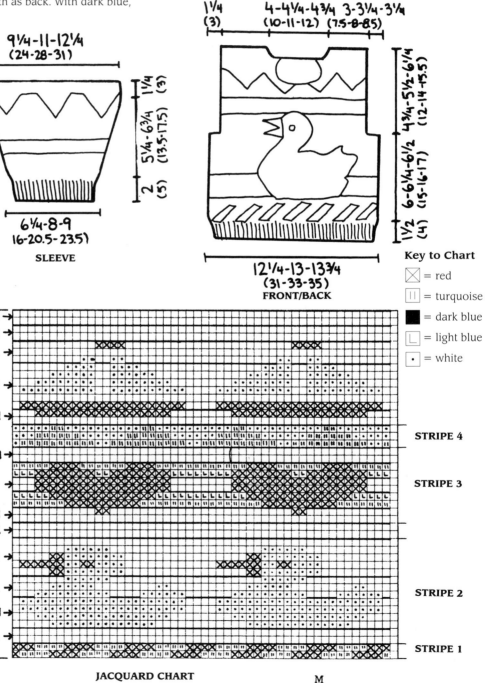

SLEEVE

FRONT/BACK

Key to Chart

⊠ = red

‖ = turquoise

■ = dark blue

□ = light blue

· = white

JACQUARD CHART

Hooded Pullover

Level: Challenging

Size

❖ Child's size 2 (4) years, chest 21 (23) in. — 52.5 (58.5) cm
❖ Finished chest measurements: 25-1/2 (28) in. — 64 (70) cm, length: 12-3/4 (14-1/4) in. — 32 (36) cm
❖ Sleeve seam: 9-3/4 (11) in. — 23.5 (27.5) cm

Materials

❖ Scheepjeswol Superwash Zermatt (approx. 99 yds per 50 g skein) 5 (7) skeins color blue, 2 (3) skeins color cobalt, 1 skein each color light yellow, ochre, red, green, gray, and white
❖ Zipper
❖ Crochet hook U.S. size F/5 (Metric size 4) or size needed to obtain gauge
❖ Knitting needles U.S. size 4 (Metric size 3.5)
To save time, take time to check gauge!

Gauge

15 sc and 19 rows = 4 in. (10 cm)

Stitches

Chain (ch), sl st (sl), single crochet (sc), half double crochet (hdc), double crochet (dc).
Stripe pat: Work in sc as foll: *7 rows in blue, 1 row in yellow, 7 rows in cobalt, 1 row in yellow*, rep * to *.
When changing colors, work the last loop of the last st with the color of the next st.
1/1 ribbing: Row 1: *K1, p1*. Rep * to * across.
Row 2 and all foll rows: Work sts as established in previous row.

Note: See "Stitches and Techniques" for detailed instructions on stitches and shapings.

Back

With crochet hook and cobalt, ch 48(53) + ch 1 = 1 sc. Row 1: 1 sc in the 3rd ch from hook, 1 sc in each of the foll ch = 48 (53) sc. Continue in sc. Ch 1 to turn. Work until piece measures 11-1/2 (13-1/4) in. - 29 (33) cm. Fasten off.

Front

Work same as back until piece measures 7 (8) in. - 17.5 (20.5) cm. On the foll row, leave the center 2 (3) sc unworked for slit and work each side separately. When slit measures 2-3/4 (3-1/4) in. - 7.5 (8) cm, shape neck. At neck edge of every row, dec 5 sts once, dec 2 sts once, dec 1 st 3 times as foll: Dec at beg of row: sl over the dec sts, ch 1 = first sc. At end of row: Leave indicated number of sts unworked. Work rem 13 (15) sts to a length of 11-1/2 (13-1/4) in. - 29 (33) cm from beg. Fasten off. Work other side to match.

Sleeves

With crochet and blue, ch 27 (29) + ch 1 to turn. Row 1: 1 sc in 3rd ch from hook, 1 sc in the foll ch. Continue in stripe pat, ch 1 to turn at beg of each row. Inc 1 st at each edge of every 3rd row 6 (9) times. Inc 1 st at each edge of every 4th row 3 (2) times = 45 (51) sts. When piece measures 8 (9-3/4) in. - 20.5 (24.5) cm, fasten off.

Muff

With crochet hook and light yellow, ch 5. Row 1: 1 sc in the 3rd ch from hook, 1 sc in the foll ch, 5 sc in foll ch, along the underside of the ch, work 1 sc in each of the foll 2 ch, 4 sc in the last ch. Sl st to join = 14 sc. Continue in rounds. Beg each round with ch 1 = first sc. End each row with 1 sl st in the first ch. Row 2: 1 sc in each of the foll 4 sc, 2 sc in the foll sc, 1 sc in foll sc, 2 sc in the foll sc, 1 sc in each of the foll 4 sc, 2 sc in the foll sc, 1 sc in foll sc, 2 sc in the foll sc = 18 sc. Row 3: 1 sc in each of the foll 4 sc, 2 sc in the foll sc, 1 sc in each of the foll 3 sc, 2 sc in the foll sc, 1 sc in each of the foll 4 sc, 2 sc in the foll sc, 1 sc in each of the foll 3 sc, 2 sc in the foll sc = 22 sc. Row 4: 1 sc in each of the foll 4 sc, 2 sc in the foll sc, 1 sc in each of the foll 5 sc, 2 sc in the foll sc, 1 sc in each of the foll 4 sc, 2 sc in the foll sc, 1 sc in each of the foll 5 sc, 2 sc in the foll sc = 26 sc. Row 5: 1 sc in each of the foll 5 sc, 2 sc in the foll sc, 1 sc in each of the foll 5 sc, 2 sc in the foll sc, 1 sc in each of the foll 6 sc, 2 sc in the foll sc, 1 sc in each of the foll 5 sc, 2 sc in the foll sc = 30 sc. Row 6: 1 sc in each of the foll 5 sc, *2 sc in the foll sc, 1 sc in

each of the foll 3 sc*, work * to * twice, 2 sc in the foll sc, 1 sc in each of the foll 6 sc, *2 sc in the foll sc, 1 sc in each of the foll 3 sc*, work * to * twice, 2 sc in the foll sc, 1 sc in each of the foll 10 sc, 2 sc in the foll sc, 1 sc in each of the foll 5 sc, 2 sc in the foll sc, 1 sc in each of the foll 10 sc, 2 sc in the foll sc, 1 sc in the foll 2 sc = 40 sc. Row 8: 1 sc in each of the foll 6 sc, 2 sc in the foll sc, 1 sc in each of the foll 10 sc, 2 sc in the foll sc, 1 sc in each of the foll 8 sc, 2 sc in the foll sc, 1 sc in each of the foll 10 sc, 2 sc in the foll sc, 1 sc in each of the foll 2 sc = 44 sc. Row 9: 1 sc in each of the foll 6 sc, 2 sc in the foll sc, *1 sc in each of the foll 5 sc, 2 sc in the foll sc*, work * to * twice, 1 sc in each of the foll 10 sc, *2 sc in each of the foll sc, 1 sc in each of the foll 5 sc*, work * to * twice, 2 sc in the foll sc, 1 sc in each of the foll 2 sc = 50 sc. Row 10: Work 1 sc in the foll 8 sc, work 2 sc in the 9th sc, *work 1 sc in the foll 7 sc, work 2 sc in the 8th sc*, work * to * twice, work 1 sc in the foll 8 sc, work 2 sc in the 9th sc *work 1 sc in the foll 5 sc, work 2 sc in the 6th sc*, work * to * twice, work 1 sc in the foll 4 sc = 56 sc. Row 11: Sc, working 2 sc in every 7th sc = 64 sc. Row 12: Sc. Row 13: Sc, working 2 sc in every 8th sc = 72 sc. Row 14: Sc. Row 15: Sc, working 2 sc in every 9th sc = 80 sc. Row 16: Sc. Row 17: Sc, working 2 sc in every 10th sc = 88 sc. Make an ear on each side of head in ochre as foll: 1 sc in 10 sc. Work back and forth, beg each row with ch 1. Row 2: Sc, beg row with 2 sc tog = 8 sc. Rows 3 and 5: Sc. Rows 4, 6, and 7: Like row 2 = 2 sc. Row 8: 2 sc tog. Fasten off. Work 1 row of sc in light yellow around the ears and the body. Fasten off. Snout: For each half snout, ch 4 with white and sl st in a ring. Round 1: 8 sc in ring, sl st to join. Round 2: Sc, working 2 sc in every 2nd sc = 12 sc, sl st to join. Round 3: Sc, working 2 sc in every 3rd sc = 16 sc, sl st to join. Round 4: Sc, working 2 sc in every 4th sc = 20 sc, sl st to join. Fasten off. Make a 2nd half snout. Lips: With ochre, ch 4 + ch 1 = first sc. Row 1: 2 sc in the 3rd ch, 2 sc in the foll ch. Row 2: Ch 1 = 1 sc, *2 sc in the

foll sc, 1 sc in the foll sc*, work * to * twice, 2 sc in the foll sc, 1 sc in each of the foll 6 sc, *2 sc in the foll sc, 1 sc in each of the foll 3 sc*, work * to * twice, 2 sc in the foll sc = 36 sc. Row 7: 1 sc in each of the foll sc*, work * to * twice. Row 3: Ch 1 = 1 sc, *2 sc in the foll sc, 1 sc in the foll sc*, work * to * twice, 1 sc in the foll sc. Fasten off.
Bow: With red, ch 12 + ch 1 = 1 sc. Row 1: 1 sc in the 3rd ch from hook, sc in each of the foll ch. Row 2: Ch 3 = 1 dc, 1 dc in each of the foll 2 sc, 1 hdc in the foll sc, 1 sc in each of the foll 4 sc, 1 hdc in the foll sc, 1 dc in each of the foll 3 sc. Row 3: Like row 2 = dc above the dc, hdc above the hdc and sc above the sc. Fasten off.

Finishing

Block pieces to indicated measurements. With knitting needles and cobalt, pick up 32 (34) sts from lower edge of each sleeve and work 1 in. (2.5 cm) in 1/1 ribbing. Bind off loosely. With crochet hook, work 1 row of sc along lower edge of back and front with light yellow. With knitting needles and blue, pick up and knit 50 (52) sts from lower edge of back and front and work 1-1/4 in. (3 cm) in 1/1 ribbing. Bind off loosely. Sew shoulder seams. Sew sleeves to armholes, matching center of sleeve with shoulder seams. Sew side and sleeve seams. *Hood:* With crochet hook and cobalt, work 1 row of sc around neck edge. Fasten off. From center front to center back, with crochet hook work 1 row of sc with blue, then work in stripe pat, beg with 3 rows of blue for larger size. At right edge of every 5th row, inc 1 st 6 times. Work inc sts in stripe pat. Work a total of 32 (35) rows = end with 1 row of light yellow. At the right edge, leave 3 sts unworked and work 4 rows of blue. The total length is 7-1/2 (8) in. - 19 (20) cm. Fasten off. The last row is the center of the hood. Work the 2nd half by rev shapings on opposite neck edge. Sew back and top seam of hood. Work 1 row of sc in cobalt along front of hood. Fasten off. Sew muff to front, using photo as a guide, leaving sides open for muff openings. Sew bow under the head. Embroider whiskers and nose on the snout in stem stitch. Embroider the eyes in satin stitch in green and the pupils in black. With ochre, work 3 stripes at top and at each side in chain st. See photo. Sew in zipper.

(Diagram on page 135)

Primary Colors Cardigan

Level: Challenging

Size

❖ Child's size 4 (6, 8) years, chest 23 (25, 27) in. — 58.5 (63.5, 69) cm
❖ Finished chest measurements: 26-1/4 (28-3/4, 30-3/4) in. — 66 (72, 77) cm
❖ Length: 14-3/4 (16-1/2, 17-3/4) in. — 37 (41, 45) cm
❖ Sleeve seam: 11 (12, 12-1/2) in. — 28 (30, 32) cm

Materials

❖ Mayflower Cotton Helarsgarn (approx. 88 yds per 50 g skein) 3 (4 ,4) skeins color red, 2 skeins each color yellow, orange, green, turquoise and blue
❖ 6 (6, 7) buttons
❖ Crochet hook U.S. size G/6 (Metric size 4.5) or size needed to obtain gauge
❖ Knitting needles U.S. size 3 (Metric size 3)
To save time, take time to check gauge!

Gauge

15 sc and 20 rows = 4 in. (10 cm)

Stitches

Chain (ch), slip st (sl), single crochet (sc).
Jacquard: Foll the chart. Use a separate ball of yarn for each section of color. When changing colors, work the last loop of the last st with the color of the next st.
1/1 ribbing: Row 1: *K1, p1*. Rep * to * across.
Row 2 and all foll rows: Work sts as established in previous row.

Note: See "Stitches and Techniques" for detailed instructions on stitches and shapings.

Body

With knitting needles and red, cast on 109 (117, 125) sts and work 2 in. (5 cm) in 1/1 ribbing, making buttonholes on right edge when border measures 1/4 and 1-1/2 in. (1 and 4 cm) from beg as foll: Work 2 sts, k2 tog, yo. On the foll row, work the yo in rib. Place 6 sts at each edge on holder. Bind off center 97 (105, 113) sts. With crochet hook, work by foll chart, working 1 sc in each knit st. Inc 1 st at each edge = 99 (107, 115) sc. The border sts are not shown on chart. When piece measures 8-3/4 (10, 11) in. - 22 (25, 28) cm from beg, divide work in 3 separate sections: Work 25 (27, 29) sc for right front, 49 (53, 57) sc for back, 25 (27, 29) sc for left front by foll chart. Work right front first. Inc 1 sc at armhole edge for border st. Work until armhole measures 3-1/2 (4, 4-1/4) in. - 9 (10, 11) cm. At neck edge of every 2nd row, wrong side facing, dec 5 (6, 6) sc once, dec 3 (3, 4) sc once, dec 1 sc twice. Work rem 16 (17, 18) sc until armhole measures 6 (6-1/4, 6-3/4) in. - 15 (16, 17) cm. Fasten off. Work left front by rev shapings and continuing pat motif. Work center 49 (53, 57) sc for back, inc 1 sc at each edge for border st. When armhole measures 6 (6-1/4, 6-3/4) in. - 15 (16, 17) cm, fasten off.

Sleeves

With knitting needles and red, cast on 32 (34, 36) sts and work 1-1/2 (2-1/2, 1-1/2) in. - 4 (6, 4) cm in 1/1 ribbing. Bind off loosely. With crochet hook, work 35 (37, 39) sc, centering jacquard chart. At each edge every 1-1/4 (1-1/4, 1-1/2) in. - 3 (3, 4) cm, inc 1 sc 6 (7, 7) times = 47 (51, 53) sc. When piece measures 11 (12, 12-1/2) in. - 28 (30, 32) cm from beg, ending with a full triangle motif, fasten off.

Finishing

Block pieces to indicated measurements. With knitting needles and red, pick up 6 sts from left holder. Inc 1 st at inner edge and work in 1/1 ribbing. Dec 1 st at inner edge. When border fits along front to neck edge, bind off border st and place rem sts on holder. Pick up sts from right holder and work in the same way, making 3 (3 ,4) buttonholes, spaced 2-1/2 (2-3/4, 2-1/2) in. - 6.5 (7.5, 6.5) cm apart. Sew borders to front. Sew shoulder seams. With knitting needles and red, pick up and knit 95 (99, 103) sts from around neck, including sts from holders. Work 1-1/2 in. - (4 cm) in 1/1 ribbing, making last buttonholes when border measures 1/4 and 1-1/2 in. (1 and 4 cm). Bind off loosely. Fold neckband in half to inside and slip st in place. Sew sleeves to armholes, matching center of sleeve with shoulder seams. Sew side and sleeve seams. Reinforce buttonholes and sew on buttons.

(Chart on page 135)

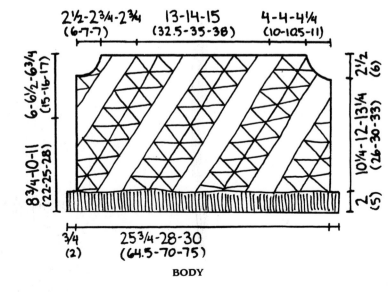

BODY

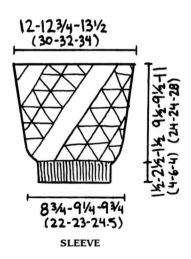

SLEEVE

Dog Motif Jacket

Level: Challenging

Size
❖ 2 (3) years, chest 21 (22) in. — 52.5 (55) cm)
❖ Finished chest measurements: 25-1/4 (27-1/2) in. — 63 (69)cm
❖ Length: 15 (16) in. — 38 (40) cm
❖ Sleeve seam: 9-1/2 (10-1/2) in. — 24 (26) cm

Materials
❖ Bulky weight yarn (approx. 110 yds per 50 g skein) 3 skeins color gray, 1 (2) skeins color light gray, 2 skeins each color black and dark gray and 3 skeins color red
❖ 5 buttons
❖ Crochet hook U.S. size F/5 (Metric size 4) or size needed to obtain gauge
❖ Knitting needles U.S. sizes 3 and 4 (Metric sizes 3 and 3.5) To save time, take time to check gauge!

Gauge
14 sc and 18 rows = 4 in. (10 cm)

Stitches
Chain (ch), slip st (sl), single crochet (sc)
Jacquard st: When changing colors, work the last loop of the last st with the color of the next st. Hold the unused yarn against the back of work. When inserting hook, work around the unused yarn so that the new sts hold it against the work. Beg each row ch 1 = 1 border st. The dogs are embroidered using double strand in cross st by foll chart.

Note: See "Stitches and Techniques" for detailed instructions on stitches and shapings.

Body
With crochet hook and black, ch 90 (98). Work 1 row of sc, work the first sc in the 3rd ch from hook. The last sc is the border st. Turn, ch 1 = 1 border st. Work 87 (95) sc with 1 border st at each edge. Work 1 row of sc in black. Foll row (right side facing): Ch 1, *1 sc

131

in black, 1 sc in dark gray*, rep * to *. Work 13 rows in sc in dark gray. Foll row, right side: Ch 1, *1 sc in dark gray, 1 sc in black*, rep * to *. Foll row: Sc in black. Foll row: Ch 1, *1 sc in black, 1 sc in gray*, rep * to *. Work 3 rows in sc in gray. Work in dot pat as foll: Row 1, right side: Ch 1 in gray, *3 sc in gray, 1 sc in black*, rep * to *. Rows 2, 3, and 4: Sc in gray. Row 5: Ch 1 in gray, 1 sc in gray, *1 sc in red, 3 sc in gray*, rep * to *. Rows 6, 7, and 8: Sc in gray. Always rep these 8 rows. Work until piece measures 9-1/2 (10) in. - 24 (25) cm. Divide work in 3 pieces. Ch 1, work 20 (22) sc, turn. Inc 1 st at armhole edge. Work in dot pat until armhole measures 1-1/4 in. (3 cm), end with 3 rows in sc in gray. Foll row, right side facing: Ch 1 in black, *1 sc in gray, 1 sc in black*, rep * to *, 1 border st in black. Foll row: Sc in black. Foll row: Ch 1 in black, *1 sc in black, 1 sc in light gray*, rep * to *, end with 1 border st in black. Work 11 (13) rows in sc in light gray. Foll row, right side facing: Ch 1 with light gray, *1 sc in light gray, 1 sc in black*, rep * to *, end with 1 border st in black. Foll row: Sc in black, leaving the last 5 (6) sc unworked, turn, do not ch, sl 1 st in black, *1 sc in dark gray (black), 1 sc in black (dark gray)*, rep * to *, end with 1 border st in black. Continue in dark gray in sc, leaving 1 sc unworked at neck edge. Work 13 (14) sc with 1 border st at each edge. When armhole measures 5-1/2 (6) in. - 14 (15) cm, fasten off. Skip 1 st and work next 45 (49) sts in dot pat, inc 1 st for border st. Work until piece measures 4-3/4 (5-1/4) in. - 12 (13) cm. Leave center 15 (17) sts unworked. Work each side separately. At neck edge of foll 2 rows, dec 1 st twice. Work rem 13 (14) sc on each shoulder. Fasten off. Work 2nd front to correspond to right front.

Sleeves
With crochet hook and black, ch 31 (33). Work 1 row of black in sc. Work first sc in the 3rd ch from hook. The last sc is the border st. Turn each row with ch 1 = 1 border st. Work 28 (30) sc with 1 border st at each edge. Work 8 (10) rows in sc in

black. Work same band as on body, inc 5 sts on last row = 33 (35) sc. Continue in dark gray for 11 (13) rows. Work black zigzag row and dot pat as on body. Inc 1 sc at each edge every 3/4 in. (2 cm) 3 (4) times. Work until piece measures 8-1/4 (9-1/4) in. - 21 (23.5) cm. Work 1 row alternating 1 sc in black, 1 sc in green, then work 1 row of sc in black. Fasten off.

Finishing
Block pieces to indicated measurements. Sew shoulder seams.
Along the front edges, with crochet hook, work 1 row of sc, matching colors of fronts. Along the right front, with crochet hook, work 1 row of sc, then on next row of sc, make 5 loops evenly spaced along front.
For each loop, ch 2, skip 2 sc. Fasten off. Along the left front, work 4 rows of sc in black for facing. Fasten off. With crochet hook, work 1 row of sc in light gray around neck, omitting

black facings. Work 4 rows in sc in black, dec 3 sc on the 1st and 3rd rows. Fasten off. Sew sleeves to armholes. Sew sleeve and side seams. Embroider as on bunting. On the dark gray band of sleeve, embroider 2 dogs using light gray with 3 sts between them at center. Sew buttons on the 2nd row from the body on facing.

Scarf
With larger size knitting needles and red, cast on 26 sts and work in 1/1 ribbing for 28 in. (70 cm). Bind off loosely.

Mittens
With smaller size knitting needles, cast on 26 sts and work 2 in. (5 cm) in 1/1 ribbing. Change to larger size knitting needles and work in stockinette st. After 2 rows, shape thumb: Right side facing, 1 border st, k12, inc 1 st in the loop, work to end of row. Purl wrong side row. Foll row: 1 border st, k12, inc 1 in strand between sts, k1, inc 1, work to end of

row. Purl 1 row. Foll row: 1 border st, k12, inc 1, k3, inc 1, work to end of row. Purl 1 row. Inc 2 sts on every 2nd row until you have 9 sts for thumb. Foll row: Work 1 border st, k12, work 9 sts for thumb, turn and purl 9 sts, place rem sts on holder. Work 9 sts for 6 rows. Dec 4 sts on foll row. Break yarn and thread through rem sts. Continue on sts for hand. Work the last 13 sts first, then purl across all 26 sts until piece measures 2-3/4 in. (7 cm) above border. Dec for top as foll: Right side facing, 1 border st, k1, sl 1, k1, psso, k6, k2 tog, k2, sl 1, k1, psso, k6, k2 tog, k1, 1 border st. Purl 1 row. Foll row: 1 border st, k1, sl 1, k1, psso, k4, k2 tog, k2, sl 1, k1, psso, k4, k2 tog, k1, 1 border st. Purl 1 row. Foll row: 1 border st, k1, sl 1, k1, psso, k2, k2 tog, k2, sl 1, k1, psso, k2, k2 tog, k1, 1 border st. Purl 1 row. Break yarn and thread through rem sts. Sew side and thumb seams. Make a cord of red yarn and sew to each mitten.

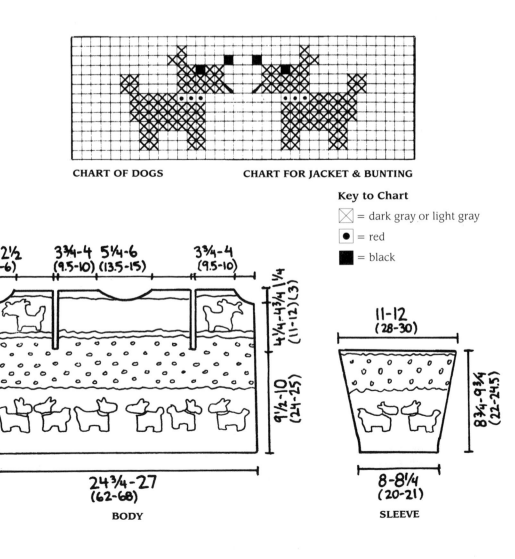

CHART OF DOGS **CHART FOR JACKET & BUNTING**

Key to Chart
⊠ = dark gray or light gray
● = red
■ = black

Bunting

Level: Challenging

Size
❖ 6 months, chest 19 in. (47.5 cm)
❖ Finished chest measurement: 27 in. (68 cm)
❖ Length: 23-1/4 in. (58 cm), sleeve seam: 7-1/4 in. (18 cm)

Materials
❖ Bulky weight yarn (approx. 110 yds per 50 g skein) 6 skeins color gray, 3 skeins color dark gray, 2 skeins each color light gray and black and 1 skein color red
❖ Red zipper 18 in. (45 cm) long
❖ Crochet hook U.S. size F/5 (Metric size 4) or size needed to obtain gauge
To save time, take time to check gauge!

Gauge
14 sc and 18 rows = 4 in. (10 cm)

Stitches
Chain (ch), slip st (sl), single crochet (sc)
Jacquard st: When changing colors, work the last loop of the last st with the color of the next st. Hold the unused yarn against the back of work. When inserting hook, work around the unused yarn so that the new sts hold it against the work. Beg each row: Ch 1 = 1 border st. The dogs are embroidered using double strand in cross st by foll chart.

Note: See "Stitches and Techniques" for detailed instructions on stitches and shapings.

Back
With black, ch 59. Work 1 row of sc, work the first sc in the 3rd ch from hook. The last sc is the border st. Turn, ch 1 = 1 border st. Work 56 sc with 1 border st at each edge. Work 1 row of sc in black. Foll row: Ch 1, *1 sc in black, 1 sc in dark gray*, rep * to *. Work 13 rows in dark gray. Foll row: Right side: ch 1, *1 sc in dark gray, 1 sc in black*, rep * to *. Foll row: Sc in black. Foll row: Ch 1, *1 sc in black, 1 sc in gray*, rep * to *. Work 3 rows in sc in gray. Work in dot pat as foll:

Row 1: Right side, ch 1 in gray, *3 sc in gray, 1 sc in black*, rep * to *. Rows 2, 3, and 4: Sc in gray. Row 5: Ch 1 in gray, 1 sc in gray, *1 sc in red, 3 sc in gray*, rep * to *. Rows 6, 7, and 8: Sc in gray. Always rep these 8 rows. At each edge every 2-3/4 in. (7 cm), dec 1 st 4 times - 48 sts + 1 border st at each edge. Work until piece measures 18-1/2 in. (46 cm), end with 3 rows of gray..Foll row: With gray, sl over first 3 sts, ch 1, *1 sc in gray, 1 sc in black*, rep * to * to last 3 sts. Leave these sts unworked = 42 sc + 1 border st at each edge. Foll row: Sc in black. Foll row: Ch 1, *1 sc in black, 1 sc in light gray*, rep * to *. Work 11 rows in light gray. Foll row: Ch 1, *1 sc in light gray, 1 sc in black*, rep * to *. Foll row: Sc in black. Foll row: Ch 1, *1 sc in black, 1 sc in dark gray*, rep * to *. Work 2 rows in sc in dark gray. Leave center 12 sts unworked. Work each side separately. Work 1 row in dark gray, 1 row alternating 1 sc in dark gray, 1 sc in black, then work 1 row in sc in black. At neck edge of every row, dec 1 st 3 times. Fasten off. Work other side to correspond.

Front
Work same as back until piece measures 5-1/2 in. (14 cm). Divide work in half. Work 28 sc with 1 border st at side seam. Dec 1 st at center edge. Work until piece measures 21-3/4 in. (54.5 cm), end with 1 row of black. On foll row, leave 4 sts unworked at neck edge. At neck edge of every row, dec 1 st 4 times. Work to same length as back. Fasten off. Work 2nd half to correspond.

Sleeves
With black, ch 28. Work 1 row of black in sc. Work first sc in the 3rd ch from hook. The last sc is the border st. Turn each row with ch 1 = 1 border st. Work 25 sc with 1 border st at each edge. Work 5 rows in sc in black. Inc 4 sts on last row = 29 sc. Foll row: Ch 1, *1 sc in black, 1 sc in gray*, rep * to *. Work 3 rows of sc in gray. Work in dot pat. Inc 1 st at each edge every 1-1/2 in. (4 cm) 3 times. Work 35 sc with 1 border st at each edge until piece measures 6-1/4 in. (16 cm). End with 3 rows in sc in gray. Foll row: Ch 1, *1 sc in gray, 1 sc in black*, rep * to *.

Work foll row in sc in black. Foll row: Ch 1, *1 sc in black, 1 sc in dark gray*, work 1 row of sc in dark gray. Fasten off.

Mittens
With red, ch 27. Work 1 row of sc, work the first sc in the 3rd ch from the hook. The last sc is the border st. Ch 1 to turn = 1 border st. Work 24 sc with 1 border st at each edge. Work 10 rows. Foll row: 1 border st, 12 sc, ch 6, skip 6 sc, work the row in sc, 1 border st. Work 1 sc in each ch in the foll row. Work 17 rows. On foll row, dec as foll: *1 sc, work 2 sc tog*, rep * to * = 16 sc. Work over the foll 2 rows, work 2 sc tog across row. Break yarn and thread through rem sts. Work 12 sc around thumb opening. Work 6 rows of sc spiralwise (do not sl st to join), then work 2 sc tog around. Break yarn and thread through rem sts.

Finishing
Block pieces to indicated measurements. Sew shoulder and side seams.
Hood: Around the neck, work 46 sc with black. Rows 2 and 3: Sc in black. Row 4: Sc in black, *work 1 sc in each of the foll 2 sc, 2 sc in the foll sc*, rep * to *, end with 1 sc, 2 sc in the last sc = 59 sc + 1 border st at each edge. Row 5: Ch 1, *1 sc in black, 1 sc in dark gray*, rep * to *. Row 6: Sc in dark gray. Row 7: Ch 1, *1 sc in dark gray, 1 sc in black*, rep * to *. Row 8: Sc in black, inc 4 sc = 63 sc + 1 border st at each edge. Row 9: Ch 1, *1 sc in black, 1 sc in gray*, rep * to *. Continue in dot pat as on body. Beg 4th row with dot pat with ch 1, 1 sc in gray, 1 sc in black. Work until piece measures 6-1/4 in. (16 cm) = 28 rows from the neck. At center back of every 2nd row, work 2 sc tog 4 times. Work in dot pat until hood measures 8 in. (20 cm), end with 3 rows in sc in gray. Alternate 1 row in sc in gray and 1 row in black, end with 1 row in sc in black. Fasten off. Sew top seam of hood. Along the hood and slit opening, work 1 row of sc in gray. Join row with 1 sl st in the first sc and fasten off. Sew sleeves to armholes. Sew sleeve seams. Sew on mittens to lower edge of sleeves so that the 7th row of mittens is at the lower edge of sleeve. Sew in zipper.

Embroider dogs with double strand of light gray in cross st on dark gray bands at lower edge. Embroider 2 dogs 3 times, beg at center back. Leave 3 sts between dogs' tongues. Make another pair 3 sts from the first with 2 sts between their tongues. Embroider with dark gray on light gray band 1 dog on each front section and 2 on back with 3 (5) sts between them.

DOGS

Size
❖ Height: 7 in. (18 cm), width 9 in. (23 cm).

Materials
❖ Bulky weight yarn (approx. 110 yds per 50 g skein) 2 skeins color light gray or dark gray, small amounts of color black and red

Dog
Work by foll chart in sc. Beg with 1 foot. Ch 8. Row 1: work in sc, working the first sc in the 3rd ch from the hook, 1 sc in each of the foll ch = 7 sc. Ch 1 to turn. Work 6 rows. Fasten off. Make a 2nd foot. Foll row: Work 7 sc of 1 foot, ch 8, 7 sc of 2nd foot. Foll foot: 7 sc, 1 sc in each of the 8 ch, 7 sc = 22 sts. Work by foll chart. Fasten off. Make a 2nd piece. Panel: Ch 6. Work in sc, work first sc in the 3rd ch from hook, 1 sc in each of the foll ch 8. Work in sc until piece fits between the front and back of the dog.

Finishing
Embroider the eye in cross stitch in black by foll chart. Sew the panel between the back and front pieces, leaving an opening for stuffing. Stuff and close opening. Embroider the nose in satin st as shown in photo. Tongue: With red, ch 6 and work in sl st. On foll row dec 3 sts. Work 1 row in sl st and fasten off. Sew tongue as shown in photo. Collar: With red, ch 4. Work in sc to desired length. Fasten off. Sew collar on. With red, make a cord and sew to collar.
(continued on page 134)

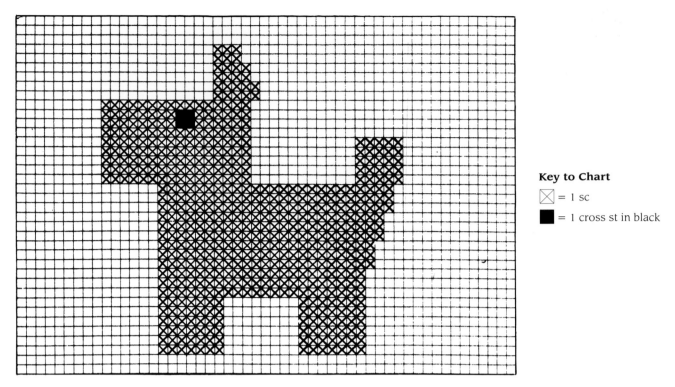

CHART FOR DOG

Key to Chart

☒ = 1 sc

■ = 1 cross st in black

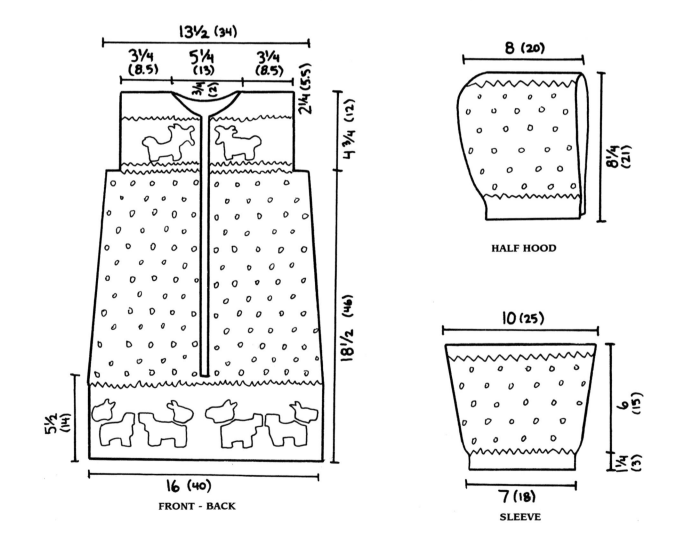

FRONT - BACK

HALF HOOD

SLEEVE

Hooded Pullover

(continued from page 126)

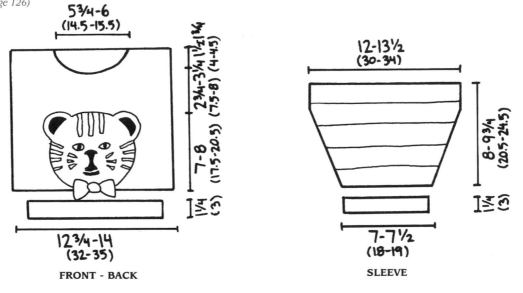

FRONT - BACK

5¾-6
(14.5-15.5)

2¾-3¾ (7.5-8)

1½-1¾ (4-4.5)

7-8
(17.5-20.5)

1¼
(3)

12¾-14
(32-35)

SLEEVE

12-13½
(30-34)

8-9¾
(20.5-24.5)

1¼
(3)

7-7½
(18-19)

Primary Colors Cardigan

(continued from page 128)

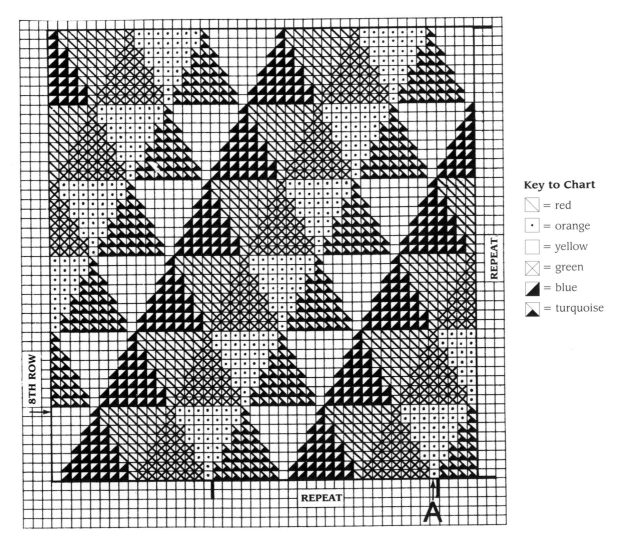

8TH ROW

REPEAT

REPEAT

A

CHART FOR CARDIGAN

Key to Chart

◻ = red

· = orange

◻ = yellow

⊠ = green

◤ = blue

◣ = turquoise

Blue Pullover

Level: Challenging

Size

✣ Child's size 2 (4, 6) years, chest 22 (23, 25) in. — 52.5 (55, 58.5) cm
✣ Finished chest measurements: 28 (28-1/2, 29-1/2) in. — 70 (72, 74) cm
✣ Length: 14-3/4 (15-1/2, 16-1/4) in. — 37 (39, 41) cm
✣ Sleeve seam: 12 (12-3/4, 13-1/2) in. — 30 (32, 34) cm

Materials

✣ Sport weight yarn (approx. 135 yds per 50 g skein) 7 (7, 8) skeins color blue
✣ 4 buttons
✣ Crochet hook U.S. size E/4 (Metric size 3.5) or size needed to obtain gauge
✣ Knitting needles U.S. size 3 (Metric size 3)
To save time, take time to check gauge!

Gauge

16 hdc and 14 rows = 4 in. (10 cm). 17-1/2 sts and 14 rows in pat st = 4 in. (10 cm). Center panel with bobbles in relief dc = 2-3/4 in. (7 cm).

Stitches

Chain (ch), single crochet (sc), half double crochet (hdc), double crochet (dc)
Front Relief dc: Insert hook around the front post from right to left, yo before inserting hook in st.
Back Relief dc: Insert hook around the back post from right to left, yo before inserting hook in st.
Relief tr: Work the same way as relief dc, but yo twice before inserting hook.
Cable pat over 5 sts:
Row 1: Wrong side facing: 5 dc.
Row 2: Right side facing: 1 front relief dc around the foll 2 dc, 1 back relief dc in the foll dc, 1 front relief dc in each of the foll 2 dc. Row 3: Around the first 2 dc, work 1 back relief dc; around the center dc, work 1 front relief dc; and around each of the last 2 dc, work 1 back relief dc. Row 4: Work 1 front relief tr around the 4th and 5th dc, then 1 back relief dc around the center dc, and 1 front relief tr around the first and the 2nd dc = cable.
Rows 5 and 7: Like row 3.
Rows 6 and 8: Like row 2.
Always rep row 3 to row 8.
Bobble: *Yo, insert hook around the post of the st 2 rows below and draw up 1 loop*, rep * to * 3 times in the same st until you have 6 loops, yo, draw through all loops.
Bobble pat: Worked over 7 hdc.
Row 1: Wrong side: Hdc. Row 2: 1 hdc, *1 bobble in the foll hdc of the previous row, 1 hdc in the foll hdc*, rep * to * 3 times. Row 3: 7 hdc. Row 4: 1 bobble in the hdc in the 2nd row, *1 hdc in the foll hdc, 1 bobble in the foll hdc in the 2nd row*, rep * to * 3 times. Always rep these 4 rows, but on the 2nd row of pat, work in the hdc of the 4th row.
Pat st: Multiple of 5 hdc.
Row 1: Wrong side: Hdc. Row 2: *1 relief tr in the each of the foll 2 hdc of the previous row, 1 hdc in each of the foll 3 hdc*, rep * to *. Row 3: Hdc in each st of the previous row. Row 4: *1 relief tr in each of the 2 underlying relief tr, 1 hdc in the foll 3 hdc*, rep * to *.
Rows 5 to 8: Like rows 3 and 4.
Row 9: Like row 3. Row 10: *Cross relief tr with the first tr in the 2nd underlying relief tr and work 2nd tr in the first underlying relief tr, 1 hdc in each of the foll 3 hdc*, rep * to*. Always rep the 3rd to the 10th rows.
Relief tr:
Row 1: Wrong side: hdc. Row 2: Work 1 relief tr in the underlying hdc. Row 3: Work 1 hdc in the underlying relief dc. Row 4: Work 1 relief dc in the tr of the 2nd row. Always rep the 3rd and 4th rows.
1/1 ribbing: Row 1: *K1, p1*. Rep * to * across.
Row 2 and all foll rows: Work sts as established in previous row.

Note: See "Stitches and Techniques" for detailed instructions on stitches and shapings.

Back

With knitting needles, cast on 62 (64, 66) sts and work 2 in. (5 cm) in 1/1 ribbing, end on wrong side row. Bind off loosely. With crochet hook, work as foll: Row 1: Wrong side facing: Ch 2 = 1 border st, work 57 (59, 61) hdc and end with 1 hdc = 1 border st. Row 2: Right side facing: Ch 2 = 1 border st, 3 (4, 5) hdc, 5 sts in pat st 4 times, 2 relief tr, 7 sts in bobble pat, 2 relief tr, 5 sts in pat st 4 times, but beg with 3 hdc in the 2 relief dc, end row with 3 (4, 5) hdc and the hdc in the border st. Work until piece measures 14-1/4 (15, 16) in. - 36 (38, 40) cm. Leave center 19 (21, 23) sts unworked. Work each side separately. Wrong side: Work the first 19 sts + 1 border st for 1/4 in. (1 cm), end on right side. Fasten off. Work to same length as left half, then work 2 rows of hdc. Fasten off.

Front

Work same as back until piece measures 13-1/4 (14, 14-3/4) in. - 33 (35, 37) cm. Leave the center 9 (11, 13) sts unworked. Work each side separately. At neck edge of every 2nd row, dec 3 sts once, 2 sts once. Work to same length as left half, but work 1 row of sc on right shoulder with 3 button loops evenly spaced on shoulder. Beg at armhole edge, work as foll: *3 sc, ch 2, skip 2*, rep * to * twice, work around neck in sc. Fasten off.

Sleeves

With knitting needles, cast on 40 (42 ,44) sts and work 2 in. (5 cm) in 1/1 ribbing, end on wrong side row. In bound off sts of ribbing, with crochet hook, work 35 (37, 39) hdc plus 1 border st at each edge. Row 2: Ch 2 = 1 border st, 2 (3, 4) hdc, 10 sts in pat st, 2 relief tr, 7 sts in bobble pat, 2 relief dc and 10 sts in pat st, beg with 3 hdc, then the 2 relief tr, end with 2 (3, 4) hdc, 1 border st. Inc 1 st at each edge of every 5th (5th, 6th) row 6 times = 47 (49, 51) sts + 1 border st at each edge. Work inc sts in pat st, alternating 5 hdc, 5 sts in cable pat = 55 (59, 63) sts + 2 border sts. When piece measures 10-3/4 (11-1/2, 12-1/4) in. - 27 (29, 31) cm, inc 1 st at each edge of foll 3 rows. Work until piece measures 12 (12-3/4, 13-1/2) in. - 30 (32, 34) cm. Fasten off.

Finishing

Block pieces to indicated measurements. Sew right shoulder seam omitting facing. Work 1 row of sc around neck. With knitting needles, pick up and knit 71 (73, 75) sts from sc around neck and work 3/4 in. (2 cm) in 1/1 ribbing. When neckband measures 1/4 in. (1 cm), work last buttonhole 2 sts from edge by k2 tog, yo. Bind off loosely. Sew ends of facing in place. Sew sleeves to side seams. Sew side and sleeve seams. Sew buttons to last row of back shoulder.

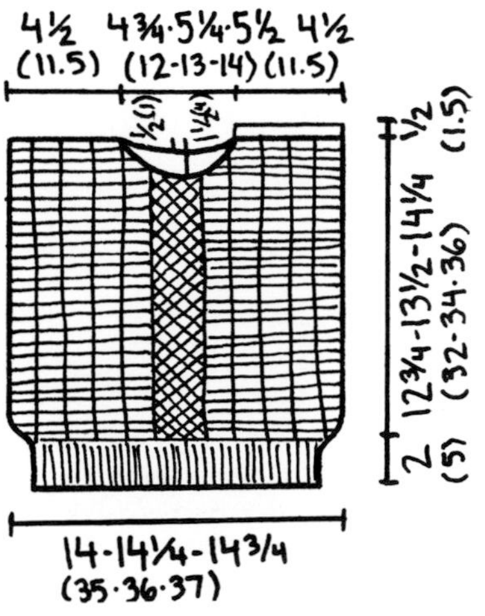

4½ 4¾-5¼-5½ 4½
(11.5) (12-13-14) (11.5)
½ (1.5)
12¾-13½-14¼ (32-34-36)
2 (5)
14-14¼-14¾
(35-36-37)

FRONT - BACK

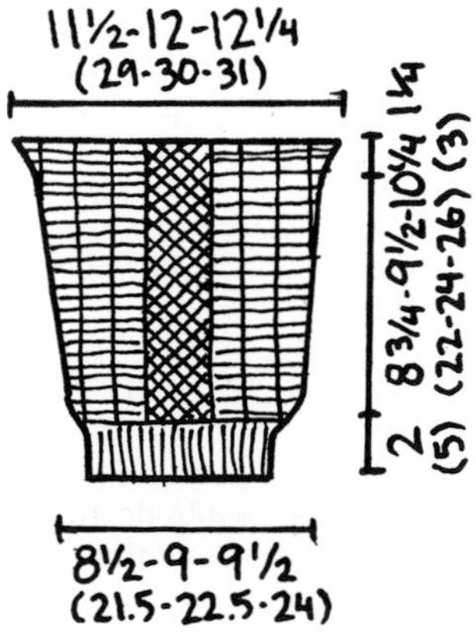

11½-12-12¼
(29-30-31)
1¼ (3)
8¾-9½-10¼ (22-24-26)
2 (5)
8½-9-9½
(21.5-22.5-24)

SLEEVE

Yellow Pullover

Level: Challenging

Size
❖ Child's size 2 (3, 4) years, chest 21 (22, 23) in. — 52.5 (55, 58.5) cm
❖ Finished chest measurements: 27 (28, 28-1/2) in. — 68 (70, 72) cm
❖ Length: 13-3/4 (14-1/2, 15-1/4) in. — 35 (37, 39) cm
❖ Sleeve seam: 11 (12, 12-3/4) in. — 28 (30, 32) cm

Materials
❖ Sport weight yarn (approx. 135 yds per 50 g skein) 7 (8, 8) skeins color yellow
❖ 3 buttons
❖ Crochet hook U.S. size E/4 (Metric size 3.5) or size needed to obtain gauge
❖ Knitting needles U.S. size 3 (Metric size 3)
To save time, take time to check gauge!

Gauge
16 hdc and 14 rows = 4 in. (10 cm). 5 sts in cable st and 5 hdc = 2 in. (5 cm)

Stitches
Chain (ch), single crochet (sc), half double crochet (hdc), double crochet (dc)
Front Relief dc: Insert hook around the front post from right to left, yo before inserting hook in st.
Back Relief dc: Insert hook around the back post from right to left, yo before inserting hook in st.
Relief tr: Work the same way as relief dc, but yo twice before inserting hook.
Cable pat over 5 sts:
Row 1: Wrong side facing: 5 dc.
Row 2: Right side facing: 1 front relief dc around the foll 2 dc, 1 back relief dc in the foll dc, 1 front relief dc in each of the foll 2 dc. Row 3: Around the first 2 dc, work 1 back relief dc; around the center dc, work 1 front relief dc; and around each of the last 2 dc, work 1 back relief dc. Row 4: Work 1 front relief tr around the 4th and 5th dc, then 1 back relief dc around the center dc, and 1 front relief tr around the first and the 2nd dc = cable.

Rows 5 and 7: Like row 3.
Rows 6 and 8: Like row 2.
Always rep row 3 to row 8.
1/1 ribbing: Row 1: *K1, p1*. Rep * to * across.
Row 2 and all foll rows: Work sts as established in previous row.

Note: See "Stitches and Techniques" for detailed instructions on stitches and shapings.

Back
With knitting needles, cast on 60 (62, 64) sts and work 2 in. (5 cm) in 1/1 ribbing, end on wrong side row. Bind off loosely. With crochet hook, work as foll: Row 1: Work 67 (69, 71) dc in bound off row, beg with ch 3 = 1 dc as the border st. Last dc = 1 border st. Row 2: 1 border st, 5 (6, 7) hdc, 5 st cable, *5 hdc, 5 st cable*, rep * to* 4 times, end with 5 (6, 7) hdc, 1 border st. Beg with ch 2 and end with 1 hdc in the turning ch. Work until piece measures 8-3/4 (9-1/4, 9-1/2) in. - 22 (23, 24) cm. Dec 2 sts at each edge for armholes. Work until armhole measures 4-1/4 (4-3/4, 5-1/4) in. - 11 (12, 13) cm. Leave the center 17 (19, 21) sts unworked. Work each side separately. At each neck edge, dec 3 sts once. Work rem 20 sts until armhole measures 4-3/4 (5-1/4, 5-1/2) in. - 12 (13, 14) cm. Work left half for 3/4 in. (2 cm) more in hdc for button flap. Fasten off. Work sts for right half to correspond omitting button flap.

Front
Work same as back until armhole measures 3-1/2 (4, 4-1/4) in. - 9 (10, 11) cm. Leave the center 17 (19, 21) sts unworked. Work each side separately. Dec 1 st at neck edge of every row 3 times. Work until armhole measures 4 -3/4 (5-1/4, 5-1/2) in. - 12 (13, 14) cm. Fasten off. Work other side to correspond.

Sleeves
With knitting needles, cast on 38 (40, 42) sts and work 2 in. (5 cm) in 1/1 ribbing, end on wrong side row. Bind off loosely. With crochet hook, work 37 (41, 45) hdc in bound off sts of row with 1 border st on each edge.

Foll row: 1 border st, 6 (8, 10) hdc, *5 sts of cable, 5 hdc*, rep * to * twice, end last rep with 5 sts of cable pat, 6 (8, 10) hdc, 1 border st. Inc 1 st at each edge of every 4th row 6 (7, 8) times, inc 1 st at each edge of every 2nd row 3 (2, 1) time. Work inc sts in pat st, alternating 5 hdc, 5 sts in cable pat = 55 (59, 63) sts + 2 border sts. Work until piece measures 11 (12, 12-3/4) in. - 28 (30, 32) cm. Leave 26 (28, 30) sts unworked at each edge. Work center 7 sts in cable st with 1 border st at each edge. Work sleeve extension for 4 in. (10.5 cm). Fasten off. Make a 2nd sleeve, making 2 buttonholes when sleeve extension measures 1-1/4 and 2-3/4 in. - (3 and 7 cm). For each buttonhole, skip the center dc and ch 1. On foll row, work 1 dc in ch 1.

Finishing
Block pieces to indicated measurements. Sew sleeve extension without buttonholes to back and front shoulders. Sew front shoulder seam of 2nd sleeve extension. Sew side and sleeve seams and sew in sleeves. With knitting needles, pick up and knit 72 (74, 76) sts around neck and work 3/4 in (2 cm) in 1/1 ribbing, making 1 buttonhole when border measures 1/4 in. (1 cm). 2 sts in from edge, k2 tog, yo. On the foll row, work the yo in ribbing. Sew on buttons.

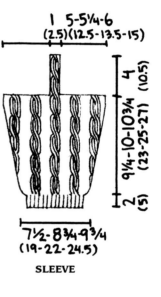

1 5-5¼-6
(2.5)(12.5-13.5-15)

4
(10.5)

9¼-10-10¾
(23-25-27)

2
(5)

7½-8¾-9¾
(19-22-24.5)

SLEEVE

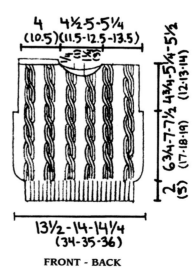

4 4½-5-5¼
(10.5)(11.5-12.5-13.5)

4¾-5¼-5½
(12-13-14)

6¾-7-7½
(17-18-19)

2
(5)

13½-14-14¼
(34-35-36)

FRONT - BACK

Red Pullover

Level: Challenging

Size

❖ Child's size 2 (4, 6) years, chest 22 (23, 25) in. — 52.5 (55, 58.5) cm
❖ Finished chest measurements: 28 (28-1/2, 29-1/2) in. — 70 (72,7 4) cm
❖ Length: 14-1/2 (15-1/4, 16) in. — 37 (39, 41) cm
❖ Sleeve seam: 11-3/4 (12-1/2, 13-1/4) in. — 30 (32, 34) cm

Materials

❖ Sport weight yarn (approx. 135 yds per 50 g skein) 7 (7, 8) skeins color red
❖ 3 buttons
❖ Crochet hook U.S. size E/4 (Metric size 3.5) or size needed to obtain gauge
❖ Knitting needles U.S. size 3 (Metric size 3)
To save time, take time to check gauge!

Gauge

16 hdc and 14 rows = 4 in. (10 cm). 10 sts of pat st = 2-1/2 in. (6 cm)

Stitches

Chain (ch), single crochet (sc), half double crochet (hdc), treble crochet (tr)
Front Relief dc: Insert hook around the front post from right to left, yo hook before inserting hook in st.
Back Relief dc: Insert hook around the back post from right to left, yo before inserting hook in st.
Relief tr: Work the same way as relief dc, but yo twice before inserting hook.
Cable pat over 3 sts:
Row 1: Right side facing: 3 hdc. Row 2: Wrong side facing: 3 hdc. Row 3: Skip 1 hdc, work around the post of the foll hdc 2 rows below: 2 relief dc worked tog: work 2 relief dc in the same st = 3 loops, yo, draw loop through last 3 loops, work 1 hdc in the center hdc of the previous row and work 2 relief dc tog in the center hdc 2 rows below, skip 1 hdc. Row 4: 3 hdc. Row 5: Work 2 relief dc tog in the center hdc 2 rows below, 1 hdc in the previous hdc in the last row, and work 2 relief dc tog in the center hdc 2

rows below. The 1st and 3rd hdc of previous row are skipped. Always rep rows 4 and 5.
1/1 ribbing: Row 1: *K1, p1* Rep * to * across.
Row 2 and all foll rows: Work sts as established in previous row.

Note: See "Stitches and Techniques" for detailed instructions on stitches and shapings.

Front

With knitting needles, cast on 60 (62, 64) sts and work 2-1/2 in. (6 cm) in 1/1 ribbing, end on wrong side row. Bind off loosely. With crochet hook, work as foll: Row 1: Ch 2 = 1 border st, 57 (59, 61) hdc, end with 1 hdc = 1 border st. Row 2: Like row 1. Row 3: Ch 2 = 1 border st, 3 (4, 5) hdc, 1 front relief tr in the foll hdc of the first row, 3 hdc, 3 sts of cable pat, *3 hdc, 1 front relief tr in foll hdc of first row, 3 hdc, 3 sts of cable pat*, rep * to * 3 times, end with 3 hdc, 1 front relief tr in the foll hdc in the first row, 3 (4, 5) hdc, 1 hdc = 1 border st. Row 4: Ch 2 = 1 border st, 57 (59, 61) hdc, 1 hdc = 1 border st. Always rep

rows 3 and 4, working the relief tr in the underlying relief dc. Work until piece measures 8 (8-1/4, 8-1/2) in. - 20 (21, 22) cm. At each edge of every 2nd row, inc 3 sts 3 times, inc 29 (33, 36) sts once = 133 (143, 151) sts + 1 border st at each edge. Work inc sts in pat st. Work until piece measures 13-1/4 (14, 14-3/4) in. - 33 (35, 37) cm. Leave center 11 (13, 15) sts unworked. Work each side separately. At neck edge of every 2nd row, dec 3 sts once, dec 2 sts once = 57 (61, 64) sts. Work for 4-3/4 (5-1/4, 5-1/2) in. - 12 (13, 14) cm, measured from sleeve end. End on right side of work. Break yarn and work 2nd half to correspond. For back button facing: Ch 18 + ch 2 to turn. Work 2 rows in hdc, working the first hdc in the 4th ch from hook. Break yarn. Beg on wrong side, work in hdc across sts of left sleeve, ch 21 (23, 25) for back neck, work 18 sts of facing and work last 38 (42, 45) sts of 2nd sleeve, end with 1 border st = 133 (143, 151) sts + 1 border st at each edge. Work until sleeve measures 9-1/2 (10-1/4, 11) in. - 24 (26, 28) cm measured from end of sleeve. Dec

29 (33, 36) sts, turn, work 57 (59, 61) sts + 1 border st at each edge. Leave rem sts unworked. At each edge of every 2nd row, dec 3 sts 3 times. Work to same length as back without border, end on right side of work. Fasten off. With knitting needles, pick up 60 (62, 64) sts and work 2-1/2 in. (6 cm) in 1/1 ribbing. Bind off loosely.

Finishing

Block piece to indicated measurements. With knitting needles, pick up and knit 38 (40, 42) sts from each sleeve end and work 2 in. (5 cm) in 1/1 ribbing. Bind off loosely. Work 1 row of sc around neck and facing. With knitting needles, pick up 58 (60, 62) sts around neck and work 3/4 in. (2 cm) in 1/1 ribbing. Make a buttonhole at 1/4 in. (1 cm) 2 sts from edge. For buttonhole: k2 tog, yo. Bind off loosely. Sew side and sleeve seams. Along edge of front shoulder work 1 row of sc, making a loop 1-1/4 and 2-3/4 in. (3.5 and 7) cm from side seam. For each loop ch 2, skip 2. Fasten off. Sew buttons to last row of back shoulder to correspond.

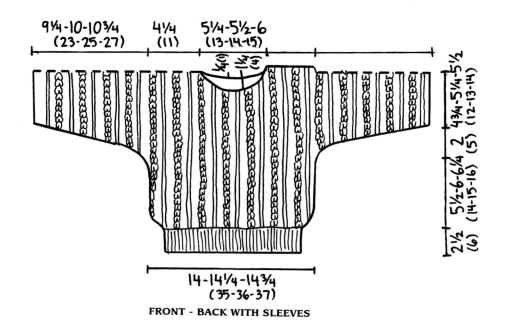

FRONT - BACK WITH SLEEVES

Yoke Cardigan

(photo on preceding page)

Level: Challenging

Size

❖ Child's size 10 (12, 14) years, chest: 28-1/2 (30, 32) in. — 71.5 (75, 80) cm
❖ Finished chest measurements: 33-1/2 (35-1/4, 36-3/4) in. — 84 (88, 92) cm
❖ Length: 22-3/4 (23-1/2, 24-1/4) in. — 57 (59, 61) cm
❖ Sleeve seam: 13-1/2 (14-1/4, 15) in. — 34 (36, 38) cm

Materials

❖ Sport weight yarn (approx. 130 yds per 50 g skein) 8 (9, 10) skeins color red, 2 skeins each color yellow and blue green, 1 skein each color loden green and teak
❖ Crochet hook U.S. size E/4 (Metric size 3.5) or size needed to obtain gauge
❖ Knitting needles U.S. size 3 (Metric size 3)
To save time, take time to check gauge!

Gauge

18 sts and 9 rows = 4 in. (10 cm)

Stitches

Chain (ch), slip st (sl), double crochet (dc).
Pat st: Foll the chart. Beg each row with ch 3 = first dc. When changing colors, work the last loop of the last st with the color of the next st. Hold unused yarn against the back of work. When inserting hook, work around the unused yarn so that the new sts hold it against the work.
1/1 ribbing: Row 1: *K1, p1*. Rep * to * across.
Row 2 and all foll rows: Work sts as established in previous row.

Note: See "Stitches and Techniques" for detailed instructions on stitches and shapings.

Body

With crochet hook and red, ch 150 (157, 164) + ch 3 = first dc (1 border st). Work in pat st. When piece measures 12 (12-3/4, 13-1/2) in. - 30 (32, 34) cm, work as foll: 1 border st, 35

(37, 38) sts, 1 border st for 1 front, (armhole), 1 border st, 74 (77, 82) sts, 1 border st for the back, (armhole), 1 border st, 35 (37, 38) sts, 1 border st for 2nd front. Dec 1 st at each raglan edge every row 4 times. Fasten off.

Sleeves

With crochet hook and red, ch 40 (42, 44) + ch 3 for the first dc. Work in pat st. Inc 1 st at each edge of every 2nd row 11 times = 62 (64, 66) sts. When piece measures 12 (12-3/4, 13-1/2) in. - 30 (32, 34) cm, dec 1 st at each raglan edge every row 4 times. Fasten off.

Yoke

With crochet hook and red, work over one front, one sleeve, one back, 2nd sleeve and the last front, leave the border sts at each armhole edge unworked = 232 (243, 254) sts + 1 border st at center edge of each front. Continue by foll chart. Rows 1 and 3: Work

without dec. Row 4: Dec 21 (22, 23) as shown on chart. Rows 5 and 6: Without dec. Row 7: Dec 21 (22, 23) sts as shown on chart. Row 8: Dec 20 (21, 22) sts as shown on chart. Rows 9 to 11: Without dec. Row 12: Dec 42 (44, 46) sts as shown on chart. Row 13: Dec 22 (23, 24) sts as shown on chart. Row 14: Without dec. Row 15: Dec 21 (22, 23) sts as shown on chart. Row 16: Without dec = 85 (89, 93) sts + 1 border st at each edge.

Finishing

Sew raglan seams. With knitting needles and red, pick up and knit 1 st from every st along each sleeve end and work 1-1/2 in. (4 cm) in 1/1 ribbing. Bind off loosely. Sew sleeve seams. With knitting needles, pick up and knit 116 (126, 136) sts along each front and work 3/4 in. (2 cm) in 1/1 ribbing. Bind off loosely. Sew neckband seam. Fold neck-

band in half to inside and slip st in place. With knitting needles and red, pick up and knit 1 st from every st along lower edge and work 2-3/4 in. (7 cm) in 1/1 ribbing. Bind off loosely. With knitting needles and red, pick up and knit 2 sts from every st around neck and work 3/4 in. (2 cm) in 1/1 ribbing. Bind off loosely.

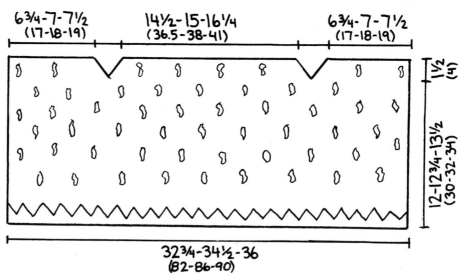

6¾-7-7½ (17-18-19)   14½-15-16¼ (36.5-38-41)   6¾-7-7½ (17-18-19)

1½ (4)

12-12¾-13½ (30-32-34)

32¾-34½-36 (82-86-90)

BODY

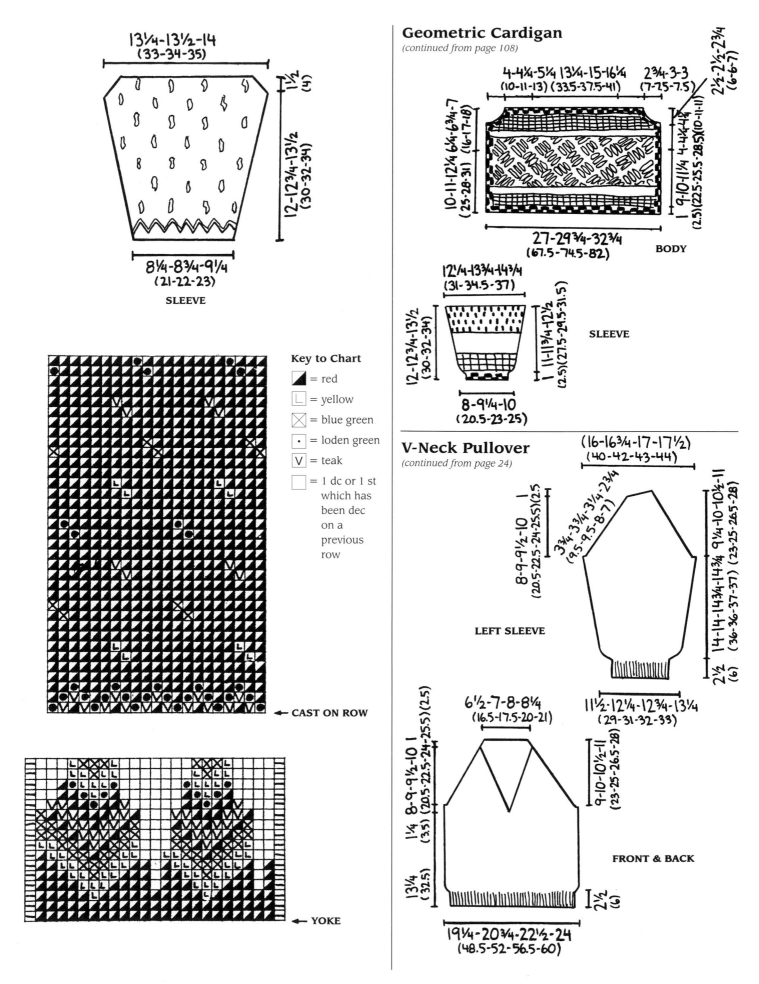

13¼-13½-14
(33-34-35)

1½
(4)

12-12¾-13½
(30-32-34)

8¼-8¾-9¼
(21-22-23)

SLEEVE

Key to Chart

◣ = red

L = yellow

⊠ = blue green

• = loden green

V = teak

□ = 1 dc or 1 st which has been dec on a previous row

← **CAST ON ROW**

← **YOKE**

Geometric Cardigan

(continued from page 108)

4-4¼-5¼ 13¼-15-16¼   2¾-3-3

(10-11-13) (33.5-37.5-41)   (7-7.5-7.5)

2½-2½-2¾
(6-6-7)

6¼-6¾-7
(16-17-18)

10-11-12¼
(25-28-31)

4-4-4¼-4½
(10-10-11-11)

9-10-11¼
(2.5)(22.5-25.5-28.5)

27-29¾-32¾
(67.5-74.5-82)   **BODY**

12¼-13¾-14¾
(31-34.5-37)

12-12¾-13½
(30-32-34)

11-11¾-12½
(27.5-29.5-31.5)

1
(2.5)

8-9¼-10
(20.5-23-25)

SLEEVE

V-Neck Pullover

(continued from page 24)

(16-16¾-17-17½)
(40-42-43-44)

8-9-9½-10
(20.5-22.5-24-25.5)

1
(2.5)

3¾-3¾-3¼-2¾
(9.5-9.5-8-7)

9¼-10-10½-11
(23-25-26.5-28)

14-14-14¾-14¾
(36-36-37-37)

2½
(6)

LEFT SLEEVE

11½-12¼-12¾-13¼
(29-31-32-33)

6½-7-8-8¼
(16.5-17.5-20-21)

8-9-9½-10
(20.5-22.5-24-25.5)

1
(2.5)

9-10-10½-11
(23-25-26.5-28)

13¼
(32.5)

2½
(6)

FRONT & BACK

19¼-20¾-22½-24
(48.5-52-56.5-60)

Index

Bibliography

Theiss, Nola. *Glorious Crocheted Sweaters*. New York: Sterling Publishing Co., 1990.

Schapper, Linda P. *Complete Book of Crochet-Stitch Designs*. New York: Sterling Publishing Co., 1985.

Schapper, Linda P. *Complete Book of Border Design*. New York: Sterling Publishing Co., 1987.